# Psychology Beyond Western Perspectives

# Psychology Beyond Western Perspectives

Kwame Owusu-Bempah and Dennis Howitt

THE BRITISH
PSYCHOLOGICAL
SOCIETY

First published in 2000 by BPS Books (The British Psychological Society), St Andrews House, 48 Princess Road East, Leicester LE1 7DR, UK.

A catalogue record for this book is available from the British Library.

Library of Congress Cataloging-in-Publication Data on file.

ISBN 1 85433 328 3

Typeset by Book Production Services, London.
Printed in Great Britain by MPG Books Limited.

# Contents

# Introduction

Three worlds of psychology in terms of research, teaching and practice are discernible. One is the world of psychological knowledge and application originating from the USA; another is that of a body of knowledge and practice developed in Western European nations; and the third comprises the psychologies of the so-called Third World nations. Of these, North American psychology has been dominant in modern times; it serves as the most important source of influence for European nations as well as the rest of the world.

The globalization of the combined European and North American psychology and the consequent negation – or at least neglect – of other world psychologies, such as African, Arabic, Asian and Native American psychologies, have resulted in calls to redefine the discipline. The argument is that a redefinition of psychology in terms of theory, research and practice is needed in order to accommodate other psychologies or world-views and to better serve humankind in all its complexity. Even within Western boundaries, the clientele of psychologists has diversified considerably owing to complex modern migratory patterns. This book is an attempt to respond to these twin pressures on the discipline. Traditionally, psychology has enjoyed the luxury of being concerned with a fairly homogenous and restricted clientele – essentially Caucasian populations. As such, psychologists have had, until recent times, little need to raise the difficult question of the interplay between culture and psychology: psychology has, and to an extent continues to be, part of Western European history and culture; it is characteristically Euro-American in nature.

The globalization of Euro-American psychology seeks to propagate Western beliefs and values as *sine qua non* for economic, political and psychological growth or maturity. A materialistic outlook on life and reality, individualism (selfishness) and competition, an attitude of consumerism (avarice), belief in autonomy of the individual, the replacement of God with science, freedom from ethical and religious control in the name of capitalism are some of the salient characteristics of the culture in which Euro-American psychology flourishes.

Few psychologists world-wide have difficulty recognizing the Euro-American foundations of their discipline. Rather, it is harder for them to appreciate that cultures can no longer be defined by national or geographic boundaries, particularly Euro-American boundaries. Notwithstanding, psychologists and other practitioners even in the West are faced with the task of explaining the thoughts, emotions, feelings and actions of culturally heterogeneous populations. The immediate issues for some practitioners may be those connected with 'race', culture or ethnicity. We would be the first to agree that psychologists need to be aware of these issues in their activities. Racism or cultural errors must be avoided at all costs in our theorizing, research, teaching and practice. Whether or not the profession has achieved all that is possible in this respect is not the issue here. Our motivation for writing this book is the realization that psychologists are ill-prepared to deal with cultural variety; the average practitioner, for example, is ignorant of the variety of cultural and religious beliefs and values (categorical values as opposed to instrumental values) which guide or profoundly influence the behaviours of their multicultural, multiethnic clientele. This often results in providing inappropriate services to them. Thus, Mays *et al.* (1996) have recommended that North American psychology, for example, educates itself about the psychologies of other nations, in order to better understand the limits of its science, practice and professional development for the betterment of all its clientele.

While this book in part documents how psychology is remiss in its grand mission and the consequences for our clientele, we do not construe the task as one of merely identifying the problem. However, suggesting appropriate directions for psychologists, be they educators, researchers or practitioners, is a huge task. The multitude of cultures to be found even within a Western practice precludes the writing of a handbook or manual for multicultural practice. The complexity of the task is not the only difficulty. As yet, explorations of psychology anywhere other than in Western cultures have been insufficiently extensive or adequate to allow such a compendium or blueprint. We see this book as being a modest part of the beginnings of culturally appropriate practice in psychology and related disciplines. As such, we provide the conceptual background and solutions from which we will benefit, given the present state of knowledge. As research and practice improve in relation to human and cultural diversity, models of good practice will almost certainly develop for specific cultural groups. Currently, these are available only in a rudimentary form.

Furthermore, such developments imply a degree of specialization that is simply not practicable at the present stage of the development of psychological and related services both within and outside Western boundaries. Many practitioners are generalists with a varied clientele; their needs are not easily solved by a multiplicity of guidelines for working with specific cultures or groups. The task is obviously too complex. In the meantime, their needs are better dealt with by providing general principles which take into account cultures beyond Western ones; this is the approach employed, in part, in this book. Teachers, researchers and practitioners in all branches of psychology and related disciplines are the primary audience, as well as their students and trainees. Users of psychological services – clinical, educational, occupational – will, we hope, be the primary beneficiaries.

Some readers might find our choice of words initially confusing when we refer to racially defined groups. We use the word 'Black' in the common political sense to apply to all groups who are victims of racism including peoples of African, Asian and Native American origins. In the context of the UK, we use African, African-Caribbean, Bangladeshi, Indian, Pakistani and similar terms to indicate broad cultural and ethnic groupings. While not universal, this is fairly standard practice among writers in the field.

## Acknowledgement

The first author would like to acknowledge the assistance of the University of Leicester in granting a semester of study leave for the completion of this book.

# Chapter 1

# Beyond the limitations of Western psychology

*By placing culture in the vanguard of our concerns, we are finally drawn to the enormous global need for a psychology of practical significance. Western psychology has had the luxury of devoting most of its research to questions of abstract theory and viewing application as a second-rate derivative. Not only are such theories largely parochial (even when supporting universality), but very little of the research has particular payoff.*

Gergen et al., 1996, p. 502

## Locating psychology

The game is between unequal players. Professional psychology, as most of the world knows it, has its historical, intellectual, organizational and financial roots in the Western nations and North America in particular. Few, if any, psychologists would gainsay this. The point of disagreement is only reached when the question of the influence of psychology's origins on its nature is posed. The range of positions is wide but can be construed as a dichotomy between two poorly defined camps. There are those who believe that in its search for the universal underlying principles of human thought, conduct and feeling, psychology is effectively one psychology and a single psychology for all peoples as a consequence. There are others who reject this view as untenable and a substantial disservice to peoples the world over. They see psychology as neglecting the vast majority of its subjects – diverse populations of people.

Furthermore, it imposes Western European and North American values world-wide in a form of cultural imperialism which is as invidious as any other, perhaps more so given the primary location of this intellectual colonialism among the economic and financial elite of economically developing nations. This is not solely an issue of what is occurring in far-flung parts of the world. It is an issue that affects psychologists in all Western nations too. As a result of migration the clients of psychologists are culturally diverse within Western nations. Yet the psychology on offer is, at best, the indigenous psychology of

White Western peoples within highly industrialized nations. It is a psychology for people who are imbued with the values of such industrialized societies. The psychology is of individuals acting with other individuals against a backdrop of society. Personal development and achievement is what gives people their sense of identity, not the welfare of the community.

Of course, there is little new in this sort of complaint against psychology. Feminist psychologists, for example, have long railed against the imposition of this value system on women to their disadvantage. They see the values of psychology as serving the power interests of White, middle-class men in industrialized societies. The reaction has been to develop an alternative psychology with alternative methods to answer fundamentally distinct research questions. These valuable contributions, however, only serve to highlight the problem we are addressing. Gender is just one aspect of human diversity and, beyond the purely biological, is diverse in its nature, form and expression in different cultures and subcultures across the world. The need is for psychology to contribute to understanding this diversity in a way that does not repeat the error of seeking for universals without question. There is reason to think that Western psychology fails many groups within the West itself. Developing out of the movement towards culturally sensitive counselling, surveys were conducted into the use of clinical services by immigrant populations in the United States. These have revealed findings that ought to cause all practitioners of psychology and allied disciplines some discomfort. Members of minority populations are the least likely to use professional psychological mental health services. Equally significant is that minority group members who use such services are the most likely to abandon treatment before completion (Sue, 1988). Whatever the reasons, the findings demonstrate the inappropriateness of service provision for minority group members.

One explanation for the reported under-utilization of such services by minorities is the cultural inappropriateness of the treatment. It is easy to leave the analysis at the level of the accusation that their own cultural perspective profoundly limits practitioners of psychology. Unfortunately, this in itself does not tell us how practice can be improved or give us confidence that anything can be done. There is a great need to eliminate the discrimination perpetrated against minorities (and possibly their alienation) by psychological workers and at the same time create a psychology which is of value to members of minority cultures in the West, as well as cultures beyond the West. The client groups of Western psychologists are patently varied in national and cultural origins and likely to be increasing as a result of migration trends. Awareness needs to be heightened that we, as psychologists, use psychology that is fit for its purpose and for all client groups.

Recognition of the problem has been most acute in the United States, despite its being at the root of the problem. Nevertheless, recognition of a problem may be widespread but the response inadequate. Numerous critiques are to be found in mental health literature of the dominance of particular value positions inherent in theories of normal and pathological human development (Foster, 1998). Foster describes this ideological foundation to theory in this area as ethnocentric or, as others would have it, Eurocentric. Based on the psychodynamic concept of countertransference, Foster writes about cultural countertransference. This involves a number of things: the thoughts and feelings expressed in the form of academically-based practice and theory which govern psychologists' activities; psychologists' personal life values which they develop within their own culture; prejudices about minorities and the feelings about their own ethnic identity which no honest psychologist can deny to have. These are active and interacting components that influence all aspects of life including a psychologist's professional life.

Dominated as they are by Western thought, psychologists have a conception of the self which involves numerous different religious and secular elements. Most of us as participants in the Western psychological enterprise either find it difficult to recognize many of these or take it for granted that this is what people are. The Western conception of self, especially as evidenced by Euro-Americans, primarily values individual autonomy and responsibility. The attainment of a fulfilled self is practically synonymous with individual autonomy. This is the ideal to be emulated and an important goal in life. Any barriers to individual autonomy are devalued, irrespective of their nature, and made part of life's problem. So academic theories of human development which have gained prominence and influence in Western psychology reproduce these elements by presenting human development as a pathway to the idealized state of autonomy from others. Foster (1998) describes how children are construed as being in a struggle for liberation from their mothers. The healthy outcome is seen as independent adults who have minds of their own and are prepared to speak their mind. Adolescence is a period of intense struggle which achieves separation from the family which otherwise would inhibit growth into the independent adult. The issue is not whether this picture is right or wrong for children of Western cultures; it is the way in which this process is overridden by the sense that this is the normal process of human development. Is it, however, merely normal for some? Is it normal for everyone? It is a necessity for psychologists to recognize that it is not human nature but Western values that define what is psychologically healthy – the way that things should be.

It is not easy to know the dominant characteristics of other cultures when operating solely from within a Western culture. However, some therapists have attempted to identify crucial differences between Western and other cultures. A good example of this is when Roland (1988) describes what he has gleaned from his clients and others, to be the salient characteristics of people from India to set against those of, in this instance, Americans:

- Their intense sense of emotional connectedness with other people communicated for the most part non-verbally;
- Symbiotic rather than exploitative social thinking, associated with a permanent sensitivity to others;
- An in-built assumption that relationships will exhibit reciprocity;
- Giving at levels which would seem unusual to Westerners;
- Indulging others continually with warmth and concern;
- A sense that other people are part of us and inseparable from us as opposed to distinct and separate.

Specifically, on marriage Indian women solicit emotional intimacy with the women in their husband's family, such as their mother-in-law. Indian men try not to appear competitive in the workplace. They try to show the virtues of loyalty, co-operation and agreeability with others. Self-esteem is evaluated in terms of the reputation of the family rather than the individual. Work is important to Indian people in the context of relationships rather than the source of one's personal identity.

This set of characteristics is merely one of many instances of how peoples from beyond Western cultures may differ from what is broadly normative in the West. When we look at each entry in the list through the lens of what we have already learnt about the Western self, we are bound to pause at times to note how curious we would regard a person presenting for treatment or counselling with these characteristics. For example, just how would we help individuals whose family had brought disgrace on itself? By telling them that they cannot be held responsible for the mis-doings of others who are old enough to be responsible for themselves?

As we shall see in Chapter 7, the literature on the psychologies of indigenous peoples throughout the world is replete with a common argument: beyond the West, conceptions of the self are radically different. Indeed, the argument sometimes goes as far as to suggest that Western psychology is not even helpful for understanding such significant groupings as women (Gilligan, 1982). This aside, the central message is that beyond the West, psychology involves a fundamental realignment in terms of how the self is defined. That is, the self and the community are only meaningfully separated and isolated within Western conceptions. There are numerous variants according to the culture in question, as we shall see in succeeding chapters. The key point is that our understanding of what is psychologically healthy is conditioned by Western culture. Consequently we risk ignoring other possibilities and, worse still, see the alternatives as in some way faulty or pathological. If the selves of peoples beyond Western psychology are alien curiosities to Western psychologists, how can psychology be in sympathy with these peoples?

## Is it racism again?

This book is primarily concerned with psychologies which do not disenfranchise peoples in the way that Western psychology does. However, there is just a small step from this neglect to the actual racism of professionals. Both of these attitudes reflect the cultural origins of currently dominant psychological ideas. It is not as if psychology had a special prerogative to be racist or ethnocentric in its outlook. Both practices come from the wider culture that nurtured and supported psychology since its beginnings, whenever we take them to be, in the West. For that reason, it is important to reprise the arguments made about modern psychology and 'race' when considering the alternatives to the present situation. The Western ethnocentric perspective of most psychology would not end entirely if psychology and related disciplines were rid of racism, but it would be more exposed and evident. As it is, psychology supports the notion that Western values are both right and natural – the roots of personal psychological health as well as a society which has as its primary concern economic growth rather than social cohesion.

Professionals nowadays rarely express crude racist sentiments at work. At the least, overt racist acts bring the risk of embarrassment; at the extreme, public notoriety and humiliation result. Because the issue of racism and racial discrimination has had a high public profile in recent times, many organizations, including professional bodies, are eager to publicly dissociate themselves from it. They work to achieve this by claiming an equal opportunities status: 'is an equal opportunities employer'; ' is committed to Equal Opportunities'; 'all applicants will be considered on the basis of suitability regardless of sex, race, marital status or disability'; 'we particularly welcome applications from ethnic minority groups who are under-represented in the organization.' Others claim to recognize that we live in a multicultural society and to be committed to providing services appropriate to the needs of such a society: 'We are committed to Equal Opportunities in employment and service delivery.' Some claim to be even more active by proclaiming an anti-racism or anti-discrimination stance. In such circumstances, racist words and deeds are open to challenge and criticism both from within the organization and from the wider community. Not surprisingly, therefore, the expression of racist views tends to be saved for private moments.

It is overly optimistic to assume that racism is eradicated from organizations simply because they have a policy stipulating that it should not be there. Much of the Western world, including the USA and

Britain, implemented legislation outlawing racial discrimination in public places as early as the 1960s. Racism remains; only the framework within which racist thoughts are expressed and deeds carried out has changed. It would be unrealistic and naive to expect legislation alone to rid organizations of racism in the absence of a resolute social and political will. Racist acts continue to be documented extensively: in housing, education, employment, the health care system and even in law, including the criminal justice system (Brown, 1984, Brown and Gray, 1985; LACRC, 1985; NACRO, 1986; NAHA, 1988; Owusu-Bempah, 1999b; Runnymede Trust, 1992; Scarman, 1981). Indeed, crude racial violence and racial abuse appear to be on the increase (CRE, 1987a,b, 1988a,b; Macpherson, 1999; Skellington and Morris, 1992). This is apparently so throughout most Western societies.

Genuine multicultural strategies stress the provision of knowledge about, insight into and respect for the cultures and achievements of all cultural groups. The public acceptance of a multicultural philosophy and strategies by organizations is, therefore, reassuring; but perhaps it is premature to suggest that all is well in our institutions. This feeling of reassurance is reinforced by the way in which personnel throughout our public institutions are increasingly conversant in anti-racist and anti-discrimination rhetoric. Such rhetoric, in turn, tempts us to believe that organizational racism is a declining, if not dead, problem. This is mistaken confidence in the effectiveness of broad policies and procedures. Vetting intended to prevent flagrant acts of racial discrimination tends to operate best in relatively narrow spheres such as recruitment. Even then no ironclad guarantee exists that racist acts have been eliminated.

The generally held belief that racism manifests itself as verbally crude and physically violent racist assaults on Black people can also stand in the way of ridding society of racism (Howitt and Owusu-Bempah, 1990; 1994). Because we often assume that racism is crudely expressed, we tend to overlook institutional racism and the subtleties of racially biased decision-making, as well as the practices of individual professionals. Vetting, screening and monitoring by organizations can be employed to ensure a measure of fairness in personnel decisions, including shortlisting and even promotion; similarly, the delivery of services may be monitored to ensure that individuals are not treated less favourably or excluded on the grounds of race, ethnicity, citizenship or nationality. However, these measures are not 'racism-proof'. Clearly putting in place provision for the fair and adequate treatment of clients from all sections of a multicultural society remains a major undertaking. It is an even more formidable task to ensure that the complex day-to-day decisions made by professionals about Black service-users are free from bias. Decision-making is rarely an open process in which the basis of the available choices is clear to everyone involved. This is compounded further by the fact that many individuals who take essentially racist decisions feel no, or are unaware of, any personal antipathy to Black people or dislike for them. Frequently, they inadvertently act racially for reasons that they feel are in the best interest of the Black client. Professionals are prone to patronizing or benevolent racism: they often act in the arrogant or false belief that they know what is in the best interest of Black people without even consulting them (Howitt and Owusu-Bempah, 1990b; Owusu-Bempah, 1994). This patronization may take place even in an environment of genuine and profound anti-racist beliefs. Such an ethos may, indeed, tend to serve the deception inherent in the situation, making it difficult to recognize or accept that racism exists in the organization and within the individuals themselves.

Revealing overt racism is simple; revealing covert racism in the thinking or actions of professionals is another matter. None-the-less, it can be achieved by examining how professionals deal with Black and White individuals in very similar circumstances. In this way, the subtleties of the processes involved become readily apparent. In the next section we will turn to some of the evidence of racism by professionals and the processes by which this form of racism is perpetrated.

## The subtlety and discretion of racist acts

*Never let the fox into the henhouse to feed the chickens.*
African proverb; Williams, 1980, p. 403

Three decades ago, Unesco declared: 'All men living today belong to the same species and descend from the same stock' (Unesco, 1967, Statement 10). Thus 'race' is a baseless, meaningless concept when applied to human beings. Nevertheless, the belief that humanity comprises different racial groups continues to dominate our thought, feelings and conduct. 'Race' has been given a social reality that transcends its flimsy existence as a biological fact. That humankind is made up of different 'races' may be gossamer in biological science, in society it is rock solid. Over the centuries, different 'races' have been 'identified' by Western 'scientists' and presumptions made about their relative worth. The discourse and rhetoric employed to describe and identify different 'races' have changed substantially over time, what remains constant is the notion of 'race' as a vital social reality. Like all socially based knowledge, 'race' is a social construction that best serves the interests of those who designed it (Howitt, 1991). That is, it provides a rationale or justification for policies which advantage some and disadvantage others; it justifies the differential allocation of power and resources among groups; it enables the acceptance of the otherwise unacceptable. This socially constructed 'knowledge' serves as a framework for professional training and practice, among other things. After all, the professions that create the knowledge also use it.

Every profession and institution is a microcosm of the wider social structure. Social work, medicine, psychiatry, nursing, law, the police and teaching all reflect and touch directly on all aspects of society. There is no sense in which they are isolated from, or immune to, the broader political and ideological forces that shape society. Significantly, these professions are subject to major interventions consequent upon government policy. Professional autonomy, to the extent that it has any meaning, therefore, refers only to a given profession's ability to control, regulate and discipline its own membership.

Prevailing social values, beliefs, myths and folklore largely influence a profession's guiding principles, values and practice. So an examination of the influence of race on specific professions will provide a better knowledge of its dynamics in society as a whole (Owusu-Bempah, 1997). Historically, psychiatry, social work and teaching, among other professions, have been underpinned by the same race theories, beliefs and assumptions that have pervaded related professions and society in general (Howitt and Owusu-Bempah, 1994). This means that, in their dealings with Black people, professionals have a long tradition of using race or culture as a frame of reference. As detailed in Chapter 5, even when the term 'culture' is used in professional discourse, it is usually synonymously with race. Thus, practitioners' perceptions, assessments and treatment of Black clients or service-users have been adversely affected or clouded by (mis)conceptions of race. Consequently, the needs of Black people have been (mis)interpreted and (mis)understood in ways that have little bearing on what would be generally helpful or acceptable to them. This does not imply that professionals have been static in their racial thinking. Rather, race has been employed as a mutable concept which alters, fluctuates and adapts to the prevailing socio-political environment. This ever-changing environment includes the thinking of professionals. A new generation of professionals may have apparently different views from those of previous generations; the question is whether these are new themes or variants of the same old tunes. Whether they are new or old tunes, race continues to influence professional training and practice in many ways. Put another way, it is often difficult to detect race thinking in the day-to-day discourse and activities of today's professionals, for such race-based discourse is couched in a mantle of reasonableness and caringness. Racism is not something done solely by racist bigots; the overt and offensive racial animosity displayed by the archetypal racist of the far right or fascists is not essential to racism. Racism is perpetrated also by people who positively value Black people. Racist bigotry may be one thing; the racism endemic in social institutions is another, more subtle matter. Take the case of a manager who rejects a Black job applicant. In an ethos antipathetic to racism, this rejection needs to be achieved in ways which do not constitute 'social gaffs'. Essed (1988), for example, has demonstrated how a rejection can be justified in a job application interview on the basis of difficulties created by the applicant's reaction to the interviewer's racist assumptions.

## Uncovering covert racism

Several studies carried out in the helping professions, such as nursing, social work and the voluntary sector, illustrate the continuing influence of race on the thinking and practice of professionals. These studies follow in the tradition of research that investigated the role of race in employment decisions in industry. In these, job applications ostensibly from a White person have been shown to receive more interest or a more favourable consideration than similar applications from a Black person (CRE, 1987a; 1987b; Esmail and Everington, 1993; Smith, 1974). Of course, the letters had been composed by the researchers so as to be as similar as possible on factors such as the qualifications and experience of the applicants. Race was the feature that differentiated them. In a typical case, the employers would receive, at random, either an application from a Black person or a White person. This ensured that any differences between the responses to the two versions of the letter were due to the race of the applicant. Others have found similar differential responses to private letters to Black or other ethnic minorities versus White people (Howitt *et al.*, 1977; Howitt and McCabe, 1978; Howitt and Owusu-Bempah, 1990b). Howitt and Owusu-Bempah (1990b), for example, sent letters to voluntary sector organizations in the East Midlands area of England. The letters simply requested information about voluntary work opportunities with the organization:

*Dear Sir/Madam*

*Would you please let me know if you have any need for voluntary workers? A prepaid envelope is enclosed.*

*Yours faithfully,*

Each handwritten letter was identical in all respects with one exception – the signature. In about half of the cases Mrs Irene Croft signed the letter, and in the other cases Mrs Arima Kumari signed it. That is, the letter was seemingly from a White person or a Black Person. At random, the organizations received one or other of the versions of the letter, thus ensuring that there were no systematic differences between the organizations receiving each letter.

In a non-racist world, the presumed skin colour of the writer should certainly make no difference, and we should expect voluntary sector agencies to be unconcerned about the race or skin colour of prospective volunteers. In this instance, the reality was rather different. Replies were received to about two-thirds of the letters irrespective of the race of the applicant. Not surprisingly, given the nature of the letters sent to the agencies, most of the replies tended to be positive; voluntary organizations, after all, need volunteers. This did not mean that all was well. There were racial differences in the rate of rejections of the offer: the Black (Asian) volunteer was four times more likely to be rejected than the White volunteer. Furthermore, positive offers of work or suggestions about other possibilities were more common in the replies to a letter from a White person than one from a Black person. Thus Black applicants tended to be treated less favourably than White applicants. Independent raters coded the replies in terms of how encouraging they were to the applicant. Once again, consistent evidence emerged that Black applicants were more likely than White ones to receive relatively discouraging replies.

The replies universally lacked direct racist antipathy. Superficially, they were civil, courteous and apparently appropriate replies. Indeed, individual Black recipients of any of the letters might reasonably assume that the replies to their inquiry contained no racist elements. Only on aggregate does the dismal racist story unfold. The cumulative consequence for an applicant who received several of these replies would be much more damaging, and the suspicion of racism stronger. The net outcome of a series of such replies would probably be much more dispiriting. In short, without the comparison of the more favourable treatment of White applicants, there is always an element of doubt about how to interpret the replies. Tasks can be found, of course, for volunteers if the motivation to do so is there.

Another worrying aspect is that the authors of these negative replies might not have perceived their actions as racially motivated; it is not known exactly what was in the minds of these letter writers. There is reason to believe from other research that to-day's professionals are guided in their actions (perhaps unconsciously) more by racial beliefs, stereotypes or assumptions than gut-feeling racial hatred. As we shall see, research on members of other caring professions confirms this interpretation. Professionals have a repertoire of beliefs and assumptions about Black people, their cultures, families and experiences which materially affects their work with both Black children and adults. Howitt and Owusu-Bempah (1994) and Owusu-Bempah (1994, 1997) provide a detailed account of the role of such racial thinking in the activities of professionals, such as clinical and educational psychologists, psychiatrists and therapists. Two particularly relevant and illuminating studies follow.

# Professional decisions

## *Psychiatric nurses*

Richards (1995) investigated the ways in which White European psychiatric nurses regarded clients of different racial origins. She created a number of fictitious case files each of which included a photograph of the putative client. Among the fictitious accounts were ones in which the gender, age, type of behaviour and the voluntary or forcible admission of the client to hospital were varied. The types of behaviour that the clients demonstrated ranged from the odd or eccentric (such as talking to oneself), through misdemeanours (various types of socially disruptive behaviours), to criminal acts. Not all the nurses received identical selections of case files. In some, these differed significantly only in terms of the client's race. For each of the people described in the case files, the nurses provided the following:

1  The diagnostic label they would attach to the client;
2  A plan for their care;
3  The nurse's beliefs about the client's most likely response to being in hospital;
4  An indication of the outside support system available to the client (e.g. family and/or friends);
5  A recommendation of the strength of medication to be given to the client (ranging from mild to strong); and
6  An evaluation of the client's long-term viability for successful return to his or her community.

In responding to these requests, the nurses did not rely on the factual material (the contents of the case studies) alone. They frequently drew upon a broad array of ideas and beliefs current in the community about Black people when reaching their decisions. As with much racism, these racial resources often had a 'taken-for-granted' or common sense tone which belied their true meaning. Furthermore, these ideas and beliefs were incorporated into the nurses' discourse as if they had come directly from the case studies, rather than from a more general race repertoire. The nurses' decisions often mirrored well-established trends in the differential treatment of Black people in the psychiatric system (Bolton, 1984; Fernando, 1989; Howitt and Owusu-Bempah, 1994; Littlewood, 1992; Littlewood and Lipsedge, 1989; Mercer, 1984; Shaikh, 1985). For example, Black clients were recommended stronger medication than the equivalent White client. This reflects mental health personnel's tendency – as demonstrated in previous research – to use physical treatments more readily on Black patients.

The case study of the African-Caribbean client, Delroy Williams, specifically and clearly included the statement: 'staff soon contacted his family who eagerly provided a detailed case history'. Obviously, this Black family was keen, if not anxious, to be of help, but the nurses tended to disregard this when forming judgements about the likely social support available to him. Indeed, they construed his (Black) family as failing a key test of a good family – solidarity in times of trouble: 'I don't think he'll get much support from his family'; 'His parents don't seem to be supportive of him'; 'Possibly friends but NOT family support whether in or out of hospital'; 'His parents don't want to know'; and 'I don't believe his support system of friends or family will be good'. Even when the nurses believed that Delroy's parents might be helpful, grave reservations were expressed about the benefits to him. That is, the family support was perceived to be so badly flawed that it was almost certain to damage him further: 'But if his parents are heavily involved in his return to the community... it is likely to make him more rebellious and agitated which will hamper his progress and lead to further breakdowns.'

In keeping with the view that there is a degree of specificity in race beliefs about different ethnic minority groups, it is noteworthy that certain minority clientele are regarded differently. So, for example, the following was written of a client's Muslim family: 'I think his family will be supportive as Muslim families tend to stick together more.' It is easy to see how the apparent specificity of racial beliefs about different ethnic groups might have provided the nurses with spurious reassurance that their racial views reflected social facts.

The stereotypic assumption of the violent and aggressive nature of African-Caribbean males appeared in the nurses' responses to Delroy. In his case history, there is a very ambiguous statement that might imply that Delroy had been the victim of violence rather than its perpetrator. This statement tended to be ossified into the firm 'fact' that Delroy's violence required urgent attention: 'He is violent.' 'He's obviously physically violent.' 'Delroy is a danger to himself and the public ... going to need his behaviour restrained to protect others.' '...protect the people around him.' 'Delroy will need strong medication to reduce his violence.'

It is startling how a very similar case study involving a White man, Johnathan Spencer-Summers, produced responses that suggested that he might be the victim of circumstances, that the problem was apart from him. This occurred despite the fact that the case history clearly described Johnathan as an arsonist! 'I don't think Johnathan will appreciate being in hospital, it might make him worse.' 'The arson offence is an indication of the frustration or fear that he feels about his studies.' 'Johnathan might have to be given medication to control his illness but hopefully drugs will be a last resort.' 'Johnathan's care plan needs to focus on counselling.' In contrast, the nurses never mentioned any factors other than his illness as an explanation of Delroy's behaviour.

The study also revealed how race plays an important part in the anticipation of problems, and not just their interpretation. Comments made about the Black youngster, Delroy, predicted that he would make a troublesome client: 'His frequent conflict with the police shows that he finds it difficult to appreciate rules and this will present problems for staff.' 'He seems quite an unsociable man ... I also think that he may have problems in communicating with others.' Such anxieties were not typical of the way in which the White youth, Johnathan, was regarded. The nurses seemed far more enthusiastic about him as a successful client who would fit in well with life in the hospital. For example, one wrote, 'I think he will respond well to the hospital environment, he seems to communicate happily with others... community groups could be helpful as he appears to want to communicate with others in the community.' 'I think he will respond well to the hospital environment in terms of his interaction with others.'

At a subsequent stage of the research, a separate group of people evaluated the psychiatric nurses' judgements. They were unaware of the racial group to which the clients belonged. Nevertheless, there were clear differences in the perceptions of the nurses' comments. The reports about White clients were rated as more optimistic, more supportive, warmer, more trusting, fairer and more concerned than the reports about Black clients. Patients of South Asian origin tended to be seen somewhere between African/African-Caribbean and White clients. When 'illicitly used' drugs were involved, they were specifically mentioned as the cause of a Black patient's illness. In contrast, illicit drug use tended to be underplayed or disregarded as a cause of illness when the patient was White. Such tendencies have been shown in psychiatrists, the police and other professionals (Howitt and Owusu-Bempah, 1995; McGovern and Cope, 1987).

Just why drugs were so readily seized upon by these nurses as a cause of psychiatric problems in Black people, but disregarded when White people were concerned, is not known for certain. It may well be that they had been taught about the so-called 'cannabis-induced psychosis' in Black people (in the 1970s, the vogue was 'cultural psychosis'). There are cases of White Western psychologists lecturing African students in an African country about this. Carr and MacLachlan (1993), for example, describe how they encouraged their Black African students to search for evidence of 'markers for Chamba (marijuana) abuse and Chamba-related psychosis'. 'Chamba-related psychosis' was promoted as a way of understanding the mental health problems of Africans. Note that there is a great deal of uncertainty about whether diagnoses of marijuana-induced psychosis are valid. For instance, McGovern and Cope (1987) describe how psychiatrists diagnose substantial numbers of Black people in Britain as having the condition. Although there are high levels of use of the substance among White people in Britain, the 'diagnosis' is never given to the latter. The use of socially fabricated diagnoses has been documented by other investigators (e.g., Fernando, 1989; Littlewood and Lipsedge, 1989; Ranger, 1989). The diagnosis is not a trivial matter since some of these researchers also claim that it is used frequently by the police, in complicity with psychiatrists, to incarcerate Black people under the mental health legislation.

## Social workers

Generally, by virtue of their training, social workers are believed to be relatively sensitive to issues of inequality, including racism. In Britain, for example, there is a clear and specific requirement for racial issues to be part and parcel of their education and training (CCETSW, 1991). Given this, social workers constitute a crucial test of our argument that professional thinking continues to be racially constructed. Recent research seems to support this contention. It seems that social workers' responses to case histories such as the following concerning a boy of 'mixed-race' parentage are determined, in part, by racial considerations:

> Stephen is a thirteen year-old boy who first came to the attention of Social Services at the early age of nine, when he deliberately set fire to his mother's bed. Subsequently his behaviour deteriorated, and he has since been in constant contact with the police and social workers for various offences, including shoplifting, stealing bikes, and damaging cars and property. Stephen (who likes to be known as Steve) is the oldest of three children in the family. Steve's mother (Angela) is a white single parent. She had Steve when she was eighteen years old, but left Steve's father when Steve was just about two years old. She remarried a year later, and has two other children, a boy aged nine and a girl aged seven. Her second marriage ended in divorce shortly after the birth of her daughter. Apart from Steve, the rest of the family are white. As far as the mother can recollect, the first time Steve started to show signs of behaviour disturbance was at the age of about eight, when he started to ask questions about his father. Until then, he was what one might describe as an ideal child. Steve has never met his father, who is Afro-Caribbean, and seems to know virtually nothing about him. And his mother is not helpful in providing him with information about his father since she claims not to know his whereabouts. Generally, Steve is very reluctant to talk about himself or his family. At home, Steve is frequently physically aggressive and verbally abusive towards his mother and his younger sister. He is, however, more favourably disposed towards his younger brother. According to his mother, he also steals from her to buy cigarettes and sweets for himself and his friends.
>
> At school, which is racially mixed, Steve has been described by his teachers as a very difficult boy: insolent, with an undisguised dislike for authority, uninterested in school, playing truant, having a low self-esteem

*which he tries to overcompensate for by bullying other children. At other times he is sullen and withdrawn. Academically, Steve is among the poorest in his class. Steve seems to think that everyone is against him, except his two best friends who are white.*

Owusu-Bempah, 1994a, p. 127

Social workers were given, at random, virtually identical versions of the above case study. The alternative versions described the situation of a White boy, Alan, or an African-Caribbean boy, Winston. Apart from this, the case histories were identical. The social workers were asked to:

1  Identify social and psychological factors associated with the boy's behavioural and emotional problems.
2  Suggest intervention(s) that might be helpful.

Superficial browsing through the recommendations of these social workers gives little immediate indication of the racially predominated nature of their views, partly because much racist discourse is effected through the rhetoric of reasonableness and common sense. It is difficult to tease out the racial meaning in relatively bland and normative pronouncements. Nevertheless, a few examples begin to show that underneath this apparent sense of reasonableness, the recommendations of the social workers were built on a set of racial assumptions. Regarding the White boy, one social worker commented:

*Social work intervention could include addressing Alan's aggression, enabling him to come to terms with 'why'. It may also mean approaching Alan's mother and requesting that she enables him to become aware of his father's character, etc.*

Notice how Alan's aggression is not held to be a characteristic of White boys in general but is assumed to have another cause. In contrast, another social worker having read identical facts about the mixed-race boy, Steve, stated:

*Steven might benefit from home personal support. A social worker might not have the skills to offer this but could act as a link enabling Steven to develop relationships with the Black community. Some form of family therapy might be possible. Steven's mother would benefit from some anti-racist training. I would also like to address the issues of Steven's sexism if he would benefit from being encouraged to join a mixed youth club. I would consider all the above because Steven's main problem is his lack of self-esteem which has driven him to become an attention seeker. Steven needs to be told clearly what the consequences of his actions are: e.g., criminal activity.*

Once again this is superficially reasonable. Nevertheless, the school's statement about Steven's lack of self-esteem has become central in the social worker's recommendations. The suggestion about relationships with the Black community reflects this given that cultural linkages dominate many modern debates about children of 'mixed-race' parentage. Also, like the nurses' differential response to the cases involving White and Black youngsters, the social workers' concern with Alan's anger is about how to help him to come to terms with its cause(s), while their concern with Steven's anger is the 'likelihood' that it will result in criminality.

One social worker wrote of the African-Caribbean boy, Winston:

*Perhaps Winston, with his whole family, needs to attend a 'family therapy centre' if one is available. Were this to happen, each could bring out his/her worries/concerns etc. to the others in a neutral environment with the help of a counsellor or facilitator. This might help bring out the underlying causes of Winston's behaviours. It might be appropriate for Winston to see an Educational Psychologist, re. his problems with school. However, it seems that the bad behaviour as noted by the school stems from matters other than school, so family therapy may be better. Winston's mother could be encouraged to speak to/contact/his father if this is possible for her – or at least to give him some details of his father's character, appearance etc. A Social Worker may be able to discuss this with her, and help in contacting him, if this is correct.*

This account dwells on the intractable nature of Winston's problems and contrasts markedly with the relatively straightforward recommendations made by the social workers about the White boy's identical problems where it is implied that a social worker will have the necessary skills to deal with the boy's problems. The point is that, in none of the above accounts taken alone, is there sufficient evidence that ideas of race greatly influence the professional judgements and recommendations. We may have suspicions when courses of action, such as facilitating contact with the Black community, are recommended despite the absence of any clear statement in the case study that 'Blackness' is a problem for the boy. After all, his school is racially mixed, so it would be safe to assume that he lives in racially mixed community. In a case conference, without awareness of the recommendations being made about other children of different ethnic origins in similar circumstances, undoubtedly the aura of reasonableness in the recommendations would prevail most of the time.

When the data were aggregated, the racial trends in the social workers' recommendations became more apparent. Overall, the lack of information about the absent parent was mentioned as a possible cause of the problems. Nevertheless, there were clear differences between the racial groups in terms of the frequency with which other factors were attributed to the boys' problems. First of all, 85 per cent of the 102 social workers who took part in the study mentioned *identity crises* as the cause of the problems of the 'mixed-race' child; 59 per cent mentioned identity in relation to the Black child; and only 25 per cent mentioned identity problems as a cause of the White child's difficulties. Second, *family circumstances* (which included such matters as financial problems and inadequate parenting) were the commonest explanation given for the problems of the White child (69 per cent) and the Black child (59 per cent). In contrast, family circumstances were substantially less likely to be mentioned as the source of problems if the child was from 'mixed-race' parentage: only 30 per cent of the social workers mentioned these as a cause of problems for the 'mixed-race' parentage child. Only one social worker saw the Black child's problems as wholly caused by the lack of information about his father. It is clear from this that the framework for interpreting the difficulties of the 'mixed-race' child tends to be identity crisis, with family circumstances rarely mentioned; White children's problems are attributed to family circumstances; Black children are seen as having both identity and family problems. Although racism was sometimes mentioned as a cause of the Black and 'mixed-race' children's problems, it was relatively uncommon. Instead, identity crises, rather than racism, were held to be responsible for their problems. This explanation is victim blaming, since it ascribes the problems to an intrinsic aspect of the child (self-identity) and excludes other possible factors besides the family.

The social workers' recommended courses of action are possibly even more illuminating: therapy was the commonest form of recommended action for the White child; children of 'mixed-race' parentage were only half as likely to be recommended for therapy; work on the child's identity problems was a common recommendation for the 'mixed-race' child; to a lesser extent, this was also true for the Black child but identity work was rarely recommended for the White child. The provision of cultural information was virtually never mentioned for the White boy, despite his mother being described as English and his father Scottish. In contrast, when considering the 'mixed-race' child, the provision of culturally relevant information was commonly mentioned. One implication of this is that White children do not have a culture about which they need to know. Similarly, although the provision of an appropriate male model was rarely recommended for the White child, it was a fairly popular recommendation to make about 'mixed-race' and African-Caribbean children. One possible explanation for this may be the general belief that Black families are matriarchal and characterized by father desertion – there are no adult males 'about the house' to interact with the children. White families, on the other hand, are said to be patriarchal and so always have adult males, including granddads and uncles, around to be emulated.

Cross-racial friendships tend to be pathologized by professionals if the child is Black or 'mixed-race'; if the child is White then such friendships are reported in much more positive terms. The following comment about the 'mixed-race' child's association with White children illustrates this tendency:

> *Steven's best friends are White, so may be confused about his identity...*
> *awareness of being different, i.e. colour, feeling of shame about his origin.*
> *Stephen has problems reconciling his own identity, he may be trying to be*
> *White.*

Similarly, of the Black child with White friends: 'Winston's best friends are White – seems to wish to repudiate the fact of being Black.' 'Winston's two best friends are White; he finds White more acceptable.'

In both of the above cases, friendships with White children are regarded as a sign of a problem. In distinct contrast, White children with Black friends are construed differently, even heroically or altruistically: 'Alan feels socially "outcast", he mixes with friends who also experience oppression – Black people. Perhaps he feels they need him owing to their position.' In this instance, there is no implication that the White child wishes to be Black, but that he has something to give the Black children.

Generally, the evidence is that, despite 'improved' training, the racial attitudes of social workers towards their Black clients have been somewhat unfavourable and resistant to change. Early in the 1970s, about one in eight social workers working with immigrant clients were hostile towards them. This figure worsened when Black clients were considered for welfare benefits, and even more so when the clients were Black immigrants (Barn, 1990). Years later, the evidence is that the caring professions still harbour racial stereotypes and, more worryingly, act upon them (Bushell, 1992; Owusu-Bempah, 1989a, 1990, 1994a; Richards, 1995).

## Are Black professionals the solution?

Does the recruitment of more Black professionals by itself improve the situation for Black clients? Common sense would suggest that the answers to the question must be in the affirmative. That is, within the context of professional and other helping relationships, many claim that Black professionals and other Black carers best serve Black clients. None the less, there have been counterclaims (e.g. Asante, 1987; Fernando, 1989; Hall, 1997; O'Brian, 1990; Owusu-Bempah, 1989b, 1990, 1994a). In therapy, for instance, it has been noted that 'Black-on-Black' does not automatically ensure that a therapist will be successful in dealing with Black clients (O'Brian, 1990; Sue, 1998). For example, Hall (1997) has noted that not all perpetrators of cultural errors or racism in therapy are White. Indeed, the study described in the previous section (Owusu-Bempah, 1994a) involved a number of Black social workers, but this did not significantly alter the situation being perceived racially. By the same token, a majority of them (70 per cent) were women, but this did not significantly affect the way in which the respondents perceived the situation in sexist terms either. Black service-users need not see a Black professional as being in any real sense 'Black' or like them. Simply because the professional is Black does not mean that they are regarded by the client as part of the Black community; the status of the practitioners may easily override racial considerations. This is clearly illustrated by the experience of O'Brian, a Black male social worker-cum-family therapist, who tried to reassure a Bangladeshi Muslim father with whom he was working. He tried to explain to the client that he knew what it is like for a Black person living in a country like Britain and having to follow its ways. The client replied:

> *Sir, with the greatest respect, you are not the same as us... It has nothing to do with religion as I would feel the same even if you were a Muslim. You see, you are in a position of authority and accepted by them. You live in a different Britain to the one me and my family live in.*

O'Brian, 1990, p. 4

This is an invaluable lesson for Black professionals in predominantly White socio-economic structures. It is naive, false, or even hypocritical, if not dishonest, for Black professionals to claim that they have not been affected by their Eurocentric primary and/or secondary socialization, their formal education and professional training. O'Brian had received a quintessentially English education in Pakistan. He had learnt English history and knew as much about the importance of the railway and canal systems to the industrial revolution as any White English child could know. Despite this, and despite being of 'mixed-race' parentage, he felt himself to be part of an ethnic minority in Britain. He admits that this early experience in his career taught him this valuable lesson: 'being a Black worker is not qualification enough to help a Black family; differences of class, position and status outweigh any similarity of skin colour' (ibid.).

To some Black service-users, therefore, having a Black skin does not necessarily confer the status 'Black' upon a person. Rather a 'Black' professional is one who not only lives their lives, or empathizes with their circumstances but is also able to formulate and articulate their problems in ways consistent with their needs, anxieties and frustrations. A 'Black' professional, to many Black service-users, is one who has a social-change outlook rather than a mere problem-solving perspective. 'Black' professionals do not focus attention exclusively on the service-user; they also regard the system as part of their ambit; they distinguish clearly between what is a personal or dispositional problem and one merely induced by the system – a structural problem (Williams, 1980). Many of the problems facing Black people in need of professional help or intervention are created by the system and must be tackled or addressed accordingly. A 'Black' professional, therefore, focuses simultaneously on both the client and the social structure. Such a person works ultimately towards social change, he or she is not content with merely delivering palliative measures to their clients.

In recent years, partly as a result of pressures from the Black community, social workers, therapists and teachers in particular have been preoccupied with 'understanding the Black culture' or acquiring a 'Black perspective'. This by itself is not sufficient to meet the needs of the Black community. It also ignores the obvious fact that to understand a culture is not the same as respecting it. Rather, practitioners need to examine and understand their own feelings about the cultures of their Black service-users. At the same time, they must expand their knowledge of the social, political and economic causes of their Black clients' problems while appreciating the role that they can play in helping or worsening those problems. The aim is to develop effective strategies to overcome the barriers to providing appropriate services to ethnic minority communities (Howitt and Owusu-Bempah, 1999; Owusu-Bempah, 1997, 1999c). We all need to examine how cultural assumptions, as well as those associated with our professions, class and gender, can interfere in our work with Black people. In short, one's cache of cultural baggage can interfere with appropriate assessment and treatment of Black clients, and we need to be aware of that. Practitioners, managers and educators of those professions involved with children and families, including social work and teaching, need to recognize and acknowledge that race is just one of the many factors impinging on Black service-users. Other social, psychological, political and economic factors may be more readily alterable. Race must not serve to deflect attention from these factors:

> *Correctly taken decisions are those for which appropriate information is sought from diverse sources, appropriately weighed against available knowledge, and whose outcomes are fed back into that knowledge to inform future practice. This requires, minimally, a more rigorous and empirically based practice than social work typically espouses.*
>
> Macdonald, 1990; p. 539

## General implications for psychology and related professions

The means by which racist work is done in professional contexts should be of crucial importance to psychologists and related professions

(Howitt and Owusu-Bempah, 1999). They are, after all, the ones whose dealings with peoples of diverse cultures need to be helpful and constructive. While, at first sight, social workers and psychiatric nurses are superficially different from psychologists, the differences are trivial in the present context. What these professionals were doing in the studies we described was to employ poorly understood cultural differences and putative cultural differences in ways that ultimately were to the disadvantage of their Black and ethnic minority clients. Can we expect that psychologists, for example, are much more sophisticated in their understanding of the cultures and family structures other than their own? Such matters, to our knowledge, are rarely parts of the curricula of psychologists in training. Indeed, the commonsense-like nature of many of the claims made about Black and ethnic minority clients militates against their being seen as problematic. These are things that we all 'know' irrespective of our training in psychology. Is this, however, not the nature of much of the knowledge practitioners employ in therapy and counselling? Just what knowledge of other cultures does the average practitioner of psychology have? To what degree does this extend beyond the crude formulas that led to the recommendations and beliefs which were disadvantageous to clients in the studies just described?

Practitioners inevitably utilize knowledge from a wide variety of sources in their practice. Some of their knowledge will be firmly based in sound theory and research, but some will have been more casually acquired and be of dubious validity and worth. So psychology has a duty to provide its practitioners with sound knowledge about different cultures and cultural diversity. This is only just beginning to be done at all systematically and there is no compendium of what this knowledge should be. However, the mere act of accepting the need will for many signal a greater awareness of the limitations and constraints imposed by interacting with clients of cultures other than our own. Even being aware of the ways in which culture has determined the manner in which psychologists think about people and their psychological health is a start.

In the coming chapters we will show some of the nature of the problem without attempting to offer a complete solution to it (Owusu-Bempah and Howitt, 1999a and b). Partial answers abound and we shall provide them as appropriate though with a sense that these may be premature. The task is awesome but necessary. The reasons why it is necessary are not simply those of applying psychology beyond Western borders but with practising psychology within national boundaries and the cultural diversity contained therein.

Perhaps an example will help us to recognize the problem, albeit in a somewhat dramatic way. It goes without saying that Chinese culture is profoundly different from Western culture. Some Chinese clients in Western settings may, of course, be virtually totally Western in culture.

However, there may be others who are guided much more by traditional Chinese cultural norms, beliefs and value systems. Such clients may adopt their indigenous social rules, which govern social interaction but express them in the Western context. The relevant indigenous interaction rules would discourage self-disclosure, emotional intensity and conflict with others in a public setting. These may be entirely missing or reduced. In the modern West, a woman who has been sexually harassed or abused would be expected to be somewhat emotional when reporting the events. In therapy and counselling it would be acceptable for her to appear tearful and depressed or openly angry, since there is a general recognition of the possible severe consequences of such abuse. However, Shiang *et al.* (1998) describe the case of a young, married Chinese woman who had been seriously sexually harassed during a business conference trip. At interview, it appeared to the worker (a woman) who was interviewing her that the client treated the matter as insignificant since she frequently smiled during the process. Influenced by Western perspectives, the interviewer interpreted the interaction as suggesting that the complaint of sexual harassment was simply not genuine. A more culturally sensitive interpretation is that the victim's behaviour was merely a manifestation of the demure, restrained exchanges that are culturally required on initial encounters with strangers. The ethnocentric interpretation made by the worker from a Eurocentric perspective led to other interpretations of events. The woman's non-assertiveness when telling the colleague who harassed her to leave her hotel room was, from the Western perspective, interpreted as meaning that she was less disturbed by her colleagues 'attention' than she implied. The question at the end of all of this is one of the extent to which any of us would be culturally sensitive enough to recognize the alternative perspectives on the victim's behaviour.

# Chapter 2

# A universal psychology

*[We] wonder what the orientation and subject matter of psychology would have been if the discipline had originated in a cultural context other than that of the dominant psychological power blocks. Imagine the English, the Dutch, the Germans or the [North] Americans being studied in terms of the criteria indigenous to African… or Asian psychologies! Such a proposition is unthinkable, though, for it is unlikely that the majority cultures would have attributed themselves the right to do so.*

Holdstock, 2000, p. 37

Holdstock raises issues that contain the essence of the debate, as have others (Howitt and Owusu-Bempah, 1990, 1994). The facts are simple. What most of us recognize as psychology has its origins in Western countries during the nineteenth century. It was developed largely in academic institutions initially in Germany, then in the United States. The professionalization of psychology came early with the foundation of bodies such as the American Psychological Association in 1892 and the British Psychological Society in 1901. Celebrations of the origins of modern psychology in Germany at the University of Leipzig in 1879 in the laboratories of Wundt continue (Holdstock, 2000). What is overlooked is that such celebrations really commemorate the gross neglect of many of the ideas of its intellectual founder by the discipline and profession of psychology that holds him in such apparent esteem. The celebration can only be of North American psychology, not what Wundt saw as a major part of the task of the discipline. According to Kim and Berry (1993), the claim that Wilhelm Wundt fathered modern psychology largely ignores the fact that his psychology had two components: a natural science versus a cultural science psychology. One component (*Naturwissenschanften*) essentially emulated the natural science model of physics, chemistry and to a lesser extent the biology of the time. However, for Wundt, this approach had only limited worth for the development of psychology. He saw the natural science model as utilizing experimentation that was useful when psychology was attempting to study the elemental or basic psychological processes involved, for example, with the individual consciousness. Nevertheless, Wundt's view was that the experimental method is of little use when studying human experience as determined by language, custom and myth: experimentation is largely useless for these aspects of human experience. The study of these would locate psychology as part of the cultural science tradition (*Geistesissenschaften*). This, he believed, would eventually dominate psychology simply because it was of greater value and importance in understanding humanity. This cultural psychology (*Volkerpsychologie*) has not dominated the history of modern psychology despite Wundt's belief (not all prophesies are fulfilled). Instead, professional psychology, as it became centred in the United States of America, followed what Wundt had seen as the lesser arm of psychology dominated by laboratory experimentation in all aspects including social and clinical areas. This phenomenon is recounted in a myriad of histories of psychology.

Usually psychology is exported to another country from the United States as a set of readymade theories and methods. The way to avert this, of course, is the creation of a psychology from within another culture, one which reflects the social realities of this other culture. Indeed, this path could be construed as merely a continuation of the traditions of psychology. Berry (1983) suggests that each society needs to develop its own blueprint for what the psychology appropriate to that society should be. After all, American psychologists took on that very task when developing a psychology fit for that culture and that industrial society.

## Psychology as a cultural science

Wundt's cultural psychology approach has some resonance in the psychology of recent years. There is a simple but core tenet of the cultural science approach to psychology which is that humanity is perpetually in a state of change and that, as a consequence, much of the knowledge about people needs to be based on theories and methods which are fundamentally antipathetic to those of the natural sciences and substantial elements of Western psychology. The search for natural laws that govern all humanity fundamentally misses the point and so is essentially futile. This is not solely because much of psychology is misdirected from the cultural sciences viewpoint, but also because some empiricist approaches to psychological understanding simply cannot cope effectively with the role of culture in human behaviour. Perhaps because of the dominance of the natural science approach, human diversity has been a troublesome theme for psychology and its institutions since the 1960s. Watts (1992) mentions the drama of the departure from the American Psychology Association by Africa-American psychologists who created the Association of Black Psychologists. They charged the American Psychological Association with failure to accommodate to the needs of Black psychologists and the Black community in general.

Cross-cultural psychology, as generally understood in psychology, is not of itself the sort of psychology which handles culture effectively. Its primary aim is to test the theories which have been developed in the West in other cultures in order to form a picture of their generalizability. Cross-cultural psychology does not involve, of necessity, the researcher to be operating within the world-view of the population in question. Using concepts derived from Pike (1966), it can be said that cross-cultural researchers may adopt an *emic* approach in which they operate from the viewpoint of an insider. Equally, the researcher may adopt an *etic* perspective in which an intellectual position from the outside world is the basic intellectual tool for developing an understanding of the culture; this outsider's perspective is usually a Western one, although not necessarily. The emphasis is on testing the cross-cultural or ecological validity of, usually, Western concepts. The search is mainly for cross-cultural universals which are presumed to be much the same in all populations. There is, then, a very real sense in which Western psychology has historically adopted an etic approach as a consequence of its emphasis on universals across cultures.

There is a developing interest in what is known as the indigenous (or cultural) psychologies approach, which has some different objectives and does not need to be comparative in the same way as cross-cultural psychology does. The core idea of indigenous psychology is: 'each culture needs to be understood from its own frame of reference and that the analysis of the historical evolution of a particular culture is fundamental to an understanding of people of that culture' (Kim and Berry, 1993, pp. 15–16).

It has to be said that within this framework there is a range of views as to the subject matter for psychology. In some cases authors concentrate on the nature of the psychological understanding which is inherent in traditional, and frequently religious, conceptions of the world. In other cases, the researchers are much more interested in the development of a psychology that will help with the implementation of national government objectives. For others, the eventual integration of indigenous psychologies using comparative methods is part of the search for the grail. Berry sees American psychology being replaced by local psychologies only if the universal goal is not pursued.

Berry (1983) explained how the cultural relativity of much of social science has been a focus for those trying to understand social science disciplines better. The conclusion often reached is that social science is culture bound and should not be applied beyond the culture which originated it. While Berry was primarily concerned about social psychology when broadly defined, one should also include most aspects of psychological practice such as therapy, educational psychology and the like by virtue of this social dimension. He sees the task of psychology as: (1) decentring the culture of psychology from Euro-American settings; (2) recentring the culture of psychology within the cultures to which it is to be applied. In addition, in the quest for a more general psychology, he recommends: (3) a move towards a universal psychology by integrating these different psychologies. Put another way, building on the emic and etic approaches, there is a need for a 'derived etic' psychology which is the integration of a number of emic psychologies in order to be applicable to a cluster of cultures or, probably unrealistically, universally. A number of writers concur with Berry's views (e.g. Marsella, 1998; Mays *et al.*, 1996). For example, Mays *et al.* (1996) stress the need for Western psychology to educate itself about the psychologies of other cultures in order to appreciate the limits of its science, practice and development.

Of course, the search for universals can only result in overarching dimensions such as individualism–collectivism. Each culture is then allocated its position on this continuum (Georgas, 1993). So, it is a universal finding that the primary source of socialization of children is the family. Furthermore, the family is the child's major source of stimulation on a day-to-day basis. Nevertheless, the family type also has profound influences on the child. The experience of a child in a nuclear family is different from that of one in an extended family, or a single-parent household or a polygamous household.

To talk of psychologies beyond the Western perspective suggests that many different psychologies are possible. Watts (1992) envisages that there may be different types of psychologies that are helpful in the endeavour to understand human diversity. These are:

1 Population-specific psychologies which currently would include the psychology of women and Black psychology;
2 Socio-political perspectives in which historical and economic issues and processes are integral, as in the psychology of oppression;
3 Cross-cultural psychology which stresses culture and intergroup and intragroup methods; and
4 Ecological psychology with its stress on the dynamic influence of specific settings.

The proliferation of numerous psychologies may be the inevitable consequence of developing the population-specific psychologies approach. There is no guarantee that any degree of integration of these would be possible, just as no one knows for certain the likely extent of the plurality of psychologies. Is there a separate psychology for each nation, for example, or is the fundamental religious philosophy of communities sufficient to unite them under one psychology? Do women in these psychologies invariably have a separate psychology? None the less, the existence and acceptance of different branches with specific disciplines and professions based on them – clinical, educational, child, occupational, forensic and so forth – are required to understand different peoples or people of different cultures. Figuratively, Watts describes the diversity as akin to the blooming of a thousand flowers.

It would be a pretence to suggest that the indigenous psychologies approach has, as yet, developed to the point that detailed accounts of the specific psychological nature of many indigenous communities are available to us. Indeed, at the present time, the literature is a little repetitive in its description and cataloguing. However, from our point of view this is less important than the role of the indigenous psychology approach in signalling to psychologists in the Western tradition the need to exercise care when dealing with peoples of other cultures either within the West or beyond. Some psychologists operating at the community level fail to recognize the cultural specificity of their ideas. Watts (1992) mentions the concepts of empowerment, coping and stressful events, which, he says, are not universals and may not be comparable in different cultures. Nevertheless, some community psychologists behave as if they were. Once again, this can be expressed in terms of Pike's (1966) differentiation of the emic and the etic in culturally based psychological work. The community psychologists are taking an inappropriate etic approach because of their imposition of knowledge from one culture onto another where it has no place. A properly emic approach would be for the community psychologists to immerse themselves in the indigenous culture. This may be through the use of participant observation in which the researcher takes the role of a member of the indigenous population or by the use of ethnography in which the researcher identifies indigenous ideas and then tries to think in their terms.

## Population-specific psychologies

Population-specific psychologies have three areas of emphasis (Watts, 1992):

1  The main elements of the culture's world-view. This enables the development of culturally appropriate community interventions: that is, the population's values are acknowledged and incorporated. In this way the existing strengths of the community form the foundation of psychology's contribution thus preventing the importation of values which may conflict.
2  The use of knowledge about culture, ethnicity and world-view to understand, predict or change behaviour.
3  The relationship between world-view, culture and oppression.

Some have recognized a grave risk in the broad indigenous psychologies approach in that, in itself, this enterprise continues to leave psychology culture bound (Kim and Berry, 1993). It is for this reason that they argue for the integration of indigenous psychologies, using comparative methods, in order to fashion a more general discipline. Indigenous psychology is valuable in its own right but is also an essential component in the development of a more universal psychology. The big difference between this perspective and previous comparative work is that the comparison is not of West with the rest of the world but between the various indigenous psychologies taken as equals. The elaboration of general principles is the desired outcome of this process. The favoured phrase among proponents of indigenous psychology is 'cross-indigenous psychology' which, they imply, can also be integrated with cross-cultural psychology. This constitutes a sort of derived etic psychology since it essentially uses both imposed etic with emic approaches. This integration is perhaps a lofty goal, and possibly inappropriate, at this stage when the resources and achievements of indigenous psychology are inevitably small in comparison with the contribution of Eurocentric psychology to Western cultures. We see matters a little differently. For us, the message of indigenous psychology is the warning not to make premature generalizations about any peoples on the basis of knowledge gained from a culture alien to it, whether it be a Western perspective or one developed outside of the West.

Indigenous psychology is built on a number of principles according to Kim and Berry (1993). In many ways these are much more useful to all psychologists no matter where they do their work than the search for universals. The key features of indigenous psychology include the following:

1 Indigenous psychology is not bound by a location outside of the West. It should *not* be construed as if it were the study of colourful peoples living in far-flung places. It is as relevant to London as the Lebanon.
2 The ecological context is essential to psychological understanding in indigenous psychology. The documentation of the ways in which people understand themselves and their environment is a primary step leading to deeper analysis of the community.
3 No perspectives of a society are inherently superior to others. The perspective of a member of the culture in question may have value, but, equally, outsiders may bring to attention matters to which the indigenous observer is oblivious.
4 Central to indigenous psychology is acceptance of the view that a plurality of different perspectives may be found in any society and that different groups within that society do not necessarily share perspectives either in their entirety or partially.
5 Indigenous psychology is method-independent and only favours methods to the extent that they contribute to and are appropriate to the particular matter under study.

6  It is appropriate for indigenous psychology to seek universals in the form of facts, principles and laws, but their existence and nature should not be taken for granted.

The task for indigenous psychology is not seen as easy by its proponents, who seem well aware of the weight placed on them by the forces of Eurocentric psychology. Kim and Berry suggest that, among other things, dominant scientific communities should exercise restraint in international work, possibly extending to retreat where appropriate. Similarly, the indigenous communities of psychologists need to eschew the personal enhancement which flows from collaboration with Western researchers and sharing in their Western spoils in the form of research funding, for example.

Roland (1997), while recognizing the possibility that there is a universal in human nature, asks us to consider what the common humanity between us all is. Does psychology emerging in the West have the capacity to deal with whatever this common humanity may be, as well as the differences so easily perceived between peoples? The search for universals among peoples risks being the search for the lowest common denominator. It may be that diversity is responsible for realizing the full potential of human nature. Some even argue that the search for universals is a peculiarly Western phenomenon rising out of the Western world-view. Hindu cultures, for example, emphasize the context rather than the core. Roland (1997) recommends relativism to psychoanalytically orientated practitioners, albeit with some reservations. Relativism, he says, involves accepting highly different conceptualizations of human nature in different cultures. Issues such as internal consistency and validity can only be addressed from within a culture, not between cultures. As a consequence there are no common concepts for evaluation, criticism and comparison between cultures. The task when comparing cultures involves the integration of Western and Eastern ideology and philosophy. This, in turn, involves the integration of the individualist Western view with the more socially and environmentally contextualized Eastern assumption. For Roland, this is a similar task to that facing feminist psychology and social constructionist approaches which are both subject to similar contextualizing pressures. He further underlines the need to develop understanding of the spiritual aspects of the self, as this area of integration transcends contextualization and the individualist views of humanity.

## Indian peoples as an illustration

One suggestion is that the psychologies of Eastern Asia are very different from those of the West (Sinha and Sinha, 1997) in that they are very ancient, spanning more than two millennia. The religious philosophies of the Hindus, Jainists, Buddhists and Caravaka in India (as well as Confucian and Tao in China and Zen Buddhism in Japan) essentially contain psychological principles. In addition, these cultures contain substantial bodies of folk knowledge and culture. Kim (1997) describes how Confucianism regards individuals as interrelated in a complex network, the prototype lying within the family. Children within families in those cultures have the expectation of being loved, being given wisdom and being treated benevolently by their parents. The children should reciprocate with obedience, respect and reverence as well as love for their parents. The parent–child relationship is much more complex than the Western view of two individual biological parents. A child's parents represent its being, its past, present and future; they represent the child's interdependent relationship with the social environment. It is this sort of extension beyond the individual self that captures much of the difference between Eastern and Western approaches.

Individualism is characteristic of Western psychology (Kim, 1997). The individual's responsibility for other people is largely limited to one's immediate family. This psychology consists of three important features: an emphasis on distinct and autonomous individuals; profound separation from family, community and religion and other relationships; abstract principles, rules and norms guide the individual in emotions, thoughts and behaviours. The individual's conception of self is discreet, autonomous and abstracted. Research suggests that these individuals have discrete boundaries demarking the self from others, self-fulfilment and freedom of choice, and a decontextualized and abstracted conception of self (Markus and Kitayama, 1991).

Collectivism is more characteristic of nations in the rest of the world: in Africa, Latin America and Asia. Collectivism involves the integration of people into communities of cohesive others which protects members on a lifelong basis subject to their loyalty. Individuals will have a conception of themselves to which terms like 'situated', 'embedded' and 'assembled' apply. These individuals are sociocentric – collective and traditional.

Just what can be said about indigenous psychologies on the basis of that which has already been observed by psychologists? The answer to this depends on the culture in question to a degree, but a good example of how different a developmental psychology would be outside of the West lies in Roland's (1988) developmental schema for the Indian self (and that of many other Asian peoples). By proposing such a scheme, Roland felt that the way psychology is stacked in favour of Western industrial self-development might be exposed. Ingrained in Indian culture, he argues, is the view that the child and its mother, because they are of the same substance, are intrinsically connected. Weaning does not occur until the child is over one or two years of age. Most of its time is spent with adults rather than in a nursery bedroom alone. Closeness with others is emphasized by the sensuous handling the children experience from adults carrying them around. In a fashion which would be anathema in Western child rearing, the child sleeps in the mother's bed whether or not alternative space is available. Last-born girl children may remain in the mother's bed until they are teenaged or married. A child is likely to progress to sleeping with other family members, child or adult. That is, togetherness as opposed to separation is a key feature of Indian families (and Japanese families too, according to Roland) The psychological ties between Indian men and their mothers follow both from the practical living arrangements as well as cultural expectations. These features of the family have been observed in Indian families living in Britain today (Hacket and Hacket, 1994).

Of course, Indian people are regarded in part as individuals, but that is not what crucially defines them. Child-rearing values emphasize that people vary widely in nature and this diversity is to be accepted. Furthermore, the development of sensitivity to the nature of relationships, their context and emotional exchanges within them, is part of the way in which a sense of the individual person is developed. Unlike, for example, Western adolescents, for whom identity development is a struggle, the 'traditional' Indian adolescent emerges from childhood to adult responsibilities largely free from these intense social and emotional conflicts. So Western conceptions of adolescence have little or no bearing on the experiences of young people or on understanding the transition into adulthood. The self that needs to develop in the Indian community primarily involves relationships and the family. This is a stage of becoming a better person due to enhancing one's qualities and inner strengths. Quite a different process is involved in becoming a distinct, autonomous individual in the Western world.

It is obvious that it is fairly easy to see how Indian child-rearing would be seen as pathological if we use the inappropriate yardsticks provided by developmental psychologists in the West. Indeed, cases have been described of how professional workers in the West may regard such developmental priorities as bad for Indian children (e.g. Howitt, 1992; Howitt and Owusu-Bempah, 1999a and b; Miatra, 1995, 1996; Owusu-Bempah, 1999c).

Similarly, Roland (1988) asserts that an American woman would be regarded as 'emotionally disturbed' if she were observed emulating the norms of Indian parenting and child development. These violate the cultural expectations of Western psychology and so are likely to be seen as pathological by Western professionals. Such a woman would appear to be failing to differentiate herself emotionally from her offspring; the child would appear to be a narcissistic extension of the woman. The expectation would be of a child growing up into a pathological adult, the offspring of a pathological mother. The task, though, for the Indian mother is to prepare her child for the family and community structure into which the child is entering. The family will be one in which there is a strong interdependence between its members. child-rearing via the Western model would be poor preparation for such a family. Western professionals risk making the error of failing to consider the psychology of the mother and the possibility that child-rearing methods apart from Western ones are both available and healthy. The Indian psychology cannot be understood without reference to its context within the Indian extended family, which itself exists within complex and hierarchical social structure (*jati*) and intergroup relationships. Nevertheless, irrespective of the importance of *jati*, the individual's primary needs of all types are satisfied within the extended family. In many cases, the family extends even beyond the members of the immediate community.

## Developing a sense of 'oneness'

In Indian cultures, as Whiting and Edwards (1988) observed, there are norms which deal with how children within the family should be treated. For example, several different families may live in a joint household which, in the West, might encourage favouritism towards one's own biological children. However, in India, a couple would be expected to treat all of the children in the household similarly. Their sons, daughters, nephews and nieces are all to be treated equally and child-care is shared as a joint enterprise. It is even known for children to be given up to childless couples within the extended family (Roland, 1997). Children are reared to think of self-regard as being built on 'we–self regard', a more extended self involving the respect for and welfare of others in the community. A child's misbehaviour at home is not so important as the consequences of such wayward behaviour on the reputation of the family.

From early childhood and for life, respect and veneration of elders and other superiors in the kinship structure is crucial. The we–self regard derives from the honour of the extended family and the community. Sons covet their father's respect and any signs of approval from them. By behaving well throughout all life stages, the positive regard they need from their father may be enhanced. Indian daughters are expected to act as carriers of both the family and the community (*jati*) culture. They regard adapting well to their in-laws' family customs as their contribution to maintaining their family honour.

For Sinha and Sinha (1997) several aspects of psychology demarcate the Eastern and Western viewpoints. They argue that Western psychology is structured around dualisms of a sort absent from Eastern thought. Among Western dualisms are those between the mind and body, the theoretical and the applied, and the subjective and objective. Perhaps the most striking of all is the West's dualism of religion versus science, which creates a conflict at many levels. While in the West we have a psychology of religion, religion and psychology are otherwise independent. Western psycholgy, originating as it did out of th science and medicine, fundamentally developed in moribund isolation from religion and philosophy for that matter.

Selfishness is essentially sanctioned by contemporary Western psychology (Wallach and Wallach, 1983). The discipline concentrates on things which form obstacles to the individual adapting to his or her environment. Having identified the obstacles, ways of defeating the obstacles are explored in order to protect the self or ego. Asian psychology has a different understanding and has as its main goal the freeing of the self (Sinha and Sinha, 1997). The quest is not to identify the self but to abandon it in the search for self-realization. Achieving control over the senses and desires frees the individual who then might achieve peace, happiness, calmness, contentment and compassion – self-realization. Traditional Asian psychology sees the problem as lying in the suffering produced by the strivings of the ego. Rid of the ego, the individual may achieve a greater sense of self-realization. Put another way, if Western psychology does its work well, it is causing harm from the perspective of traditional Asian psychology. Western psychological knowledge is regarded as being a tool for exploitation and achieving material gains. One focus of modern Western psychology is the control of people by finding ways to control their behaviour. Under this umbrella can be placed consumer psychology, industrial psychology and communications psychology. The understanding, explanation and prediction of behaviour have been the tripartite goals of this psychology's development. Sinha and Sinha (1997) identify this with Francis Bacon's view that knowledge is power. In contrast, according to the Asian tradition, knowledge is for liberation.

Western psychology dichotomizes and polarizes aspects of human experience. We speak of 'man' and society, or 'man' in nature or 'man' and the environment. The alternative is to regard each part of these dichotomies as inseparable from the other – a symbiotic relationship of mutual interdependence. Rather than speaking of 'man' and society, the eastern concept is of 'man–society'. In the two traditions the notion of a fully functioning or competent person differs. The Western view is that the competent person obtains, exercises and utilizes control over resources, including other human beings. The Eastern view is that competence is the ability or capability of developing and retaining a satisfactory and peaceful relationship with the environment, which includes the social, the physical and the spiritual.

In Sinha and Sinha's view, Eastern psychology and Western psychology differ in terms of their contents , allowing the possibility of a fusion to supply to each what the other lacks. Thus many Western theories stress individual achievement, the scientific method and rational evidence, whereas traditional Asian psychologies are concerned with corporate welfare, the evidence of experience, intuition and religious/ philosophical methods.

There appears to be profound differences in the way that different cultures regard the fair distribution of resources including rewards. The Western psychology of justice differentiates distributive justice, as these procedures are called, from procedural justice, which is about the fairness of the procedures followed in the process of distribution. Krishnan (1997) describes the traditional Hindu view of justice in India as requiring outcomes to be dependent on the individual's actions. Doing good things should result in positive outcomes and doing wrong should result in negative outcomes. Justice requires these outcomes and if they do not emerge then injustice is perceived. The outcomes of rewards or punishment may not always be immediate, in fact may not even occur until the next life. Research has shown that Indian peoples are more inclined to regard a person's need as the determinant of whether they should be financially rewarded or punished financially (Murphy-Berman *et al.*, 1984). American participants in the research tended to regard equality in the distribution of rewards and so forth as the crucial criterion, while the Indian participants tended to apply the principle of equity. Collectivism in Indian culture would seem to explain these findings.

Page and Berkow (1991) and Rosemont (1997) regard the concept of self in Eastern psychology as having crucial points of difference from Western conceptions despite some overlaps. In Buddhism, personal growth and self-examination are intertwined. Self-esteem and self-efficiency are part of the aims of modern psychotherapy. They are achieved through increased understanding of the self. Page and Berkow suggest that this understanding could be enhanced by the study of how Eastern cultures have regarded the self. In Buddhism, the self ends when there is a change in identity. When the individual has reached a view of self which involves the totality of reality as it can be experienced, then identity is not over but changed from the previous identity which, being detached from reality, is delusional or a partial experience of reality. The constructed self in Buddhism is an imaginary thing, based on a wish to have a sense of permanence in a changing reality.

Both Eastern and Western psychologies and philosophies involve attempts to identify the nature of the self. Allen (1997) argues that traditional philosophy holds that the self is objective, universal and authentic. Both philosophical perspectives are forced to regard the self as historically and culturally constituted. These are distortions of the true self and are therefore subjective or illusory. According to Allen, the majority of modern Western concepts of self have their roots in Descartes' writing. The Cartesian approach to self includes the following features:

1  The mind is a separate, individual self which can be known in isolation, independent of other human beings.

2 Knowledge of the essential self (which is regarded as a separate think-ing entity) comes from observation and analysis. We do not create our selves, and the self is not historically and culturally determined.

3 The mind – the thinking thing (*res cognitant*) – can be more aware of the reality of itself than the reality of anything else. Consequently, knowledge of one's self as a separate, distinct being is the starting point of the philosophy.

4 The mind's existence or knowledge of the mind is not dependent on or related to the existence of the body. Thus there is a separation of the mind from the body in this philosophy.

This view of the self as distinct and primary is common in Western philosophies. Allen argues that Hobbes' and Locke's influence can be seen in the concept of isolated and insular individuals, fragmented souls who come together in some form of social contract to form the basis of the state. We in the West are then indoctrinated with a view of ourselves as separate from the community and the environment. We are encouraged to see success in terms of an individual rather than a collective achievement, epitomized by conspicuous consumption and material possessions. We regard these things as natural and objective and with universal applicability. We fail to see the cultural and histori-cal basis of our view and its limited applicability. Allen (1997) sees this as the basis of the way in which Westerners have regarded other cultures. Other cultures were devalued because they lacked a concept of self as separate, autonomous, independent. Allen argues that the Western conception of self 'serves neo-colonial and imperial goals of domination'. (p. 9)

As we have seen, the Western sense of self is seen as an inadequate state in other philosophies. Hinduism sees the concepts characterizing the Western view of self as actually referring to false or illusory entities. Spiritual liberation follows from liberating oneself from the sort of self that the Westerner sees as core of his or her being. In Buddhism, the concept of the separate self is illusory and results in our construing the world in a way which leads and intensifies our consequent suffering. Liberation requires going beyond the self or its illusion. The selfish self is characterized by issues such as pride, conceit and egoism and matters of 'me and mine'. It is not merely unfortunate and immature but produces the troubles of the world at all levels.

Indian people can therefore be seen as having to develop in a social context which is more a totality than that required in the West (Kakar, 1978; 1979). They lack the individualistic orientation that serves as the overriding goal in Western conceptions of development. This means that they are interdependent and interreliant on each other. Their think-ing does not involve the abstract and decontextualized form that is required by the individualist model. This can be misinterpreted, from the Western psychoanalytic viewpoint, according to Roland (1997), as evidence of their lack of full superego development. Their ethical norms are dependent on the context of interrelationships rather than fixed, abstract rules. The demarcation between oneself and another is weaker than expected in the Western ideal. Since psychoanalytic approaches to personality are based on studies of Westerners, it is not surprising that classic theories, such as that of Freud, are founded on the bedrock of individualism and universalism. This is not to neglect approaches such as those of Erikson, which involved the study of culture in the framework of psychological development. Psychoanalysis, for many Westerners, irrespective of its current status within professional psychology, consists of a description of 'healthy' psychological development; with the warning that if this is not followed, psychopathology will result. Furthermore it is claimed to be a universal so that people from cultures not following the universal ideal risk being regarded as inferior.

This description of Indian peoples is clearly about existence in traditional as opposed to modern industrial cultures. It nevertheless captures something of the spirit of Indian peoples living in modern industrial cities. However, it is important to note the tendency of writers to idealize the traditional as reflecting a somewhat superior and more 'natural' state. For example, Allen (1997) expresses this sentiment aptly:

> For those of us in the modern, technological, industrialised West, complex nonoppressive encounters with other concepts of self can reveal new worlds of meaning: new ways of freeing our imaginations and of being more in touch with our emotions; of experiencing nature and the cosmos; of relating to death, time, and history; of understanding and creating our own selves and our relations to others
>
> Allen, 1997, p. 21

As a result, our basic problem is made more difficult since we need to understand indigenous psychologies of both traditional and modern cultures.

## More problems

As we have stressed, Western psychologists should regard the issue of indigenous psychologies as not merely being an issue of the Western world versus the rest of the world. Such a dichotomy would be culpably ignorant of the nature of culture and community in the West. One can sympathize with Gergen *et al.*'s (1996) view that much of Western psychology is worthless when faced with the needs and problems of vast numbers of people throughout the world. Psychology, to them, is merely the ethnopsychology of the industrialized West and mostly of the White middle classes and men specifically. They claim that culturally sensitive research into health, ethnic and religious conflict and the consequences of technological change is profitable but in short supply. Above all it is crucial to the agenda. However, this is essentially to ignore the day-to-day work of the personnel employed in psychology and related professions within the confines of the West where the issue of the Western ethnopsychology's relevance to many communities and cultures within Western boundaries is in doubt. Just how fit Western trained psychologists employing such a limited ethnopsychology are to deal with the many indigenous cultures with which they come into contact is problematic.

For example, that there is good reason to accept the view that what most of us have been trained to regard as a universalistic psychology is perhaps best regarded as a specific United States ethnopsychology. Consequently, it might be asked just how well even this view can cope with populations within the geographical boundaries of the USA. The 'melting-pot' that historically underlies American culture contains peoples of diverse cultural origins whose needs might be presumed to be of great importance if the value of such diversity is recognized by the Western ethnopsychology. In particular, we may question this particular ethnopsychology's ability to help psychological researchers and practitioners when involved professionally with Native American peoples – American Indians in the old terminology. For Timble and Medicine (1993) the answer is that this psychological knowledge is ineffectual and ineffective when applied to Native Americans. Part of the reason is that many different peoples and cultures are subsumed in the category of 'Native American people' and they do not share unifying concepts that would provide understanding of their minds. Using mainstream ethnopsychology will only produce flawed knowledge. Conceiving or treating such peoples as a homogenous group will obstruct understanding since this involves recognition of their complex diversity. Treating diverse peoples as one has its historical roots in how European colonists over the centuries treated all aboriginal peoples as if they could be understood in the same way – as if they possessed a single mind. Although it is not possible to compare effectively the values of all Native American peoples with those whom mainstream ethnopsychology has studied so intensively, it is possible to do so for those of North and South Dakota:

1 Mainstream psychology studies people who are strongly future-orientated in terms of what it will bring and the need to plan for the future. In contrast the native peoples of Dakota are orientated primarily to the present.
2 Mainstream psychology's subject matter is people for who time is a crucial dimension and for whom punctuality is highly valued. Time, for the peoples of Dakota, is not constrained in this way – time will always be available to get things done even if this is not immediate.

3 Mainstream psychology's subject matter is people who value them-selves in terms of material possessions and their material achievements. The native people of the Dakotas regard giving rather than possessing as the basis of status. Accumulation of possessions is for the purpose of giving.

4 Mainstream psychology's subject matter is people who value youth primarily. The Native Americans of the Dakota's culture respect older people for their knowledge of the world and of people.

5 Mainstream psychology's subject matter is people who value competition as a means to progress as well as being part of a culture which attempts to control and conquer. The Native Americans of the Dakotas see co-operation and conformity as vital parts of interactions with others. They seek harmony with the world of nature of which they are part and do not need to control and conquer it.

Other Native American groups would not necessarily be the same. For example, Pueblos would demonstrate traits such as submissiveness, humility and anonymity (Zint, 1963).

On the assumption that psychological practitioners and researchers wish to extend their practice beyond their own cultures, it is inevitable that most new contacts will raise difficulties of interpretation and understanding for which psychologists simply have not been prepared in general. It is clearly better to recognize the complexities rather than simply deny them and process these interactions through conventional Western models of psychology. While this recognition is better, what does it necessarily offer by way of solutions? The following are some of the dilemmas facing clinicians attempting to deal with situations involving people from cultures other than their own:

*How do we understand the inner world of a Japanese woman who silently waits for her therapist to intuit all that she feels?*

*How do we evaluate the impulse management of an anxious, encopretic immigrant boy from the Caribbean, whose early toilet training did not include indoor toilets? Would the vicissitudes of anal cathexes and its implications for character formation as delineated by the Freudian drive position apply for a child who was not reared in the bathroom habits of Western culture?*

*And how do we figure out the deep self-experience of a Middle Eastern man from a religious sect, who feels that without the tribe he was trained to lead, his self-esteem is unformed, non-existent? Do we view this client through the American self-psychological terms of a narcissistically derailed self, through the Ego Psychology lens of a poorly differentiated self? Or rather, as a person centred in the ensemble self-experience of his Eastern culture; where bonding to family and group kinship render individuals who throughout life are deeply identified with others?*

Foster, 1998, pp. 259–60

Being able to deal with these issues needs a different approach to psychology in which practitioners are able to incorporate detailed and specific cultural knowledge into their work (Shiang *et al.*, 1998). This would contribute to the effective provision of services for people of cultural origins beyond the West wherever they were living. It is a responsibility of practitioners to engage with clients regarding the matter of culture and the associated beliefs affecting the client (Shiang *et al.*, 1998). The issues are simple enough at the basic level. Just how do beliefs held by members of the cultural group relate to their problems? Are those beliefs typical or normative for the cultural group or would they be seen as diverging from the normal within that culture? In this way, the practitioner would understand better how cultural beliefs and expectations lead to specific cultural practices and how those specific cultural practices are maintained and reinforced. This is a matter of therapeutic competence rather than something which is merely useful or desirable in the work of practitioners: 'Only after these types of assessment are completed would the clinician be competent to consider treatment issues'(Shiang *et al.*, 1998, p. 183).

Systematic and integrated research is needed to assess cultural beliefs and behaviours among a wide variety of client groups. This might lead to understanding of the role of culture in the life experiences which eventually result in a client's coming to the attention of the practitioner. Equally important, such knowledge would help rid psychological practice of its fundamentally Eurocentric perspective on clients of psychological services. This emphasis on culture is again not an emphasis on the exotic but potentially of benefit to client groups of diverse cultural, class and religious backgrounds.

# Chapter 3

# The familiar stranger in psychological practice

*We have seen a growth of interest, curiosity and research on the black family. A new 'blame the victim' form of explanation has taken hold of the black family as the primary locus of social pathology, the cycle of depriva- tion and the culture of poverty*

Mercer, 1984, p. 25

Psychologists who accept the need for their work to cope with cultural diversity are critical of the ethnocentrism (Eurocentrism), individual- ism and the contextual naivety of much of their chosen discipline (e.g. Kagitcibasi, 1984). This is not merely a criticism of Western psychology, but the dependence of psychologists from the economically growing regions of the world on Western psychology for inspiration. This has many facets including the devaluation of applied psychology in favour of pure science, which, in its turn, has the function of decontextualizing, and universalizing psychology. The net result is the dispersal of work to develop indigenous psychology among the more traditional enter- prises of psychology. Generally speaking, the study of the socialization of children in Western psychology is child focused. It may seem to be a commensensical approach, but that is a danger since it results in an underplaying of research which attempts to study psychosocial devel- opment in a broader context in terms of child–family–community– society. Even within that psychology there is a concentration on the socialization of children from the more advantaged families. As we saw in the Chapter 2, it is largely meaningless to study children of diverse national and cultural origins as if they were part of a small and separate unit of biological parents and their offspring. Children in traditional families in many parts of the world are reared as part of a much wider community in such a way that the community as a whole substantially determines their values and views. Such arrangements, even after migration to new cultures, may continue to apply albeit sometimes in modified forms. An individualist and child-focused psychology can only cope poorly with these community and ecological aspects of tradi- tional child-rearing. One large study (Kagitcibasi, 1984) explored the qualities which parents in a variety of countries preferred in their children. Issues to do with the autonomy of the child were mentioned very commonly in the different countries. This does not, however, mean that parents shared identical desires in this respect. Westerners in the United States valued independence very positively but generally valued obedience to parents fairly poorly. In contrast, parents in Indonesia, Thailand, the Philippines and Turkey valued obedience to parents very positively whereas self-reliance was generally given a low value. Modernization and the capitalist economy seems to change the pattern since countries like Korea and Singapore, experiencing rapid and major economic growth, were more like the West in valuing independence positively.

Considerations such as these renew the questions emanating from any attempt to apply psychology to cultures from beyond the West (Kagitcibasi, 1984). The question of relevance raises further issues. For example:

1  Can Western psychology study non-Western child-rearing without addressing the issue of autonomy directly?
2  Will Western psychology see traditional socialization in other cultures in ways that judge it as somehow pathological errant, or inadequate?
3  What conceptual tools do psychologists have to deal with traditional communities and their child-rearing practices?

The answers to these questions and similar matters are already available. Psychology, along with related disciplines, has a bad record in terms of judging indigenous families within the West. The family must be seen as the central unit of any culture. No cultures exist which do not have families although their structure varies radically across societies and, to a lesser extent, within a given culture. So the way in which Western psychology addresses the issue of families is testament to the way it deals with more general issues to do with culture. The fears raised by those committed to the indigenous psychologies approach are seen as realized within Western geographic boundaries without stretching beyond. This is especially evident in the way professionals perceive and treat ethnic minority families in Western societies.

## The webs of 'dysfunction'

Ideological affronts to ethnic minorities have a long history (Howitt and Owusu-Bempah, 1994). Social policy has been deployed in ways which concretize this unrelenting assault. Key social policy issues are usually fixed in public concern by seminal events which not only focus attention but also define matters as a social problem (Howitt, 1992). For example, the intensification of 'concern' about Black families in the

Western world arose from the publication of a report commissioned by the US government in the 1960s. The report (Moynihan, 1965) typified Black single-parent families in ways which begged the phrase 'a tangle of pathology'. In other words, the problem with Black people lay not so much in their genetic inferiority, as much professional racism had previously held (Howitt and Owusu-Bempah, 1994), but in their family structure – the keystone of any culture. The report held the nature, structure and dynamics of Black families to be at fault. Notwithstanding the numerous criticisms of the idea that Black families are pathogenic (e.g., Littlejohn-Blake and Darling, 1993; Ryan, 1976), the 'tangle of pathology' notion has continued to dominate studies and accounts of Black family life. It has enabled politicians and the media, professionals and academics, and members of the general public to construe Black families as dysfunctional. Racially biased interpretation has become a 'truth' to be discussed as, literally, a matter-of-fact. Black families and their children are construed as a problem in all important spheres – psychologically, socially, morally, educationally, culturally and economically.

A classic example of the objectification of the 'tangle of pathology' notion and its influence on professional thinking and practice in Britain and other Western nations is to be found in the work of the paediatrician, Lobo, himself of Indian origin. His interpretation of child-rearing practices in African-Caribbean families incorporates a sequence of assumptions which are nothing short of damaging:

> *The curiously cold and unmotherly relationship between many West Indian mothers and their children has been noticed by observers in Jamaica and in London...The child is not cuddled and fussed over by the mother. There is a distinct lack of warm, intimate, continuous relationship between the children and their mothers from which both would get satisfaction and enjoyment. There is also no tradition of the West Indian mother playing with her young child as a toddler and pre-school child and giving him or her undivided attention for regular periods during the day.*

Lobo, 1978, p. 36.

No empirical evidence was deemed necessary to support such serious claims about African-Caribbean child-rearing practices. They are presented as social facts despite their being based, at best, on hearsay or anecdotes. This, apparently, warranted further unsubstantiated, damaging assertions: 'these poor child-rearing practices are known to be able to cripple a child's development' (p. 37).

He goes on to provide professional childcare workers with the *coup de grâce* for the African-Caribbean family, but ties it with a seemingly 'understanding' position which holds the problem to be a perennial legacy of slavery times: 'The father in the West Indian culture is not the central, stable, providing person that he is in the Asian or European cultures. The loss of African child-rearing practices and their inadequate replacement by European practices are ascribed by most observers to the destructive effect of slavery' (p. 37).

Contained within this passage is a clear stereotype of the irresponsible, absent or missing African-Caribbean father or, where present, who spends his welfare money on booze, drugs and gambling, while the best his neglected children can hope for is not to be beaten or abused in other ways. Furthermore, African-Caribbean mothers are held not to meet the standards of their European and Asian counterparts. Lobo's view is that the effects of the paucity of African-Caribbean mothering skills, and the African-Caribbean family as a whole, warrants only one comparison: 'Some of the "maternal deprivation" effects of the West Indian child *living at home* is matched only by other children brought up in old-fashioned orphanage-institutions' (p. 37, emphasis added).

In the 1970s and 1980s, this comparison would have hit a nerve. At the time, childcare professionals were increasingly anxious to deinstitutionalize the care of children. Also concerns about the problems of inner-city living had encouraged initiatives to provide enriched learning environments for pre-school children. Not only this, simple mother–infant physical contact like that deemed important between even monkey mother and child (Harlow and Harlow, 1969), and continuity in mothering, deemed vital by the then influential psychiatrist Bowlby (1944; 1951), are missing in the African-Caribbean family, according to Lobo's account. The consequences of such deprivation for the child's well-being were (and still are) believed to be detrimental: 'When deprived of maternal care, the child's development is almost always retarded – physically, intellectually and socially – and that symptoms of physical and mental ill-health may appear' (Bowlby, 1951; p. 15).

Thus, at the time, it would have been impossible to imagine a much worse environment for a child than Lobo's portrait of African-Caribbean families. It is impossible to assess the extent to which this picture of the African-Caribbean family has influenced childcare professionals – health visitors, teachers, social workers, school psychologists, child psychiatrists and therapists. One shudders to think how historically it has affected the interactions of professionals with the Black community, and their decisions concerning African-Caribbean children and their families. (We have seen already that racially biased beliefs still affect childcare decisions, and will see evidence of the differential childcare placement decisions for Black children). Could the sentiments so clearly enunciated by Lobo be responsible for the often-reported over-representation of Black children in the childcare system and their exclusion in schools? Similarly, what have been the effects of such beliefs among, for example, teachers on the relationships between them and their Black pupils, and on the pupils' consequent academic performance?

# Justifying a myth

According to Moynihan (1965), the 'pathology' of the Black family orig-inated in slavery times when family disintegration, forced by slavery, became webbed into Black family structure and continued into the modern period. Professionals have continued to reproduce this argu-ment, as we saw in Lobo's comments. Professionals in training are particularly prone to such interpretations (Figueroa, 1991; Owusu-Bempah, 1994a; Richards, 1995). There are other consequences of such victim-blaming stances, besides their tendency to make superficially less necessary explanations based on racial discrimination in health care, employment, housing and education. By blaming the Black family for the structural problems experienced by their children, the impact of the abuse that Black children are subject to in the street, school play ground or the classroom is minimized; their home background, held to be appalling, overwhelms other considerations. This may partly explain why much racism against Black children is ignored, or played down by teachers and other child care workers (e.g., CRE, 1987a and b; 1995). Assertions of Black family pathology also convey the message that there is little, if anything, teachers, psychologists and social workers, for example, can do to improve the lot of African-Caribbean children.

As we have seen, sometimes the specificity of racial claims creates the illusion that they reflect reality, albeit crudely. While the focus so far has been on African-Caribbean families, other racial groups in other circumstances can be singled out. Each of us has an everyday knowl-edge of, if not belief in, racial stereotypes (Devine, 1989; Howitt and Owusu-Bempah, 1994). Within that repertory we will find different constellations of stereotypes associated with different racial groups. We know that the stereotype of African-Caribbean children, for example, is that they are boisterous and uncontrollable in class, whereas the stereo-type of South Asian children is that they are well disciplined – if anything, over controlled (Howitt, 1992; Owusu-Bempah, 1999c). The irony is that in situations where South Asian children form the predom-inant ethnic minority (i.e. in the absence of African-Caribbean children), we find applied to them those stereotypes associated with African-Caribbean children (Ogilvy *et al.*, 1990)

The influence of the 'Black family pathology' thesis on the race thinking of professionals involved with Black children is too complex to trace completely. Nevertheless, there are numerous examples of its direct and indirect influence from research built on its assumptions. It has been argued that textbooks often serve to provide ideologically based beliefs or ideas unfounded on 'fact' for trainee professionals. Examples of these have been provided showing how textbooks deal with a number of controversial areas (Howitt, 1991; Howitt and Owusu-Bempah, 1994; Owusu-Bempah and Howitt, 1994). A further example involving nursery children is an influential textbook for nursery nurses (Brian and Martin, 1983). Its authors, a teacher and a health visitor, discuss Black children, specifically, under the heading 'children with special needs'. They discuss the following categories of children under the same heading: premature babies; children with handicaps (whom they define as children 'whose development is impaired by disease or injury', p. 232); deprived and disadvantaged children; materially, environmentally and socially deprived children; and intellectually, culturally and educationally deprived and disadvantaged children.

The authors resort to myths about African-Caribbean families when recommending ways of 'helping' their children. They draw special attention to: (a) the 'problems' of a lack of educational encouragement at home; and (b) disciplinary problems presented by African-Caribbean children as a consequence of their upbringing. Regarding educational encouragement, they write: '[West Indian] Children may need special guidance in handling and caring for play materials or books, as these are often lacking in their homes' (p. 246). When dealing with problems of discipline, Brian and Martin again use stereotypes concerning the children's 'lack of self-control' and 'sense of rhythm':

> *They find a great deal of choice bewildering, as they are not encouraged to be self-regulating at home. Strict discipline and sometimes corporal punishment at home can mean that softly spoken restraints and explanations about behaviour limitations go unheeded at nursery; perhaps the children even regard the adults as 'soft' or weak...Their responsiveness to music makes it almost impossible for them to remain still when music is being played.*
>
> pp. 246–7

Contrast this with the textbook's account of Chinese families and their children:

> *Young Chinese children may be involved in the family business if there is one, because this is their culture – that* all *contribute to the family income. If the business is catering, hours may not be compatible with ideal children's bedtimes, and in the nursery hours the children may appear fatigued... Children are encouraged in the home to be docile and hard-working. Education is rated very highly. The children are often* intelligent *and learn quickly. They are usually quiet and extremely polite and well-behaved.*
>
> (p. 247, emphasis in the original)

The sympathetic understanding communicated to readers about the circumstances of Chinese families contrasts markedly with the way in which African-Caribbean families are blamed for their children's upbringing and 'inferior intellectual make-up', 'emotionality' and 'lack of discipline'. That Chinese children of nursery age supposedly 'contribute to the family income' seems to raise no concern for the authors.

It would be dangerous to dismiss this kind of material as history. In Chapter 5 we provide further evidence of the underlying influence of the Moynihan report. Racist assumptions are endemic in White European cultures. At the very least, such textbook pronouncements do nothing to counter the racist attitudes, assumptions and stereotypes of the readers. Worse still, they may well cultivate and reinforce ideas hostile to the well-being of Black children in the minds of students and practitioners dealing with Black children. We have documented further examples of such hostile views of Africans and other peoples being reproduced in textbooks in edition after edition over decades (Howitt and Owusu-Bempah, 1994; Owusu-Bempah and Howitt, 1994; 1995).

As a result of the proliferation of such works – writings and research – psychologists, social workers, teachers, health workers and other professionals working with Black children can readily find 'evidence' to support the view that these youngsters and their families are a problem, and treat them accordingly. That is, it seems largely uncontroversial that Black children are disproportionately associated with problems, be they educational, social or behavioural. Professionals and the institutions they represent tend to ignore the structural problems facing these children and their families. Instead, they find it more convenient to seek the causes of their difficulties in their culture, especially their family structure. This is more evidence that the image of Black youngsters as 'problem youngsters' is ingrained in folk stereotypes of Black families and Black communities. Common notions that the lives of Black people are pathological in significant ways are reinforced, in part, by claims made by the academic community and orchestrated through politicized attacks on Black people, their families and their communities. The twinning of Black people with pathology takes a multiplicity of self-reinforcing forms. For example, the idea that African-Caribbean families are 'fatherless' and that the children are consequently damaged by the father's desertion is a common one (e.g. Coleman, 1994; Russell, 1994; Schoenfeld, 1988).

As we have seen, the major impetus for the belief in the degeneracy of the Black family came from the USA. However, without further investigations, the Moynihan report was readily seized upon elsewhere, including Britain, by the academic community, politicians and professionals, and presented as applicable to Black families almost globally. It is not surprising, then, that the patterns of treatment of Black children by British professionals, especially social workers and teachers, appear remarkably consistent between Britain and the USA. In the childcare system within social work, for example, research suggests that, compared to White children, Black children in the USA and elsewhere who enter the childcare system spend rather more time in care, are moved about to more foster families and are less likely to be adopted (e.g. Barth, 1997; Courney *et al.*, 1996; Longres and Torrecilha, 1992).

Contrasting these findings with those of a number of studies carried out in the United Kingdom reveals disturbing similarities. One early study (Batta *et al.*, 1975) suggested that children of 'mixed-race' parentage especially were at least eight times more likely to be admitted into care than native White or African-Caribbean or Asian children. Follow-up studies a few years later found once again that these children entered care more often; that their average age of entry was younger; and they spent longer periods in care (Batta and Mawby, 1981). Barn (1990; 1993) reviewed studies of Black children entering local authority care. Barn's studies indicate that Black children are disproportionately more likely to be admitted into local authority care than their White counterparts. This trend does not seem to have improved since the 1970s (Barn, 1993; Bebbington and Miles, 1989; Dean, 1993). In short, Black children typically spend more time in care than White children do. Furthermore, they enter the care system much more quickly – Black children are about twice as likely to be admitted into care in the four weeks following referral to an agency (Barn, 1990; 1993). This pattern has also been observed in New Zealand. For example, Hamill (1996) has noted Maori people's expressed concerns about New Zealand Social Services. These concerns include: (1) the disproportionately high numbers of Maori children in care; and (2) the heavy over-representation of Maori families on social work case loads.

As we will see in more detail later, research indicates that Black children enter care for different reasons from those for White youngsters. Such evidence suggests also that Black families, especially African-Caribbean families, are more likely to voluntarily place their children into care because of monetary problems or because of difficulties in family relationships. Contrary to popular myth (e.g. Brian and Martin, 1983; Lobo, 1978), Black children are less likely to be admitted into care because of abuse (including parental neglect) or delinquency. The point of this is that head-count evidence suggests that the offspring of Black families are over-represented in the care system. This is seen by many as a confirmation of the popular belief that Black families have problems which require the help of White professionals. We all tend to believe this because it has been drummed into us unrelentingly via the literature, the media and political propaganda. Father absence, single-parent mothers, working mothers, matriarchal family structures, divorce, lackadaisical discipline and so forth are believed to typify the Black family. The list of myths is long. Of course, this is the stereotype of African-American (in the USA) and African-Caribbean (in the UK) families. The list for Asian families is equally long, including patriarchy and oppressive over-protection of their children.

It is easy for racist beliefs to masquerade as facts in a racist world. Take, for example, the argument of the psychiatrist Schoenfeld (1988).

Like Moynihan (1965), Schoenfeld attempted to explain the high rates of Black men in US violent crime statistics in terms of a lack of a proper family structure emanating back in 'slavery times': 'Yet if, as has been stressed, the fathers of black slave families were often unrecognized or absent, the consciences of their sons would have been, to such an extent, seriously incomplete' (p. 276).

Such writings are pervaded by the belief that the slave family is the archetypal Black family with father absence rife. In this we have a perverse (but eagerly accepted) explanation as to why relatively more young Black men in Britain, especially those of African-Caribbean origin, are arrested by the police (e.g. Landau and Nathan, 1983; Macpherson, 1999; NACRO, 1986; Scarman, 1981). This 'explanation' amounts to the claim that young Black men lack a conscience due to father absence mixed with a pseudo-historical explanation based on slavery. Such an explanation effectively leaves the matter as a failure on the part of Black families. This becomes clear when Schoenfeld adds: 'Little wonder, therefore, that poorly educated and unemployed blacks brought up in fatherless homes in the squalor of urban slums commit so many violent crimes' (Schoenfeld, 1988, p. 291).

To cure this social malaise, to subdue these 'violent criminals', Schoenfeld prescribes that: 'we must... make sure that violent criminals are apprehended and punished... it is the *sine qua non* of helping blacks cope with the fires that rage within them as a result of more than 300 years of physical and psychological abuse' (p. 297).

In other words, a punitive regime to deal with Black youngsters is demanded by their historical and family circumstances – to quell the fire that has been raging within them over the centuries, beset by physical and psychological abuse, Black youngsters must be subjected to more abuse! This sets the scene for the treatment of Black youths and children by professionals such as the police, magistrates, social workers, teachers and therapists. It is not dissimilar to that set by such writers and professionals and practitioners as Brian and Martin (1983).

The crudity of Schoenfeld's argument is plain to see. It is little more than an assertion masquerading as something substantial. Others have propagated the same kind of message but couched in less explicit language. The pseudo-scientific aura surrounding such assertions makes it difficult to see it for what it is – racism. Thus even those whom one would expect to be sensitive to such forms of racism often reproduce it in different versions. For example, Coleman (1994), a Black female practising psychologist, provides a variant of the Black family pathology thesis in which parenting skills are harmed by slavery and parental migration. She argues that emigrant parents from the Caribbean temporarily left their children with grandparents. According to her, this engendered resentment and alienation in the children towards their mothers in particular. She particularly stresses the adverse inter-generational effects of this form of parental 'neglect' on the children: 'This, in turn, may inhibit healthy parenting on the part of the mother to her own child. A pattern of ambivalent and inconsistent parenting can therefore be established' (p. 5).

The basis of this assertion is uncertain. Also noteworthy is the exclusion of the father in Coleman's account; like other writers (e.g. Lobo, 1978), Coleman appears to regard it as taken-for-granted that he will be absent. She adds a further chapter to the Black family pathology thesis by highlighting informal adoption as yet another means of undermining Black children's psychological integrity, their self-concept. By combining little knowledge of history with psychoanalytic or psychodynamic concepts, Coleman, like those discussed above, produces a cocktail of ideas inimical to the well-being of Black children and their families:

It is important to recognize that society's endemic racism, often reinforced by psychological ideas and 'research', provides a fertile bed-rock on which racist assumptions, damaging to proper professional practice with Black children of African descent in particular, can flourish. There is a relatively simple set of myths about Black families, which essentially start with the archetypal beliefs about the rampant and prodigious sexuality of Black men especially (Sue, 1998), and end with a view of Black families which detracts from their well-being. Claims about Black people's sexuality date back centuries, but boil down to Black men, especially those of African ancestry, being indefatigable studs with gigantic genitals. Few, if any, of us are unaware of this culturally endemic legend, if only since it has been the butt of endless jokes and ribald comments. The net effect is to portray Black people, men and women, as genital animals (Bennett, 1990; Katz, 1996), as opposed to cerebral and cultural human beings. Bennett (1990) identified a number of different myths about African-American families, many of which are founded on this familiar racial stereotype. For Bennett, these myths amount to a 'vast propaganda campaign against the black family' (p. 168) and include the following:

1  Black family problems arise from Black people's naked and unbridled sexuality;
2  Black people are morally 'loose';
3  Black people lack a tradition of family life which provides moral standards and models of stable sexual relationships;
4  Slavery destroyed Black family bonds;
5  The emancipation of slaves led to the destruction of the Black family;
6  The migration from the South in the USA following the end of slavery and industrialization destroyed the Black family;
7  The dysfunctional structure of Black families is the consequence of the welfare dependency culture consequent on White paternalism;
8  Black families have traditionally been matriarchal and dominated by strong women; Black men are weak and absent from this matriarchal family structure;

9 Black men are unreliable sexual partners; and
10 Black women make uncaring mothers prone to 'fussing and fighting'.

Many of these myths run through the works we have reviewed above.

## Other perspectives

There are, of course, other perspectives to the understanding of Black families in predominantly White societies and the difficulties facing them. The structural-functional model is one such perspective. This model regards the structures of Black families as a means of dealing with oppressive social forces. It sees the involvement of the extended family as a means of surviving in adversity (e.g. Hill, 1972; Hylton, 1997; Littlejohn-Blake and Darling, 1993; McAdoo, 1988;). The 'emergent model' (McKenry and Fine, 1993) regards Black families as possessing positive and adaptive features. Unlike the 'problem perspective', this approach ascribes the positive and adaptive features of African-Caribbean or African-American families more to African elements of their culture interacting with the European dominant culture of the Western world.

Some of the positive features of the extended family structure common to Black and other ethnic minority families in Western societies are demonstrated by McKenry and Fine's (1993) study of the consequences of divorce on Black and White single-parents in the USA. They took a large sample of divorced women, each of whom was the custodial parent of at least one child under 18 years of age. The sample reflected US national trends in that the Black and White women were similar, except for the following variables: (1) income, (2) educational levels and (3) numbers of children. The lower ends of these factors were associated with the Black women. In reporting their findings, the researchers made appropriate adjustments for the social and economic status of the sample, and the amount of time which had passed since separation. Overwhelmingly, it was difficult to differentiate the self-reported parenting behaviours of the two 'racial' groups, for example: (1) physical punishment, hugs, shouting, praise and the children's involvement in setting household rules were much the same irrespective of race; (2) the amount of time spent by the parent with the child, in terms of leisure activities, playing together and helping with reading or homework, did not differ by race either. None-the-less, the following differences emerged. The Black single-mothers had higher expectations of their children on matters like controlling one's temper and obedience to the mother's requests. The Black single-mothers also believed that their children were having a higher quality of life than the White mothers did. Such research findings as these objectively question the mythology surrounding 'Black family pathology' – 'inadequate' and 'pathologizing' Black child-rearing practices that continue to be propagated by politicians and psychologists alike. That this is not generally acknowledged may be due, at least partly, to the fact that much research, including psychological research, on Black people is largely guided by racist ideology.

Still in the USA, Littlejohn-Blake and Darling (1993) reviewed studies concerning the strengths of the Black-American family. They suggest, among other things, that:

1 There is a religious and spiritual commitment in some Black families which provides a purpose and orientation in life and faith that things will improve.
2 Black families are more capable of absorbing other people into the household; this is one of the mechanisms by which economic and moral assistance can be provided. Informal adoption may provide a community social service in times of difficulty or in difficult circumstances; the informal network provides strength, stability and guidance within the community.
3 Black parents are ambitious for the economic and educational advancement of their children.
4 Children in Black families develop pride and a strong sense of self- or personal identity including self-esteem as well as ethnic awareness.

An important British study (Hylton, 1997) describes similar findings. The study, carried out on the behalf of the Joseph Rowntree Foundation, suggests that ethnic minority families who uphold collectivist values cope better with most social and personal problems. The study reported also that ethnic minority families preferred solving problems for themselves to voluntary or statutory solutions. It also found that a majority of the ethnic minority women interviewed were adapting to life in the UK but preferred to stay within their own cultural traditions.

Lyles and Carter (1982) provide an analysis of the mythology surrounding Black families and contrast it with the strengths of the families. They point out that stereotypical images of racial minorities are everywhere in White racist societies throughout the Western world, and that it is virtually impossible not to be influenced by them in some way. Some of the following myths, then, will be familiar to most of us:

1 The families of Black children are fragmented due to desertion by men. That may be the myth, but in the USA for example, according to Lyles and Carter, the evidence suggests that Black families most typically are intact in having two parents at home; single-parenting is much more typical of the lower socio-economic sectors.
2 Black families are matriarchal in character, with men being relatively

powerless or missing. The truth behind the myth is that Black families tend to be egalitarian (Littlejohn-Blake and Darling, 1993; McAdoo, 1981b; 1988).

3  Children in Black single-parent families are at risk of serious psychopathologies because they are socialized inappropriately or inadequately. This is the myth, but, according to Lyles and Carter, Black youngsters from single-parent families, for example, are just as likely to go to college or university as children from two-parent families. This rather invalidates the idea that they are socialized inadequately or are academically unmotivated.

Clearly, the notion of Black family pathology does not withstand scrutiny from unbiased researchers. To be sure, output measures such as crime may over-represent the children of Black families; nevertheless, it is difficult to judge the extent to which this is due to factors irrelevant to the characteristics of Black families, such as police over-vigilance and racial bias on the part of the courts. The stereotypical image of the nature and structure of the Black family in White socio-economic structures continues to be an important subject of scientific study and political debate. Since the notorious Moynihan report, academics, politicians and professionals have linked Black family structure to persisting social, cultural, economic and psychological malaise and disadvantage. However, the overwhelming majority of supporting studies have focused on the urban Black family (Horton *et al.*, 1995). The findings of these studies are often reported as representative of Black families. This is clearly not the case viewed from an unbiased perspective.

## Why the persistence of the 'tangle of pathology' notion?

One of the reasons for the belief in Black 'family pathology' is that the judgements of professionals, psychologists, therapists, social workers, nurses and teachers are predominantly distorted by racial or racist assumptions about Black families. Although these assumptions are regarded as factual to those who hold them, empirical research relevant to those families has tended to be rather sparse. Much of the pertinent research is not readily available to practitioners who may have more pressing priorities. Also, Black and ethnic minority families have been largely ignored in constructive research of families and family life. One researcher found, for example, that less than a fifth of articles in a long-established American journal on marriage and the family dealt with Black families (Demos, 1990); only one in fifty studies dealt exclusively with Black families. This carries the implication that Black families are not merely neglected in research but tend to be considered relative to

White and other families when they are studied: that is, ethnic minority families are not studied in their own right but as something to be compared and contrasted with White families.

As we have already shown, even helping professionals, for instance, social workers and nurses, problematize Black families and relate to them in ways which adversely affect them and their communities. This happens in many areas of their work with the Black community. For example, on the basis of a number of surveys of child sexual abuse, rates of abuse of Black children are no greater than for White children. Indeed, some Black children may be less likely to be abused. This is illustrated by an important and seminal study of incestuous abuse (family sexual abuse) in the USA (Russell, 1983). This study showed that the rates of childhood abuse were similar in White, African-American and 'Latin' girls. Asian girls were only about half as likely to have been familially abused as these other groups. Another study found that childhood abuse was more common in White families than African-American ones (Wyatt, 1990). Also, the study found no differences in terms of intra-familial abuse. Yet another study found African-Americans more likely to rate various forms of abuse as more serious than White people (Giovanni and Becerra, 1979). It seems clear from that there is no particular problem with Black families and communities with regard to the rates of sexual abuse of their children.

These are surveys taken outside of the intervention system. When one looks at studies of public interventions in the area of sexual abuse, a radically different picture in which Black families are over-represented, emerges. For example, studies carried out in New York suggest that Black people are more frequent in known physical and sexual abuse cases than could be accounted for by the proportions of Black people in the area. One such study found that Black children were over-represented by about 50 per cent in admissions to hospital emergency rooms (Watkins, 1990). In a similar vein, Black children were less likely than White children to be returned to their homes after attending an emergency treatment centre for abuse (Segal and Schwartz, 1985). Could this be another racial factor in the over-representation of Black children in the childcare system?

Howitt (1992), in a study of false allegations in child abuse cases, describes the case of an East African-Asian woman who had married a Frenchman in Britain. After a brief period of cohabitation, they separated and she shortly after conceived her only child, a boy, with an old childhood friend. She lived alone with her son and disliked the standards of the White community around her:

> *I wasn't very happy with the school and the headmaster because my son was bullied. And one day he came with his front tooth broken and it was bleeding...I went to the school and [the headmaster] went mad – he banned me from going there, he sent the police here, and he issued an injunction that he*

*will not allow me to go ...near the school and things, because I have made complaints and he didn't like that... he thinks, him being a white person, a graduate and a headmaster, I am being rude to him by making complaints... I complained about his inefficiency to look after my son. Like I said, I'm very outspoken and open person, so I told him on his face and he didn't like that a bit. He said to me ...'You being a Paki, what do you know about what?'...And I said I have seen people like you sweeping the streets in India.'... [I]t happened the third day... after this row... And also there are two women, they have...[a play scheme centre]... and I have complaints against a woman who was running it, whose name is Mary Granger... and I went with complaints because I don't like son to mix with rough people who were rough and speak bad language... the social worker... said I'm a very fussy mother.*

Howitt, 1992, p. 165

The case against this mother was that she had sexually abused her 7-year-old son. The context is one in which the mother is seen to be an over-protective and somewhat odd Indian woman. Such a view is merely the extreme of a stereotype of Indian families which regards the children as over-protected and over-socialized. So, although the mother's description of her child-rearing practices did nothing to undermine such a stereotype, her behaviour was used as a way of pathologizing such practices, compared to a more open system of child-rearing in which the child is allowed to explore and develop unrestricted by such concerns. In a sense, it is a variant of the theme in racist thinking which uses polar opposites in order to stigmatize Black people. As the above case study illustrates, Indian children, especially girls, are typically viewed by professionals as over-controlled or oppressed by their families. The obverse is believed about African-Caribbean children: that their families have no control over them, resulting in their delinquency – drug taking, promiscuity, educational under-achievement and criminality. Paradoxically, professionals seem to recommend the practices of each group for the other: for Indian families to be lax in the socialization of their children and for African-Caribbean families to restrict and control their children.

The majority of the instances and arguments we have dealt with in this chapter are firmly local issues for Western psychology operating within its own geographical boundaries. They reaffirm the widely held concerns about psychology's inability to deal well with issues associated with culture (Hall, 1997; Landrine, 1992; Miatra, 1996). Beyond Western geographical boundaries, the issues begin to appear even more complex. Different cultural groups have their own distinctive needs in terms of research relevant to those needs.

# Chapter 4

# Interactions between cultures: the social construction of failure

*The cross-race paradigms used to assess minority students' achievement and the explanations of their findings are insufficient for several reasons. They ignore the factor of racism, thus failing to take into account evidence that black and white children receive quite different educational experiences even when they are sitting in the same classroom*

Pollard, 1989, p. 299

Little is known about the day-to-day operation of racism and cultural stereotypes in the activities of professionals such as psychologists, psychiatrists and related disciplines (Howitt and Owusu-Bempah, 1999). What is very clear is that racism plays a role in their professional activities. This can be seen from studies which consider the differential outcomes of their decision making and in the racist nature of some professional writings (e.g. Owusu-Bempah and Howitt, 1994). In other words, we have every reason to think that these professions operate to the disadvantage of Black peoples, politically defined, and generally to the advantage of White Westerners (Esmail and Everrington, 1993; Richards, 1995). Knowing that racism permeates these professional activities gives us no insight, in itself, into the role of racism in the day-to-day interactions between professionals and their clients. Research traditions in the social sciences including psychology have tended to ignore the activities of professional elite in favour of studies of those who receive their services. Psychologists and allied professionals have it in their power to refuse to participate in research and, more importantly, guide what issues are to be researched. Nevertheless, it is important to understand what the processes involved appear to be. For that reason, we have chosen the school system as a case in point. The school system is very relevant, as it is one in which decisions about individual children are made by a variety of professions – the teaching profession and educational psychologists in particular in this context – and where psychological explanations and considerations will be to the fore. These do not have to be carefully researched matters and may be little other than examples of lay psychology or relatively naive beliefs about what affects and determines a child's conduct. These beliefs may involve racial or cultural matters that are erroneously understood or little other than stereotypes. There is probably little in this which would be seen by the professionals involved as malevolent but the outcome of the processes is at best discriminatory.

Professional carers see in educational failure, reasons why some youngsters get into social and behavioural difficulties: problems at school are regarded by them as caused by or intimately related to other problems outside the education system. If this is so, then poor performance in the education system is a warning that needs to be heeded. However, to begin with, we need to challenge the routine assumption that difficulties at school are the result of factors brought to the classroom by some children: that they are not bright enough; they are not supported by their family; they are poor; they come from a 'broken' home; they have been abused; and so forth. While not denying these as contributory factors in some cases, this chapter specifically looks at the ways in which racism in the school system can create these problems and educational underachievement. Instead of presenting professionals in the education system as struggling to overcome problems caused by social disadvantage, it discusses the ways in which they create underachievement and exacerbate the disadvantage facing these children. It is a salutary lesson for those professionals who see themselves as part of the problem rather than its solution. Such an examination is critically important also because teachers and others in the educational system are routinely in contact with other professionals involved with children.

It is uncontroversial to say that Black ethnic minority children, notably African-Caribbean children, generally fail to achieve their full potential in the British educational system. The usual turn of phrase holds that they are underachievers, and a vast range of explanations have been put forward to account for this. Nevertheless, it is also claimed that certain groups of ethnic minority children, such as those of oriental or South Asian origins, are among the highest achieving groups. Even the most rabid racist writers nowadays repeatedly temper their claims by stressing the putative academic/IQ superiority of Asian peoples compared to those of African ancestry and White peoples, a ploy which should not take us in. For us, this is little more than a variant of the good-Black/bad-Black theme. The belief in genetic differences between Black and White children has formed the basis of much of the early history of the debate concerning their differential educational performance (e.g. Eysenck, 1971; Jensen, 1969). If we were writing thirty years ago, no doubt this would be the focus of our discussion, but not nowadays. To be sure, since the nineteenth century, and before, educationalists, psychologists and other professionals have been manufacturing flawed evidence to prove the presumed genetic inferiority of Black pupils, their poor learning ability and their suitability for little other than menial tasks (e.g. Bache, 1895; Burt, 1937; Terman, 1916; Thorndike, 1940). The sea change that has occurred since the Second World War has led to such genetic views being unfashionable. While there have been the occasional forays into this area of troubled waters by psychologists and educators (e.g. Eysenck, 1971; Jensen, 1969; Rushton, 1992) in the relatively recent past, overwhelmingly, the response to these pronouncements has been negative and deriding (e.g., Kamin, 1977, 1981). This does not mean that beliefs about the genetic 'inferiority' of people of African descent are rare; it merely means that they have tended to become associated with the outpourings of extreme right-wing and Nazi-style parties, exemplified in Britain by the National Front. It has been pointed out by a number of authors that overt racism has been overridden by a rather different form of racism (Barker, 1981; Barnes, 1980; Howitt and Owusu-Bempah, 1999a, b; Owusu-Bempah and Howitt, 1994, 1995). This alternative racism implies that the problem with Black people lies not in their genetic potential but in their cultures, which produce children unsuited to take full benefit from schooling. Both the genetic and cultural accounts of the underachievement of Black children in schools place the responsibility on Black children, their families and their community. In contrast, it is our belief that ideology and racism are significant determinants of the handling of Black children by professionals. Furthermore, rather than responding to a clearly defined problem, professionals create the very problem that they are there to tackle.

It has become fashionable to regard the problem of Black children's general academic underachievement as one of the curriculum and educational methods being unsuited to their needs. This may be the case to a degree. However, despite literally thousands of research studies identifying various claims about what needs doing, it remains to be shown that multicultural education or different teaching styles in themselves reduce educational underachievement among Black children. Nevertheless, emphasis continues to be placed on these factors:

> *Teachers of low income black students.... must function as (or become) cultural translators. That is, they should be bicultural – thoroughly knowledgeable and sensitive about African American children's language, style of presentation, community value, traditions, legends, myths, history, symbols, and norms. Under no circumstances should teachers of African American children view them from a deficit perspective... the problems facing African American children's success cannot be solved by 'restructuring schools' or other educational fads. The problems will have to be solved by examining the type of instruction and the nature of the curriculum. The instructional issue requires that educators look at themselves for solutions instead of expecting problems to be solved by whatever the latest educational trend might be.*
>
> Swick, et al., 1994, p. 189

This ignores the racism of educators (Polard, 1989). The point is not that multicultural education and sensitivity to children's cultures are bad things (this would be patently absurd). However, emphasis on instructional and curricular issues, and the consequent neglect of racism among teachers, leaves the analysis of the problem incomplete. More consideration should be given to the role of classroom interaction and professional racism in actively creating the educational underachievement of Black children. The race thinking which guides the activities of professionals dealing with Black children is present in the classroom just as much as it is anywhere else in a racist society (Connolly, 1998).

## Behavioural apartheid

The exclusion of children from school for disciplinary reasons may seem a straightforward process. However, it shows how the interplay between national politics and the activities of professionals can work to deny Black and ethnic minority children justice and education. Changes in national educational policy in Britain have increased the pressure on schools to do well in order to meet performance and efficiency criteria (Bourne *et al.*, 1994; Lyle *et al.*, 1996). These changes have also resulted in an increase in the number of children excluded from the classroom for disciplinary reasons, the burden of which seems the greatest for African-Caribbean children. Traditionally exclusion meant expulsion, but now it can be either temporary or permanent. It is a tough punishment for both children and their parents, so its misapplication is no trivial matter. Evidence suggests that Black children are overrepresented in exclusion rates. Bourne (1994) provides some basic statistics on exclusion in British schools. Although African-Caribbean children comprised only 2 per cent of children in schools, Bourne found them to be overrepresented by a factor of four in the figures for children excluded *permanently*. Other figures for exclusion range from about three to five times overrepresentation of Black children in different areas of Britain, according to a variety of sources. These findings might at first appear to confirm the stereotypical image of Black children as troublesome or to illustrate the problematic behaviour of Black children in schools as asserted by such writers and Dwivedi and Varma (1996). This is unlikely to be the case for several reasons. To start with, there is evidence to suggest that punishments are associated disproportionately with many forms of social disadvantage. For example, in the USA, a study of over 4,000 discipline files from nine schools in one state revealed that more severe (physical) punishments were disproportionately administered to Black, male and 'handicapped' children (McFadden *et al.*, 1992). Checking the sorts of misdemeanours involved, the researchers found that rather milder punishments were given to children of other social groupings for identical types of offence.

Another reason for believing that exclusion in British schools has racist underpinnings is to be found in the details of some of the cases. Careful documentation indicates that exclusion is frequently imposed on Black and ethnic minority children for non-disciplinary matters, or where other aspects of the situation are ignored. That is, it is affected by factors which go well beyond the needs of discipline.

## Religious/cultural 'non' conformity

In the literature on racial discrimination in employment there are numerous examples of people from ethnic minorities being discriminated against on the basis of their culture, including their religion. A number of 'classic' illustrations of this exist, for example, where a Sikh's turban, which is a religious requirement, is held by employers to violate uniform requirements, or where only Christian religious holidays are treated as holidays. The net effect of such 'insensitive' treatment is that the individual is denied employment, dismissed or constructively dismissed for observing the requirements of their religion. While it has long been established that such discriminatory actions are illegal, remarkably similar circumstances have led to the exclusion of Black children from school: 'A Sussex school temporarily excluded two students for breaking school uniform rules. The boy had a beard, the girl was wearing a headscarf, both of which are signs of devotion to Islam' (Bourne, 1994, p. 29).

Episodes such as these are even more remarkable given the extensive debate and materials on 'multiculturalism' in education (Mahoney, 1988).

## Medical or educational problems ignored or misdiagnosed

Although it is increasingly accepted that Black people may have special health care needs, generally this has been construed as a problem of pandering to the whims of Black people. This would include matters like the provision of specialist services to treat illnesses commoner in Black people, such as sickle-cell anaemia, or being culturally sensitive in the provision of female health workers to cater for the needs of women whose culture and religion make it difficult for them to have intimate dealings with male personnel (McAvoy and Donaldson, 1990). However, in the case of exclusion from school, explanations of a child's behaviour on the basis of racial stereotypes (such as aggressiveness and uncontrollability) override obvious medical explanations.

*A 5-year-old African-Caribbean boy was suspended indefinitely from school in Harrow, following an epileptic fit during which he struck two teachers.*

*According to the head teacher, he was suspended because of a general dete-*
*rioration in his behaviour. She refused to accept that he was actually having*
*a fit when the teachers were struck... On the night of the incident... he had*
*been so ill that he had to be kept in overnight at Northwick Park hospital and*
*had been heavily sedated...*

Bourne, 1994, p. 31

## Educational/learning difficulties ignored

Similarly, educational and learning difficulties may be overlooked in
favour of explanations based on racial stereotypes. Instead of obtaining
the requisite back-up specialized services for the child, action directed
towards sorting out a conduct or behavioural problem is preferred.

*A 6-year-old boy at a Catholic school on the borders of Lambeth had a habit*
*of kicking. The school, instead of seeking help for him, merely confiscated his*
*shoes every day. Because he walked around in his socks, he was frequently*
*teased and mocked by the other children. One day when he went to the boys'*
*lavatory, a white girl followed him in and began to play with his penis. He*
*was furious and hit her. The girl ran out crying. The caretaker found her and*
*heard her allegations that the boy had hit her. Despite the fact that the boy*
*had been provoked and the girl had no business to be in the boys' lavatory,*
*the black boy was permanently excluded from school and the white girl*
*received no punishment at all.*

Bourne, 1994, pp. 32–3

In contrast to this, we can take another case in which a 6-year-old
African-Caribbean boy was excluded from his school for 'sexual
harassment' because, it was claimed, he had lifted up a girl's skirt. The
family had to enlist the help of a community worker before the school
was persuaded to remove the phrase 'sexual harassment' from his
records (Bourne, 1994).

## Racial elements of incidents ignored

One of the curiosities of racist society is its persistent attempts to hold
the victims of racism responsible for that racism simply for being its
victim. Thus a lifetime of exposure to racism and racist abuse might
result in hostility and anger, but the victim is blamed for having 'a chip
on their shoulder'. One of the implications of this is that racism or racial
abuse is insignificant; it is for Black people to control themselves and
remain calm despite their painful experiences. Similar thinking underlies some exclusion of Black school children.

> *A Russian boy walked up to an African-Caribbean boy in the playground and started a quarrel. The black boy ignored him. The white boy then shoved him in the back and called him 'Nigger'. The black boy spun round and hit the white boy. A deputy head saw this from a school window and rushed onto the playground, in a rage. He grabbed the black boy by his shirt, forced him up against the wall and manhandled him out of the playground. The black boy explained that he had tried to avoid a quarrel and that he had tried not to get involved... The black boy was suspended... but no action was taken over the white boy.*

Bourne , 1994, p. 33

There is, naturally, little documentation of the detail of how disciplinary problems are created through interaction between teachers and students. Generally, as in all unequal relationships (Owusu-Bempah and Howitt, 1990, unpublished), the pupil is held to blame. An important illustration is the observational ethnographic study by Wright (1987). She reports the following exchange between a White metal work teacher and African-Caribbean boys in his class. The teacher was not happy about the noisiness in class and threw a piece of chalk at an African-Caribbean boy, although he was largely innocent. The teacher then told a South Asian boy to retrieve the chalk, at which point an African-Caribbean boy asked why the teacher did not use black chalk.

> *Teacher [turning to the researcher]: Did you hear that? Then I would be accused of being racist... I had a black girl in my class. She did something or another. I said to her, if you're not careful I'll send you back to the chocolate factory. She went home and told her parents. Her dad came to school, and decided to take the matter to the Commission for Racial Equality. It was only said in good fun, nothing malicious.*
>
> *Keith (Afro-Caribbean)[aggressively]: How do we know that it's a joke. In my opinion that was a disrespectful thing to say.*
>
> *Teacher [raising his voice and pointing his finger at Keith]: If I wanted to say something maliciously racist, I wouldn't have to make a joke about it. I'd say it. I've often had a joke with you, haven't I?*
>
> *Keith [angrily]: Those so-called jokes, were no joke, you were being cheeky. I went home and told my mum and she said that if you say it again she would come and sort you out... My father says that a teacher should set a good example for the children, by respecting each one, whether them black or white...*

p. 112

Keith was eventually sent to the headmaster for being insolent! Afterwards the teacher described the students as 'remedials' with chips on their shoulders! (Wright, 1987).

Not surprisingly, there are some that prefer to regard the lot of Black and ethnic minority children in the educational system as the consequence of anything other than racism. Peagam (1994), who asserts that the overrepresentation of African-Caribbean children in figures for educational and behavioural difficulties and exclusion from school is attributable largely to their social class, provides a good example of this. He bases this claim on his own study in which he found that African-Caribbean children were *over*represented by a factor of at least three on educational and behavioural difficulties, whereas those of South Asian descent were *under*represented by a factor of up to four.

> *By the yardstick of children whose behaviour was seen as uncontainable in mainstream schools, Afro-Caribbeans were up to four times more likely than white European children and more than ten times than black Asian children to be identified as presenting such difficulties. Such a disparity requires an explanation, which simple allegations of teacher racism fail to supply.*
>
> Peagam, 1994, p. 34

So, is this sufficient to support Peagam's claim that the 'working-class-ness' of the Black children explains their less favourable treatment in school? Are African-Caribbean children essentially treated equitably with their social-class equivalents of any colour? For obvious reasons, while it is true that African-Caribbean children are more likely to be working-class than White children, it is difficult to explain the differential treatment of African-Caribbean and South Asian children, such as Pakistani and Bangladeshi children, on this basis. Despite his reliance on extensive statistics and statistical tables, Peagam fails to provide convincing data to support his thesis. He superficially supports his claim by citing his survey of racial groupings of children whose teachers believed them to be experiencing 'emotional and/or behavioural difficulties'. There were very few differences between them either in terms of their presenting problems or their socio-economic status, such as the low occupational status of the main provider.

Peagam's own data cast doubt on his simple theory that social class is responsible for the substantial overrepresentation of certain groups of Black children in special schools or streams. If the judgements of their teachers are anything to go by, the behavioural and emotional problems of African-Caribbean children in this study were not too serious since they did not recommend special or segregated school provision for them. Nethertheless, they receive such provision much more readily. According to their teachers' judgements, the problems of South Asian children were much more in need of special provision. On this basis, the South Asian children should have been overrepresented in special schooling provisions. Perhaps confirming that the problem lies with the school, somewhat more African-Caribbean parents than White parents believed that their children's problems were confined to the school. In short, the more one explores Peagam's data, the less convincing is his argument; all too many factors suggest that the

African-Caribbean children should *not* have been overrepresented in the special schools he studied. There are examples of leading theorists making similar intellectual contortions (see Howitt, 1992; Howitt and Owusu-Bempah, 1994 for further examples). In short, it is hard to see how the extensive racial elements in the studies we describe throughout this chapter boil down to matters of social class and demographics, apart from the fact, of course, that middle-class schools are better resourced in terms of staff and facilities than working-class schools. As we are about to see, there is convincing evidence that problems are not simply being brought to the classroom; they are actively constructed through teachers' interactions with Black children.

## Making failures

Punishing them is not the only way in which African-Caribbean and other ethnic minority children are disadvantaged by the teaching profession. Much more concern has been expressed about their lack of educational achievement over-all. Teachers who put across superficially friendly messages about the educational underachievement of African-Caribbean children can do as much harm as those who blame the children's failure on 'inferior Black genes'. Blame, for example, has been placed on the problematic nature of Black families, the incompatibility of their African learning style with Western education, the internalization of racism by Black children or any one of a myriad of other explanations which ultimately lay the blame and responsibility at the door of the Black community, the Black family, and the Black child.

Is it possible that educational failure is constructed in classrooms and staffrooms? Researchers argue that there are a number of myths about Black children which are sustained rather than challenged by the educational system (Connolly, 1998; Figueroa, 1991; Olgivy *et al.*, 1990). So, instead of suggesting that African-Caribbean children underachieve and Asian children overachieve, one should look at the unequal placement and exclusion rate of ethnic minority students within the educational system. This implies that there are socially constructed views of Black students that are amplified in the classroom and elsewhere within the educational system. The role of 'experts' in this process should not be neglected either, for it is they who provide respectability to racial prejudice; it is they who turn racial myths into a reality.

*The constant emphasis on their supposed educational 'underachievement' can itself be seen as part and parcel of the dominant negative and narrow frames of reference regarding them, and as part and parcel of their unequal location within the society. More generally, the unequal structural realities, and the processes and frames of reference integral to them, are fundamental in accounting for the situation and performance of Black ethnic minority pupils, as well as in understanding the dominant modes of perceiving, conceptualising and relating to this situation and this performance.*

Figueroa, 1991, p. 193.

One conclusion to be drawn is that educators are damaging to the success of African-Caribbean children. Unfortunately, however, much research tends to be distanced from the day-to-day processes involved in creating failures, the processes whereby professionals within the educational system damage Black pupils. To find that output measures of achievement reveal that, generally, ethnic minority and Black children do relatively poorly can tell us nothing about the process by which children with potential become failures; quite the reverse, in fact. Without the detail of what happens within the school system to create the failure of these children, it is all too easy to pathologize the children themselves, or hold it to be their own or their families' fault.

The role of classroom processes in the creation of failure is illustrated by Wright's (1987) study. She showed that the placement of African-Caribbean students in classes, streamed according to ability level, was lower than objectively ought to have been the case. Although these children tended to do as well in school examinations as their White and Asian counterparts, they were put into lower streams in English, maths, French and physics for national examinations, contrary to what their objective performances had indicated. Clearly, in this case, the African-Caribbean children were less favourably treated. Wright reports one teacher's comment on one such 'misplaced' student: 'her attitude to the teachers is not at all good, she can be a nuisance in class' (p. 124). Wright found also that the African-Caribbean students were well aware of their teachers' low expectations of them and their abilities. They were aware also that they had been precluded from taking examinations for which they were suited. A statement by a Black student epitomizes the way in which such experiences can sorely affect a child's commitment to the education process.

*I was even doing well, so well that I even wanted to be a vet until my teacher and the career adviser found out. They reminded me about my family's poverty and my race. Strange that was the only time they both spent some time talking about Black people and what we can do. Anyhow I was advised to aim for the domestic Arts College in the town centre if I wanted to make it to college. I gave up, they had to be right, I have never seen a Black vet in England. They even switched me from the O-Level class to the CSE one, I couldn't be any good. I just wanted to fail...*

Maximé, 1993, p. 103

There is other evidence of the disregard of measures of performance when coming to judgements about the achievements of Black children.

For example, a standard measure of verbal reasoning can be used to provide a baseline of the achievements of Black children at a particular point in time. Kysel (1988) obtained such standard measures about school-age children and compared them with their head teacher's ratings of their verbal reasoning ability. The sexes were considered separately. White pupils tended to be assessed by the head teacher as slightly more able than their objective scores indicated. However, for children from ethnic minority groupings, their head teachers' ratings were consistently lower than indicated by the objective test scores. The worst served groupings were South Asian, African Asian, Pakistani, South East Asian and African children. Only in the case of the African-Caribbean children did the head teachers' ratings and objective test results match at all well.

The explanation of why these 'errors' are made is naturally complex. The simplest level of explanation is to suggest that teachers have expectations of Black children which may even pre-date their entry to the teaching profession. The origins of these ideas are probably in the race thinking which is endemic in the Western world. An example of research which illustrates this is Figueroa's (1991), which simply asked a cohort of student teachers to describe their ideas about South Asian and African-Caribbean children. When responding to the open-ended statement: 'When I think of Asians I think', there emerged a number of stereotypes and clichés. Forty-five per cent of the trainee teachers mentioned areas such as trade and business. For this group, there were not very many negative images. In contrast, when asked about African-Caribbeans, a rather different set of evaluative beliefs emerged: they were described in such stereotypical terms as 'care-free', 'having rhythm', 'cricket' and 'suffering inner city depression due to high levels of unemployment'. Perhaps even more illuminating were the matchings of the two ethnic minority groups to a list of adjectives supplied by the researcher. The dominant images of African-Caribbean children were 'musical' (83 per cent of student teachers), 'noisy' (69 per cent), 'good at sports' (67 per cent), 'educational poor achievers' (34 per cent) and 'behave badly' (27 per cent). In contrast, the dominant images for South Asians were markedly different: they were described as 'musical' by only 24 per cent of student teachers, 'noisy' (1 per cent), 'good at sports' (9 per cent), 'badly behaved' (2 per cent) and 'educationally lowly' (6 per cent). It is also worthwhile noting that over a half of the student teachers felt that there was at least some racism among teachers, although this was rather less than the 92 per cent who recognized racism among the British population in general. This means that they minimized the extent of racism as a particularly important problem within the profession as compared to the racism in the general population.

That African-Caribbean children and children of South Asian backgrounds are regarded differently by teachers suggests that teachers discriminate against them not only *vis-à-vis* White children, but also treat the two groups of ethnic minority children differently. Such treatment is often based upon racial stereotypes which abound in folklore as well as the 'scientific' and professional literature (e.g. Brian and Martin, 1987; Lobo, 1978; Varma and Dwivedi, 1996). Lobo, for example, objectifies the following stereotypes about African-Caribbean pupils:

> *The West Indian boys and girls are very fond of and very good at sports, athletics and music. This is an area where their inborn physical and rhythmic talents help them win over their English competitors... The rhythms, the noise, the flashing lights of the disco seem so much closer to the African culture... they probably find in the music and dance a release of their frustrations and pent-up emotions.*
>
> Lobo, 1978, pp. 92–3

Such stereotypes as these are readily available to teachers and students. Thus, they are frequently reproduced within the classroom. There is evidence of the ways in which children of South Asian origin and African-Caribbean children are treated differentially within the classroom. This, among other explanations, is because different (often polar opposite) stereotypes are attached to the two groups. For instance, South Asian pupils, especially girls, are seen as timid, bashful and quiet, while African-Caribbean pupils are seen as boisterous, hyperactive and uninhibited (Brian and Martin, 1987; Lobo, 1978). Wright (1992) provides a good example involving children of South Asian origin. In a class of 5- and 6-year-olds, a teacher was taking the children one by one for reading. One Pakistani girl, Rehana, who had recently arrived in Britain, was called to the front but appeared not to be able to cope with the situation or the word 'flower'. The teacher then called another girl of South Asian origin, Zareeda, to come to the front.

TEACHER: What is the Urdu word for 'flower'? (*Zareeda fidgets nervously*) Tell her in Urdu that this is a flower.

ZAREEDA: (*looks very embarrassed, refuses to speak. A few children gather around the teacher's desk. Zareeda hides her face from them*).

TEACHER: Zareeda, if you're embarrassed, whisper the word to me.

ZAREEDA: (*no response*)

TEACHER: (*visibly irritated*) Well, Zareeda, you're supposed to be helping, that's not the attitude in this school, we help our friends. You're supposed to be helping me to teach Rehana English. (*to the Asian girls*) Go and sit down, both of you... I'll go next door and see if one of those other Asian children can help me. (*Teacher leaves the room*)

Wright, 1992, pp. 16–17

Wright reports that while this was going on, White children in the class began to make disparagingly racist remarks about 'Pakis'. Whatever else one makes of this exchange, it is pretty clear that it was predicated on beliefs that South Asian children are shy and uncommunicative in class. Otherwise the teacher would have wondered what she was doing wrong rather than reproaching the girls. Wright suggests those teacher–Black pupil interactions, based on racial stereotypes, produce feelings of 'insecurity' in the children and encourage their unpopularity with other children in the class.

The experience of Marcus, an African-Caribbean boy of 4 years, is the polar opposite of Rehana's. In this scenario the teacher was playing a song game involving counting, and at the end of each verse, the boy put his hand up and tried to give the correct answer. The following are some of the exchanges between the teacher, Marcus and the rest of the class:

MARCUS: [Afro-Caribbean boy with his hand up] I know.

TEACHER: (*talking to the group*) Is she right when she says 'two little leaves on a tree'...

MARCUS: [Afro-Caribbean boy, waving his hand for attention] Five.

TEACHER: Don't shout out Marcus, do you know Susan? [white girl]

MARCUS: (raising his hand enthusiastically) Four.

TEACHER: (*to Marcus*) Shush. Let's count, one, two, three, four.

Wright, 1987; p. 20

Other children within the class received much more positive feedback when they contributed a correct or even incorrect answer at the request of the teacher. All this amounts to repeated negative strokes, likely to curtail the Black child's lust for education. Central to the process is the belief that Black children, boys especially, are boisterous and difficult to control within the classroom situation.

## Instances when stereotypes are reversed

Similar problems are reported by Ogilvy *et al.* (1990) who studied interactions between staff and children in multicultural nursery schools in Scotland. The study was ingenious in that, in each of the classes studied, a child of indigenous Scottish origin was matched with one of South Asian origin of the same sex and/or similar age. All the teachers were White women. Four-fifths of the teachers claimed to have difficulties with ethnic minority Asian children, and two-thirds of these attributed this to 'the language barrier'. None-the-less, many of them failed to seek help from their South Asian language-speaking colleagues to deal with the problem.

Given the different stereotypes and judgements about African-Caribbean and Asian children described earlier, it is interesting to note how children of South Asian origin who constituted the 'Black children' at these schools were regarded. These children tended to have attributed to them characteristics which elsewhere in Britain are virtually reserved for African-Caribbean children:

> *About a third of the total sample described Asian children in terms of a variety of negative characteristics, e.g. 'aggressive', 'loud', 'lazy', 'disobedient' and 'stubborn'. Such problematic characteristics were attributed either to language: 'The ones with good English have quite good behavior; the ones with less are more aggressive to get what they want'... or to misperceive differences in cultural norms and values: 'Boys can be very stubborn... they don't like to be told what to do by a woman'... 'Their attitude is pretty aggressive, the way they're brought up, push other children out of the way'... 'Bit more disobedient, bit more aggressive. Maybe because at home there are a lot of children and a lot of adults – grannies, aunties and so on. They're not looked after the same as in a family with just two parents, more free to do what they want'....*
>
> Ogilvy et al., 1990, p. 6

It is interesting to note that the schools with lower proportions of ethnic minority students tended to be the most negative in certain respects. For example, low ethnic-mix schools predominantly viewed the South Asian children as aggressive!

The following anecdote is a case in point. It involved a 6-year-old Gujarati boy, Mikesh (fictitious name). For two terms, Mikesh returned from school almost weekly with damning reports about his behaviour at school. This obviously caused his young parents (of lower socio-economic status) great distress. One of the present authors is a very close friend of the family (of two children). Upon speaking to Mikesh, it became apparent that the author of the reports was either a trainee or an inexperienced teacher. The parents were helped to compose the following reply to his teacher:

> *Thank you for your letters... Concerning our son's behaviour at school; both have caused us great distress. We are particularly concerned that his misbehaviour and the resultant actions taken by the school may hinder his learning.*
>
> *His apparent misbehaviour at school is out of character compared to his behaviour at home. We would, therefore, support you in any way possible to*

*identify those factors within the school environment that may trigger such behaviour in him.*

*We welcome your suggestion to discuss his behaviour at school with the school psychologist. However, if he is to be interviewed by the psychologist, then we will consent* only *if one of us and a family friend (a psychologist himself) can be present to minimise any anxiety he may feel in the situation.*

*cc:Headteacher*

This was five years ago. Since then, every report Mikesh has returned from school with has been positive. So, whose attitude or behaviour needed modification – the school's, the teacher's or Mikesh's? What would have been the school psychologist's assessment had Mikesh been referred to him/her?

One should not underestimate the incredible adroitness of racism. It can flex tirelessly in form but ultimately to the disadvantage of Black and ethnic minority groups. Consider the stock racist phrases such as: 'to work like a Black', and 'as lazy as a Black' to appreciate the stark inconsistency or plasticity in the application of racial stereotypes. It should come, then, as no surprise to find that a stereotype of one race can be applied to another without shame or recognition of the inconsistency. While racist thinking is skilful at presenting itself as something else, ultimately the function of racism is to keep Black and ethnic minority people 'in their proscribed place'. Indeed, the image of children of South Asian origin as hard working, co-operative and motivated may have very little bearing on how they are treated in the long run. For example, a study of the employment of university graduates from ethnic minorities shows that there are differentials in the employment rates of African-Caribbean and Asian graduates in Britain (Brennan and McGeevor, 1987). The study found that African-Caribbean graduates and graduates of South Asian origin tended to stay on in education, following graduation, more frequently, compared to their White counterparts. Nevertheless, there were larger proportions of South Asian graduates than White graduates out of employment a year after graduation. This was the case despite the fact that their degrees were from courses which traditionally had few employment difficulties. So, for example, when ethnic minority and White graduates were matched in terms of course type, sex and degree classification, graduates of South Asian origin had greater difficulty in obtaining work in professions such as electrical and electronic engineering. Furthermore, it would seem that African-Caribbean graduates were rather more successful than their South Asian counterparts in the job market. In this case we may ask what good has the stereotype of hard work and diligence done these South Asians?

There is more. The South Asian children in Ogilvy *et al.*'s study, described earlier, were more than twice as likely as White children to be described as having behavioural difficulties by their teachers. Furthermore, they were nine times as likely to be seen as having attention or motivational difficulties, such as being easily distracted, or being reluctant to speak to staff. They were also four times more likely to be described as showing social or interpersonal problems, such as not mixing or not sharing with other children. Finally, they were twice as likely to be seen as possessing problematic emotional or behavioural characteristics, such as nervousness and laziness. The stereotyping of these South Asian children in terms that suggest that they are shy or reserved had further adverse consequences for them, despite the fact that it contradicts the stereotype of them as disobedient, loud and aggressive; but that is the logic of racism. In particular, it provided a pseudo-explanation of the children's behaviour within the classroom. For example, just a minority of the staff saw the South Asian children's limited skills in English as a problem; mostly the view was that the children understood a great deal but chose to say little. Apparently, the staff saw nothing problematic in the children's quietness. However, this was mistaken when the children's performances on a standardized measure of ability were examined: 90 per cent of the South Asian children in these assessments were found to be in the bottom 20 per cent of ability in either expressive or receptive English, or both. The contrast between the South Asian children's low objective performance on English language tests and the teachers' belief that they were really proficient in English, but reluctant to show it, is marked and important. Basically it shows that the teachers failed (or refused) to acknowledge a problem because of a racial or cultural stereotype: 'While most... acknowledged that ethnic minority children generally had language difficulties, they appeared to underestimate the extent of the problem when referring to specific children'. (Ogilvy *et al.*, 1990, p. 10).

It should be added that there was relatively little interaction to be found between the staff and the South Asian children in any case. Such a lack of communication with ethnic minority children can only exacerbate or amplify the 'language barrier'. 'One of the dangers inherent in this situation is that quietness in Asian children is perceived as a 'natural' stage in second language development and not as a reason for intervention, particularly since it conforms to the stereotyped view of Asian children as withdrawn'(p. 11). Furthermore, Ogilvy *et al.* suggest that the individual needs and educational requirements of ethnic minority children are much less likely to be met than those of White children. They argue that, on the whole, interaction between White teachers and ethnic minority children is much more 'controlling' and applied in a universal fashion, ignoring the children's individual needs.

# Yes, blame the victim

It is widely acknowledged that many accounts of the underachievement of Black and ethnic minority children within the educational system are victim-blaming. Rather than holding teachers and the rest of the educational system responsible, the problem is held to be primarily to do with the children and their families. Professional racism is hardly ever seen as a casual or, at least, contributory factor. Worse still, there are few elements of the experience of Black and ethnic minority children which are not held to be pathological. Ogilvy *et al.*'s study is a good illustration of some of the many ways in which these children, their families and cultures are pathologized and victimized in the educational system, even at the nursery level, as a consequence of our overreliance on Western psychological notions of 'normal' families and 'normal' development.

Another example is what Frisby (1993) describes as 'myths of black cultural learning styles'. Basically the notion of Black (i.e. African) cultural learning styles holds that there are cultural differences which underlie the statistics on the underachievement of Black children, that Black children's learning styles are rooted in their culture. In the USA, for example, it is claimed that African-American children's thinking, feelings, behaviour and mode of learning have been shaped differently from White children's because of their African ancestry. According to this view, therefore, education must take into account these cultural learning styles in order to remedy the problem of Black children's educational underachievement; or so the story goes. Certainly it is possible to list dimensions upon which African- and European-based cultures may differ, and there are many instances in this book. For example, it has been suggested that African cultures, like most collective cultures, are much more spiritual and communal and less materialistic or acquisitive than European cultures, that they seek harmony with nature rather than its domination, that African cultures prefer co-operative to competitive learning situations. A preference for co-operative learning environments has been observed also in school children in Japan, Korea, India and China (e.g. Allen, 1997; Kim, 1997). It is important and desirable to attempt to identify and describe the characteristic values and worth of African cultures. However, we must avoid the danger of overgeneralizing the influence of these characteristics to people who have never had direct contact with these African cultures: for example, African-American children.

Thus, Frisby is right in suggesting that underlying the idea of Black cultural learning styles are a number of dubious assumptions. Some of these assumptions are:

1  That within the Western world, Black and White cultures are incompatible, and that this cultural incompatibility is disadvantageous to

Black children's learning. However, for Frisby, the fact that African nations and their cultures have themselves experienced Westernization (and vice versa) suggests that this idea of incompatibility is an overstatement. He also points out that no evidence is available which shows that differences in pupils' cultural styles are related to academic achievement.

2 That the characteristics of Black culture 'determine' Black children's learning styles. This smacks of an excuse for Black children's educational underachievement, since many of the learning styles or characteristics attributed to Black children have also been attributed to other ethnic minority children, and also to gender differences.

Frisby claims that there is little to suggest that immersion in African-American culture by schools has much to do with enhancing the educational achievement of Black children. He supports this claim with the fact that Afrocentric schools in the USA have not been shown to achieve better standards than general integrated schools or Black schools which have no Afrocentric ethos. He also points out that the Afrocentric schools seem not to differ in terms of their techniques of education once the Afrocentric content of the curriculum is disregarded.

One study of particular significance, in our view, is that of Sowell (1986). This looked at the factors that made some Black schools (in the USA) effective at producing academically successful children. The study highlighted the unimportance of instruction in Black history. Rather, successful students reported that the dedication and strong personal interest shown in them by their teachers and the school as a whole were seminal in creating feelings of confidence and a desire to succeed. One is compelled to agree with Frisby that the notion of Black cultural learning styles leads to the very situation which its advocates seem to want to avoid.

Pollard (1989) puts forward a similar argument to Frisby's. She argues that it is hardly profitable to concentrate resources on attempts to describe and explain the failure of some Black children in the educational system. She distinguishes between two sets of variables: 'static variables' and 'alterable variables'. Factors such as poverty are in the main unalterable by educationalists, so she regards them as 'static variables'. Static variables function to stigmatize individuals, and so discourage change. More important for professionals, in her view, is to understand the nature of the 'alterable variables' which lead to success. The notion of 'alterable variables' would seem to be a more profitable direction towards the understanding of Black pupils. Certainly it is a more positive strategy than the damaging tendency to concentrate on such relatively 'static variables' as poor self-identity, family circumstances and social class, all of which function, in the main, to pathologize some children and further disadvantage them. The 'alterable variables' approach would, as Pollard has suggested, do the following:

1  Identify those children who do not seem to be particularly adversely affected by the system and determine what factors are associated with their psychological well-being and academic success.
2  Seek to identify and remedy those factors (e.g. racism) within the system which deleteriously affect as well as those which enhance their psychological well-being and academic performance.

In the absence of a constructive approach, such as the one suggested by Pollard, teachers and other professionals run the risk of doing Black and ethnic minority children more harm than good, of doing the harmed more harm. Indeed, the idea that institutions can cause the problems they sometimes try to solve is not a new one. Coard (1971) recognized this in his seminal work: *How the West Indian Child is Made Educationally Subnormal*. In this, he presented the evidence that African-Caribbean children were wrongly placed and overrepresented in institutions for the 'educationally subnormal' for the remainder of their school careers, thereby restricting their life-chances. In social work and education, for instance, the same seems to be true of the care system in which children of 'mixed-race' parentage and African-Caribbean children are overrepresented, and from which they take longer to exit (Bebbington and Miles, 1989; Barn, 1990, 1993; CRE, 1995; NSPCC, 1999). It is generally accepted that the care system is an unfavourable environment in terms of the child's social, emotional, psychological, educational and behavioural development and life prospects (Bowlby, 1944, 1951; Owusu-Bempah, 1997; Rutter, 1991; Tizard and Phoenix, 1993). However, instead of seeking the causes of the children's problems from within the system, professionals, including psychologists (e.g. Dwidvedi and Varma, 1996), as dictated by Western individualism, continue to concentrate on the individual child's personality or family as an explanation for their difficulties.

## The role of psychological theory

While there may be a temptation to regard the examples in this chapter as merely bad practice on the part of educationalists, educational psychology and others, this does not capture entirely the detail of what is happening in these cases. However viewed, it seems that mainstream Western psychology contributes little, either by omission or commission, to correcting the situation. Given the discipline's presence in the training of these individuals, the discipline in general shares responsibility with the individual practitioners. For example, take the entire sub-field of developmental psychology. Study or training in this particular area should provide students with a deeper understanding of the intimate relationship between culture and individual psychology. Nevertheless, the most popular theories in developmental psychology are those which originated in a particular culture – Western culture. Many tenets of these theories lack universal validity, and so are largely inadequate for understanding children from beyond Western boundaries (Enriquez, 1993; Holdstock, 2000; Lesser, 1996; Miller, 1997; Owusu-Bempah, 1999b; Page and Berkow, 1991). These are the theories of child development which form a central part of the education and training of such child care professionals as educational psychologists, child psychiatrists, and teachers.

Ma's (1997) critique of Kohlberg's theory of moral development is especially pertinent (see also Chapter 7). Kohlberg (1969) suggested that the developmental stages of cognitive moral development are universal and would operate the same way in all cultures. As most will know, so familiar is the theory, Kohlberg argues that moral development progresses through six different stages. The first four stages do appear to be universals in that they have been found in a variety of cultures. The problem lies with Kohlberg's fifth and sixth stages since these contain ideological elements which seem to undervalue moral development in some cultures. The sixth or final stage of moral development, according to Kohlberg, essentially describes individuals who not only make moral choices but are also responsible for directing their own destinies, the autonomous and self-directing ideal self of Western industrial society. People are responsible for their own actions. Ma explains how different this is from the crucial concept of *jen* in Chinese morality, emanating from Confucius's concepts. *Jen* involves a positive regard and affection for kinfolk but extends to all people. 'Collectivist' is a term that could be applied readily, but this cultural ideal is much more akin to the fifth stage of Kohlberg's theory that is concerned wit utilitarianism and basic rights. At this stage, the happiness and well-being of the majority is the dominant feature of moral reasoning – the rights of individuals do not have priority. In cases of conflict between the majority and the individual, the Chinese resolution would be that the individual defers to the interest of the majority. Primary socialization of children in collectivist cultures is about inculcating a strong sense of interdependence and human relatedness in them. These cultural values have been reported in diverse cultures in Africa, Asia, Indonesia and Polynesia. For example, Enriquez (1993) describes *kapwa* in the Philippines, and in Africa Holdstock (1999) describes *ubuntu*. Both concepts represent cultural value systems which emphasize a strong sense of human relatedness, the unity of the self (or individual) with others; they stress a shared identity as opposed to individual identity. In these cultures, human connectedness forms the cores of human values. *Kapwa* or *ubuntu* determines a person's personality and personhood. Without *kapwa* or *ubuntu* a person ceases to be human.

It is noteworthy that much the same case has been made from the feminist perspective (Allen, 1997). Gilligan (1982) critiqued Kohlberg's writings, pointing out that women of the West tend to achieve only the lower levels of moral development in Kohlberg's rankings. Women, if we are to take this at face value, simply do not have the moral sophistication of men. However, the much more tenable alternative is that there is something wrong with Kohlberg's notions. In keeping with the frequently expressed view that women in the West subscribe much more to a social and community ethic than men, Gillian argued that women's morality is social and concerned about interpersonal relationships. Its aim is the maintenance of caring relationships and how moral choices will affect everyone else. This is different from the individualistically orientated morality of Western men, with its emphasis on abstract principles at the expense of consideration of consequences for others.

In this sense, the responsibility for doing something about the failings of psychology spreads much more widely than the individual practitioners to a much broader group who actively promulgate, through teaching, Western ideology as science, as the given and universal. In order to broaden our understanding of human development and behaviour, we must venture beyond our horizons by studying and respecting alternative perspectives.

# Chapter 5

# Race, culture, and the family: implications for policy and practice

*To be born into an ethnic minority in Britain – particularly... whose origins are in Bangladesh, Caribbean or Pakistan – is to face a higher risk of leading a life marked by low income, repeated unemployment, poor health and housing... than someone who is white.*

Amin and Oppenheim, 1992, p. 63

These risks are positively correlated with low educational achievement. It is also almost a truism that children from these ethnic backgrounds do not achieve their potential in the educational systems of the West. It is evidently true of the British education system. This was fully recognized by the Swann report as long ago as 1985. Although many deny it, a major cause of ethnic minority children's (especially African-Caribbean children's) underachievement in the school systems of the West is racism, both within the school system and within society as a whole. In recent history, psychologists and educationalists propagated the idea that people of African descent are intellectually inferior and educationally problematic. Notable examples were Jensen (1969) and Eysenck (1971). For those who hold this view, a group's 'race' determines its educability. Concerned psychologists (e.g., Kamin, 1974) quickly intervened with attempts to counter this belief, but the idea had already taken root in somewhat fertile soil. The deleterious impact of this view on the educational attainment of Black children in Western societies is immeasurable. In Britain, Coard (1971) provided chilling evidence of the influence of Jensen and Eysenck on curriculum and pedagogy for Black children. Modern day followers of such ideas include Rushton (1991). For these psychologists, Race = IQ, and IQ = Humanity.

That societies of the West are racially and culturally heterogeneous is publicly acknowledged and sometimes lauded as a positive benefit. In Britain, as elsewhere, this recognition is encaptured in a sequence of legislation (the Race Relations Act 1976, the Children Act 1989 and the NHS and Community Care Act 1990). The challenge of the third millennium is how we put into operation the challenges of the legislation. Are we prepared to formulate polices or design procedures to ensure the provision of services appropriate to such a society? Will we ensure that, regardless of race or ethnicity, all children have an equal chance of unfolding their potential; that all citizens – adults and children – have equal access to services and facilities?

Britain, as many other Western nations, has long been a multicultural nation. British culture consists of Welsh, Scottish, Irish and English cultures, not to mention other European (Western and Eastern) cultures, or regional and class cultures. The issue is no longer of culture or ethnicity as such, but rather the cultures or cultural practices of groups who are perceived by the majority group to be racially different – people who are not White. In this chapter, the important issues about race and culture are highlighted, and their implications are noted for policy and practice with ethnic minority children in today's (and tomorrow's) Britain, children of different racial and/or cultural backgrounds to our own.

## Race

What, then, is race? Many, including psychologists and allied professionals, now recognize race as socially fabricated; race is a social and political entity with no scientific basis. Montagu (1974, 1997) regards it as fallacious, as 'Man's most dangerous myth'. Not only is race a biologically meaningless concept to apply to people, but even the artificial divisions between the so-called racial groups are nebulous and unstable, biologically, socially and politically (Davis, 1991; Dummett, 1984; Howitt and Owusu-Bempah, 1994; Montagu, 1974, 1997; Owusu-Bempah, 1997; Owusu-Bempah and Howitt, 1999a, b). Notwithstanding, the quest for the notion of race and the search for its meaning continues. This is because race is a social construction that best serves the interests of those who designed it (Howitt, 1991). It provides a rationale or justification for policies and practices that would otherwise be unacceptable; it enables its inventors to justify their control over others, to rationalize their monopoly over power and resources. As Appiah (1985) adroitly said 'there is nothing [else] in the world that can do all we ask "race" to do for us' (pp. 35–6). He points out, however, 'What we miss through our obsession with [race] is, simply, reality' (pp. 35–6).

Reality in the present context, the reality facing us, is that race has acquired social significance far beyond anything imaginable or justifiable on its meagre biological foundations. Race implies not just a superior–inferior dichotomy, but rather a 'trichotomy', distinctions between intellectually, culturally, morally and socially superior, not-so-inferior and inferior groups. It serves as a cue to more significant attributes of a group, including its culture, whereby one group's culture or way of life is presumed to be superior (or not so inferior) to those of others. The discourse and rhetoric employed in the service of race, to identify and describe different racial groups and their worth have changed substantially over time; but the notion of race as a vital social reality endures. We seem to have difficulty in abandoning our belief in race because it is fabricated specially to justify or assuage our conscience about our differential and unfair treatment of groups on the grounds of their skin colour. It provides us with the 'be-all and the end-all' justification for racial inequality and its concomitant social inequalities, principally political and economic inequalities. Owusu-Bempah (1999) has argued that the belief in race, like IQ, class, gender, and so forth, enables the oppressors to justify oppression, and the victims to rationalize their submission to victimization.

We have seen that the idea that human beings can be categorized into discrete racial groups with the resultant differential perception and treatment of people is not novel. The idea spans several centuries. There is an overabundance of historical and contemporary evidence of it for both real and artificial groups (Esmail and Everington, 1993; Howitt and Owusu-Bempah, 1990b; Owusu-Bempah, 1994; Richards, 1995). In Chapter 1, we discussed empirical demonstrations by various investigators of the enduring influence of the myth of race on the thinking and practice of professionals such as social workers and nurses. Such research evidence is unsurprising, given that prevailing societal values, beliefs, myths and folklore largely influence a profession's guiding principles, values and practice. Racial myths and stereotypes still pervade Western society and its institutions. Why then should it be unusual, in view of the fact that professions, including psychology, are all cultural products, socially, ideologically, politically and economically based? Psychology receives and transmits the history and ideologies of the culture in which it developed and is practised. In their dealings with ethnic minority children and families, for example, psychologists have a long tradition of using race as a frame of reference, as a means of providing one group, via discourses, with the power or conviction to classify or categorize other groups and exercise control over them. In post-modern terminology (Foucault, 1979), it enables the agents of one group (Caucasians) such as psychologists, psychiatrists and therapists to abstract Black and ethnic minority groups from their day-to-day realities. Then they are labelled as pathological or problems that can only be dealt with by White experts or professionals (Rossiter *et al.*, 1998).

Warnings against the dangers of this belief and practice (Howitt and Owusu-Bempah, 1999; Owusu-Bempah, 1997; Owusu-Bempah, 1999; Owusu-Bempah and Howitt, 1999b) seem, so far to have gone unheeded. However, others recognize the problem:

> *Psychotherapists in public practice in settings that are closer to state power and social control must assume that therapy has the potential for malignancy on the basis of the history of mental health and the state. Therefore, they require a conception of ethics that acknowledges the relationships of therapists and clients within a state apparatus.*
>
> Rossiter *et al.*, 1998, p. 9

Rossiter *et al.* discuss the work of Foucault (1979) in relation to the link between professional knowledge and power. They maintain that mental health professionals – psychiatrists, psychologists, and therapists – are empowered by society to separate the 'abnormal' from the 'normal', the 'sick' from the 'well', and the 'good' from the 'bad'. Practitioners often achieve this through the power of discourse, by convincing their clients, through talk that they are not 'normal', and that only professionals can help them to become 'normal'. Our view is that this is what therapy for identity, for instance, is about. Maximé (1991a, b) provides a clear example when she assumes that Black children experience 'identity crises' because they have favourable attitudes to White people and the White community. For example, she describes a 10–year-old Black girl as psychologically disturbed, simply because she preferred 'a white family placement as black ones are all too poor' (p. 103). Describing this girl's choice as astute, based upon reality, would be more helpful, even though it may not be 'politically correct'. However, such an interpretation would not be in society's interest. Society demands that these children and their families be seen as defective, a burden, in order to justify marginalizing and disenfranchizing them, at least with regard to access to services and other resources. It would also seriously implicate Black and ethnic minority professionals; it would challenge them to work towards the elimination of those structural barriers which hinder Black and ethnic minority communities from providing foster homes to their young members who are in need of such and other help. In this case, one may detect a coalition of interests, perhaps.

There is further contemporary evidence indicating that professionals have a repertoire of beliefs and assumptions about ethnic minorities and their cultural practices, especially their child-rearing practices, which adversely affect their work with Black and ethnic minority clients (e.g., Owusu-Bempah, 1994; Richards, 1995). This is in spite of the fact that many professionals today avoid the term 'race'. Although they try to distance themselves from race, they still use it as a mutable concept, a concept that alters, fluctuates and adapts to the prevailing socio-political environment. For instance, the term 'culture' or 'ethnicity' is often employed euphemistically by politically correct professionals to signify the more contentious term 'race' or 'racial', to denote 'Black' (with all its negative connotations) or, at best, exotic. For example, Maitra (1995) has noted that the children of immigrants from

Western and Eastern European countries tend quickly to lose their ethnic or cultural minority status, while second or even third generation South Asians, Africans and African-Caribbeans remain ethnic minorities. Even children and adults of 'mixed-race' parentage are regarded as ethnic minorities. Professionals see them as out-groups, and are expected to be like 'us' in order to receive appropriate services, be they education, health care, or even justice. The Stephen Lawrence Enquiry provides vividly disturbing evidence of this (Macpherson, 1999).

## Culture, ethnicity, and the child

Any meaningful professional intervention, including psychological interventions, should be guided not only by clients' needs, but also their cultural beliefs and values (Owusu-Bempah, 1999c). In the case of children in Britain, the 1989 Children Act actively encourages workers to 'include the wider family and friends in situations where shared care of children is the cultural norm'. Besides, many also recognize that attention to the cultural context of the child's environment and experiences, especially his/her child-rearing experiences, is necessary for a better understanding of their developmental needs (Boushel, 1994). Yet, childcare practitioners still fail to appreciate, for example, the African adage: 'it takes a whole village [community] to raise a child'. They fail to accept, for example, the fact that adoption and fostering within the extended family or the larger community, a characteristic of collectivist cultures, constitutes a normal childcare arrangement (Owusu-Bempah, 1999c; Roland, 1988; Whiting and Edwards, 1988). Similarly, Maitra (1995) has observed that with ethnic minority children, parenting assessments are often required by professionals when the cause of the conflict appears to be parental authority, the parents' insistence on traditional practice. They tend to disregard the fact that such family conflict is a common feature of all families, irrespective of culture or ethnicity. How many White families have not been in conflict with a son or daughter over whom they date in terms of age, colour, religion, sexual orientation or class? That is, family conflict assumes greater salience or significance for professionals when it involves ethnic minority families. May the tendency of professionals to overreact to or misconstrue ethnic minority cultural practices be due to a lack of respect for, or at best misunderstanding of, ethnic minority cultures?

Culture has been variously defined by the social science disciplines. The consensus, however, is that the term 'culture' refers to a composite structure of the corporeal, the symbolic and the mythical: objects, institutions, artefacts, beliefs, ideas, mythology, religion, rituals and so forth, transmitted and internalized in varying degrees by members of that culture. The culture of a given group is the sum of the shared ways of thought, reactions, rituals, customs and habits or behaviour acquired directly or vicariously by its members. It includes child-rearing practices, kinship patterns, marriage rites, diet, dress, music and art; it also includes interpersonal relationships. Thus, Rhoner (1984) has described culture briefly as an organized system of meanings which its members attribute to the persons, objects and ideas that constitute that culture. Artefacts aside, most of the elements of a culture are intangible, such as beliefs, values, and ideas which its members incorporate into their selfhoods; as such they are a potent force in moulding and shaping their dreams, aspirations and conduct. In short, one's cultural background is hardly separable from one's psychological processes. Although its members share a culture, each member experiences it in a unique way, resulting in individual personalities.

The term 'ethnicity' (which nowadays seems to carry the same meaning as 'race') is relatively new in mainstream psychological writings. Both culture and ethnicity are frequently used synonymously, but there is a conceptual distinction between them, as the following definitions of ethnicity illustrate. Phinney (1996, p. 918) views ethnicity as a 'multidimensional construct consisting of cultural norms and values... and the experiences and attitudes associated with [a given group]'. Weidman (1978, pp. 16–17), on the other hand, defines ethnicity as a 'culturally transmitted meaning structure' which 'can be determined by taking into consideration linguistic terms, marriage patterns, ethnic friendship networks, socialisation in established ethnic enclaves, and self definition in certain instances'. Montagu (1974, 1997) similarly describes an ethnic group 'as one of a number of populations which individually maintain their differences (physical and cultural) by means of isolating mechanisms such as geographic and social barriers. An ethnic group may be a nation, a people, a language group, or a group bound together in a coherent cultural entity by a religion' (1974, p. 186). An earlier definition of ethnicity by Morris (1968, p. 167) portrays an ethnic group as a 'distinct category of the population in a larger society whose culture is usually different from its own... the members of such a group are, or feel themselves, or are thought to be bound together by common ties of race or nationality or culture'.

In short, these definitions imply that there is no single criterion by which an ethnic group can be defined, explaining its persistently interchangeable use with related terms: race, culture and nationality. They show also that it is not only Black and ethnic minority groups who have ethnicity. In fact, combined, they suggest that a person may have not just one ethnicity, but rather a multiple ethnicity, in terms of age, geographical region, sex or gender, occupation, religion, and so forth, besides race, colour and nationality.

# Individualism versus collectivism

Attempts have been made to classify cultures according to whether they are individual-orientated or group-orientated, whether they are characterized by individualism (independence) or by collectivism (interdependence). For example, Triandis (1995) and other investigators (e.g., Markus and Kitayama, 1991) have suggested four attributes which distinguish individualist cultures from collectivist cultures. These features are:

1 *Conceptions of the self*: collectivist cultures define the self in terms of group identity, interdependence with the members of one's group or community; individualist cultures conceive of the self as autonomous and independent of others.
2 *Setting of goals*: in collectivist cultures, group goals have primacy over individual goals; individualists, on the other hand, give priority to their personal goals and accomplishments.
3 *Norms and attitudes*: collectivists tend to use cultural or group values as determinants of their social behaviour; individualists give more importance to attitudes or personal standards as determinants of social behaviour.
4 *Meeting needs*: in collectivist cultures, the needs of the community predominate. For example, if a relationship is desirable from the point of view of the group (e.g., the family), but costly from the point of view of the individual, the individual is likely to stay in the relationship. In contrast, individualists engage in exchange relationships ('What is in it for me?'), so that if the 'costs' of being in a social transaction exceed the benefits, individualists terminate the transaction.

These features indicate that cultures differ in their perception of the individual's relation to others. Triandis (1995) and others (e.g. Markus and Kitayama, 1991; Owusu-Bempah and Howitt, 1995) claim that, generally speaking, Western cultures are individualist, whereas most other cultures are collectivist.

Others classify cultures in terms of their perception and use of time. For example, Hall (1983) and Levin and Bartlett (1984) distinguish between cultures that view time as a scarce commodity and cultures that view time as a limitless resource. According to these investigators, individualist cultures view time as a precious resource which can be 'used', 'saved', 'bought' or 'wasted', ideally a resource which must be rationed and controlled through the use of schedules and appointments, for instance, by doing only one thing at a time. In contrast, time abounds in collectivist cultures; individuals have a flexible attitude to time. The elasticity of time enables them to service their various relationships, to meet their obligations to the various members of the community to whom they are bound. In the West, an obvious implication for psychologists, working with individuals from collectivist cultural backgrounds is that strict adherence to schedules and appointments may impede therapy. It may partly account for the reported reluctance of ethnic minorities to enter therapy, and their high dropout rates when they do so (e.g., Moncayo, 1998; Sue, 1998).

The literature reviewed earlier (Chapter 2) suggests that a uni-dimensional analysis may not be sensitive enough to enable us to distinguish between cultures or groups on the unipolar individual-ism–collectivism dimension. Both individualism (a sense of autonomy) and collectivism (interdependence) may be found in the same culture, albeit in varying degrees. Hence, we concur with Azuma (1984) in suggesting that this criterion be replaced with, at least, a bi-dimensional criterion. A given culture may occupy a certain position on each dimension at a given point in time, and a member of that culture may exhibit either characteristic in a given situation and time.

## Culture, the family and the child

*The caretakers of young children [of all societies] do have goals that are universal (e.g., protection, socialisation), there are societal differences in the behaviours of caretakers that are related to the community's ecology, basic economy, social organisation, and value systems.*

Whiting and Edwards, 1988; p. 8

That is, we derive our meaning or understanding of childhood from our culture. This evidently gives rise to cultural variations in the meaning of childhood and child-rearing practices. The way a group perceives childhood, and hence, brings up its children, is determined by the group's culture. For example, in Western (capitalist) societies, as we have seen, a high premium is placed upon loyalties to the 'self' (oneself), so that children in these societies are brought up to be indi-vidualistic; they are taught to see themselves as autonomous, distinct agents, self-reliant and independent. By contrast, many other societies (like some White working-class and rural communities to an extent) are collectivist. They place great emphasis upon group loyalties, chil-dren are socialized to see themselves in terms of their relation to both the physical and social environments, to relate interdependently or coexist with their environment (Enriquez, 1993; Fogel, 1993; Landrine, 1992; Marsella *et al.*, 1985; Miller, 1997; Owusu-Bempah, 1999c; Owusu-Bempah and Howitt 1995, 1997; Rosemont, 1997; Triandis, 1995). Members of these cultures feel psychologically empty or incomplete without a sense of belonging (to the family or the commu-nity).

Collectivist cultures inculcate a strong sense of family loyalty that often extends beyond the 'nuclear' family of parents and their children. Family obligations extend to distant cousins, in-laws, and others who are made a part of the family, such as sponsors and close friends. In these cultures, the extended family forms the basic social and economic nucleus. Within the extended family (which may be 'as long as a piece of string'), there is mutual sharing of resources and good fortunes, and despair and disappointments are also equally shared; there is a community of fate. Such cultural values have been reported in diverse cultures in Africa, Asia and Indonesia. For example, Azuma (1984), among others, describes *amae* among confucians; Enriquez (1993) describes *kapwa* in the Philippines; and in Africa, Holdstock (1999) describes *ubuntu*. As previously discussed, in these cultures, human connectedness is *sine qua non*. These basic values are cultivated at a very early age by the family. They are manifest even in second generation members of collectivist cultures living in societies characterized by individualism, such as Britain (Heuvel *et al.*, 1992; Marsella *et al.*, 1985, Owusu-Bempah, 1999a, c).

## Culture and family function

To reiterate, no group's culture is superior or inferior to that of another (Montagu, 1974; 1997). The differences observed between cultural groups are due to the simple fact that each group lives in a different physical and/or social environment. This means that there is no justification for professional concern about the (adverse) psychological effects of another cultural group's child-rearing practices, as demonstrated by a recent British study (Hackett and Hackett, 1994) which examined the differences in child-rearing practices between two groups of mothers (Gujarati mothers and indigenous White mothers). Specific areas of interest were discipline, feeding, sleeping arrangements and toilet training. In the area of discipline, for example, there were similarities in the use of smacking and withholding privileges. However, the Gujarati mothers, compared to their White counterparts, employed emotional methods of discipline, such as threats to send the child away (for misbehaviour), withdraw love and affection from the child or bring in an outside authority figure – a teacher, doctor, social worker or police officer. The Gujarati mothers' tactics of child discipline may be at odds with Western received wisdom. That is, many childcare practitioners, trained in the Rogerian, Bowlbian, or Ericksonian tradition, might be inclined to disapprove of these methods. However, it must be noted that the study found the Gujarati children to be better adjusted emotionally than their White counterparts.

Hackett and Hackett's study clearly cautions against ethnocentrism, or 'professionocentrism' – the belief or assumption that in the professional–client encounter, professional (Western) values are the only values; the belief that there is only one opinion, the professional opinion; the assumption that the professional text is the only text (or knowledge-base) – in short, the professional arrogance that the practitioner always knows best what is in the client's interest.

In most cultures outside the Western world, one seeks to advance the family rather than oneself; a member's concern is for the welfare and happiness of the family as a whole. Thus, one engages in secondary control. That is, individuals are changed, adjusted and acted upon until they fit more harmoniously within the family, relationship or community; alternatively, the entire group is changed to improve the quality of life of all of its members, rather than for any individual. Family therapy based on this philosophy is appropriate in this setting. Unfortunately, professionals in the West, including therapists and counsellors, often misinterpret this radically different understanding of family function. They tend to see some members of these families as displaying submissiveness, passivity or helplessness. Miatra (1995) has cautioned against providing, for example, assertiveness training to individual members of a collectivist family perceived to be submissive. It is misguided and inimical to satisfactory therapeutic outcomes, in so far as family and self are a single, internal unit.

A study carried out on the behalf of Joseph Rowntree Foundation (Hylton, 1997) suggests that ethnic minority families who develop values which oppose the materialism and individualism of the UK majority community, who uphold collectivist values, cope better with most social and personal problems. In this study, it was found that ethnic minority families preferred solving problems for themselves or within the extended family or the community to voluntary or statutory solutions. Indeed, most of the ethnic minority respondents expressed concern about the actions of professionals, such as schoolteachers and social workers. They saw them as interfering and undermining parental authority. It was also found that a majority of the ethnic minority women interviewed were adapting to life in the UK, but preferred to stay within their own cultural traditions. These findings reinforce the call by many (e.g. Owusu-Bempah, 1999; Silavwe, 1995) for caution in the application of Western principles or values in cross-cultural work with children and families.

It must be emphasized that even though most of the West's ethnic minority communities may be described as collectivist, each has identifying characteristics. Culturally, they differ in many important features, including child-rearing practices. These variations, in turn, differ from the majority culture that is often placed above the ethnic minorities. These differences unfortunately lead professionals to misinterpret and pathologize minority cultural beliefs and habits, including their child-rearing practices. For example, South Asian children, especially girls, are typically viewed by professionals as over-protected, over-controlled or oppressed by their families and their socialization process as a whole. The obverse is believed about African-Caribbean children: that their families have no control over them, resulting in their 'delinquency – drug-taking, promiscuity, educational underachievement and criminality'. Ironically, these very same professionals seem to recommend the practices of each group for the other. They advise South Asian families to be lax in their socialization of children: 'the social worker I had... prior to my son was taken into care... said the child should not be taught, he should be allowed to go out and play and that's how they learn' (Howitt, 1992, p. 165)

African-Caribbean families, on the other hand, are advised to lock up their children. The material previously discussed in connection with the influence of the Moynihan report must not be dismissed as history. Apart from being current, the ethnicity and professional standing of the authors of the following text makes it a special case in point. Writing in the middle of the 'politically correct' 1990s, Dwivedi and Varma (1996), both of South Asian origin, give the following description of African-Caribbean families and their children's developmental and educational needs: 'West Indians [in Britain] tend to be unaware of the emotional needs of the growing child...[Consequently] Many West Indian children now attending secondary schools are grossly retarded educationally' (pp. 43–4).

The authors, a child psychiatrist and an educational psychologist, in the following recommendation deliver a body blow to the educational aspirations of African-Caribbean children: 'We... need to think in terms of planning, for the children... the type of curriculum which would aim at exploiting their particular interests, with emphasis on... woodwork, metalwork, handicraft, art... For this group particularly we would need a reorganization of the traditional remedial class within the school, if we hope to sustain their interest in class, and reduce the degree of difficult behaviour seen at school' (p. 47).

As previously shown, it appears that being Black or an ethnic minority *per se* offers no immunity against the influence of racist literature, so long as one practises psychology. The arguments advanced by the authors of 'a tangle of pathology' tradition, irrespective of their skin colour, all present versions of the Moynihanian problem approach to the study and understanding of Black families. They disregard, and encourage others to ignore, other perspectives to the understanding of Black and ethnic minority families, and the difficult circumstances in which they live. Sadly, such literature, reinforced by the media and political propaganda, is seen by many as an authoritative confirmation of the popular belief that ethnic minority families are problem-ridden. Father absence, single-parent mothers, matriarchal family structures, divorce, lackadaisical discipline, lack of educational aspiration and so forth, are believed to typify the African-Caribbean family. Again, the list for South Asian families is different but equally long, including:

overcrowded households and academically unrealistic expectations for their children.

It has been argued that psychologically, much of the (unconscious) professional urge to influence ethnic minority children and families to toe the majority cultural line stems from the assumption that they would be 'better off' if they experienced themselves and the world as Westerners (or the professionals themselves) do. There seems to be a long tradition of this urge among those concerned with child welfare. For example, Wagner (1979) remarked of Dr Barnardo: 'he was fighting to retain custody, not principally to prevent children returning to cruel parents, but to prevent their being brought up as Roman Catholics'. (quoted by Forsythe, 1995, p. 7)

This is not to suggest that negative aspects of an ethnic minority family should be accepted as normal and used as an excuse for a non-intervention stance when a child desperately needs intervention and protection. Simple adherence to banal 'ethno-sensitivity' (i.e. sensitivity to ethnic minority cultures) may assume, for example, that abuse (seen as such even by members) is acceptable in the child's culture. The consequence of such over-sensitivity may be at least as harmful as that of insensitivity.

To be fair, it must be acknowledged that in recent years, partly as a result of pressures from ethnic minority communities, social workers and other professionals have made efforts to 'understand' Britain's ethnic minority cultures. Nevertheless, this by itself is not sufficient to enable them to meet the needs of ethnic minority children. To achieve this, they need also to respect their cultural backgrounds. Additionally, they must expand their knowledge of the social, political and economic causes of their clients' problems, while appreciating the role that they can play in helping or worsening those problems. The aim is to develop effective strategies to overcome the barriers to providing appropriate services to ethnic minority children and families. Current attempts to address these issues have tended to be preoccupied with the establishment of Black 'experts' within the relevant professions (Owusu-Bempah, 1997). As indicated already, even those whom one would expect to be more understanding or sympathetic towards ethnic minority children and their families' circumstances sometimes propagate ideas or perspectives damaging to their well-being. This raises the pertinent question as to whether the recruitment of more ethnic minority professionals by itself will improve the situation for ethnic minority clients. We have shown that both British and North American studies suggest that this is not necessarily the case (e.g. Barth, 1997; Courtney *et al.*, 1996; Hall, 1997; O'Brian, 1990; Owusu-Bempah, 1989a, 1990, 1994, 1997). Thus in the area of fostering/adoption, for example, Barth (1997) suggests, on the basis of research evidence, that the power of the ethnic matching preferences be reduced in the interest of the children: 'distasteful as this may be to many adoption specialists of all ethnic backgrounds, reducing the emphasis on racial matching must be a component of any serious plan to provide equal rights to a family for African-American children' (p. 302)

In cross-ethnic therapy, Hall (1997) declares that 'not all the perpetrators of cultural errors [read racism] are White' (p. 645). Such views seriously question the usefulness of the notion of 'Black perspectives' (which are in reality White perspectives) in social work and therapy, for instance. Its utility is further questioned by its proponents' (e.g., Ahmad, 1990; Robinson, 1995) failure to define it. No group of workers, be it social workers or psychologists, can claim a professional status on the basis of ideas which cannot be defined. It appears, therefore, that this notion only serves to muddy the waters. To borrow Wakefield's (1996) suggestion in relation to eco-systems, 'Black perspectives' proponents confuse the field's intellectual discourse by trying to force their ideological agenda on the profession. In practical terms, one cannot guarantee the effectiveness of a practice based upon fuzzy ideas, so that the claim that therapists need so-called 'Black perspectives' in order to ensure their effectiveness appears to be baseless. Indeed, Owusu-Bempah (1994, 1997) has argued that the only utility of such untested ideas as 'Black perspectives' (or more to the point, professional perspectives) which derive from the notion of race (itself unfounded), is in further disadvantaging ethnic minority children (and adults) in the provision of services and facilities.

This is by no means to suggest that ethnic minority members have no part to play in the child welfare professions, including mental health, and educational psychology. The argument here is that, as far as helping ethnic minority children and families is concerned, their most valuable contribution would appear to be one of helping other colleagues to develop an understanding of, and respect for, ethnic minority cultures and cultural practices. Individually, they cannot claim expertise in all matters cultural or ethnic. Some (e.g. Owusu-Bempah, 1990, 1999b; Owusu-Bempah and Howitt, 1999a; Stevenson, 1998) have warned against the temptation to use 'ethnic minority specialists' to 'ghettoize' services to ethnic minority communities and their children.

It goes without saying that provision for ethnic minority children, for example, must vary according to the child's individual requirements. No standard package is available which could be expected to meet the needs of all children. However, as a group, these children have a shared pool of needs or experiences that are distinct from children from the dominant culture. Their experiences of racism is one of the most salient of these; being on the receiving end of racial prejudice, abuse and discrimination are inevitably influential in ways which simply do not apply to other groups of children. Furthermore, research (Brown, 1984; Modood *et al.*, 1997; Skellington and Morris, 1992) shows that racism is experienced by the significant people in their lives –

parents, siblings, uncles, aunts and grandparents – in virtually every important sector of society.

The racial injustice experienced by their significant others is directly and vicariously experienced. It is quite easy to see how the inter-generational effects of racial disadvantage operate. For example, parents who were discriminated against in education are more likely to transmit negative feelings about schooling to their offspring; bad childcare decisions made by professionals may cause both the parents and the children to suffer a sense of injustice; a child whose mother received inadequate or inappropriate antenatal care due to the racism within the health care system may carry the effects for life; parents who have been allocated poor housing on racial grounds have little choice but to live in deleterious circumstances with their children. The list is endless. Dummett (1984) has described the process by which racism takes its toll as being a pattern rather than a simple accumulation of experiences: 'each instance of discrimination against you increases the likelihood of discrimination working against you in some other instance' (p. 134).

## Recommendations

Addressing fully the needs of Black and ethnic minority children particularly requires recognition of, and solutions to, racism's injurious effects on them. Such solutions, however, will not be found without a genuine desire and concerted political will to change. Furthermore, the necessary change can only be effected if childcare professionals and policy-makers have accurate information about ethnic minority children upon which to base decisions and practice. Racially and culturally unbiased messages in which there is no room for myths, assumptions, stereotypes and conjecture are crucial to this important task. None of this is outside our collective will or individual power. 'None is totally without power; all groups have... and, therefore, the capacity to veto business as usual' (Willie, 1993, p.454). The issue, then, is whether we are prepared to exercise our power in ways that benefit ethnic minority families and children.

Obviously, the necessary changes require a new approach not only to practice or policy but, more importantly, education. In other words, to enable practitioners to be effective, and policy-makers to formulate the right policies, their education and training, including the literature to which they are exposed, should be empowering. Their education ought to equip them with:

> ... the means to critically appropriate knowledge existing outside their immediate experience in order to broaden their understanding of themselves, the world, and the possibilities for transforming the taken-for-granted assumptions about the way we live.
>
> Spring, 1994, p. 27

As Spring has suggested, practitioners are empowered to empower the powerless when they change their mode of thinking, when they become aware that they can exercise political power to bring about changes in their social and economic conditions and those of their clients. In short, at the core of empowering childcare practice should be an untiring quest for, or a burning desire, to eliminate racial injustice, thereby promoting every child's well-being, regardless of his/her race, culture or ethnicity, creed, gender or class. This objective can only be achieved by our being prepared to extend our horizon beyond that provided to us by the Western world, by being prepared to respect and learn from other psychologies.

# Chapter 6

# Race, self and culture

*The reasons for expecting blacks to have lower self-esteem were thus almost overwhelming. There is just one problem with this reasoning, however, namely, that it isn't true.*

Rosenberg, 1989, p. 362

From the perspective of White racist societies, their treatment of ethnic minorities, Black people of African ancestry in particular, is not only fair, but also natural (Howitt and Owusu-Bempah, 1994). The passage of time has produced many overlapping variants on this theme and, although once dominant views may have faded, they persist in people's minds and in society at large – in the collective unconscious. They resurface in an altered guise in a different time or, maybe, in a different place. In modern times, there has been a trinity justifying Black people's social disadvantage. This trinity consists of an assault on the intellect of Black people, an assault on the morality of Black people and an assault on the integrity of the Black soul (or personality) (Owusu-Bempah and Howitt, 1999a, b; Howitt and Owusu-Bempah, 1999). In other words, Black people are flawed psychologically, morally and socially. Of course, the assault extends beyond the individual psychology of Black people into the disparagement of their cultures, including their family structures and child-rearing practices. These assaults make it difficult for a racist society to conceive of Black families (and their children) as healthy, whole and functional.

Analysis of discourse would suggest that the racism to be found in the practices and writings of professionals and academics reflects everyday racist thinking or racism within society at large (e.g. Billig, 1988; Van Dijk, 1987). In this way, professionals reify and amplify the existing racism in society. Actually, things are sometimes worse than that; professionals and academics frequently create, legitimize and articulate fundamentally racist ideas. In relation to Black children, the role of professionals in the conceptualization of Black identity as problematic is more than just a small mischief. It is bad enough that the idea was thought of in the first place, worse still it has survived for decades, despite only the crudest of empirical support put forward for it and frequent criticisms against it. It is the way in which such unacceptable ideas linger in psychology without serious challenge that supports the view that psychology, as a discipline, is racist to the core.

The idea of Black 'identity problems' came to professional attention through the works of sociologists Park (1928, 1931) and Stonequist (1937) and their notion of the 'marginal man'. Both Park and Stonequist defined the 'marginal man' as a person who did not fall 'naturally' into one or the other major social groupings (i.e., Black or White) in the USA at the time. Marginal persons were the offspring of 'inter-racial' sexual unions. Thus, they objectively belonged to both communities. None-the-less, they were not accepted as such by either community; often communities rejected them. Marginal status was claimed to entail a whole range of disadvantages and difficulties in economic, social, cultural, spiritual and psychological matters. Culturally and socially, the marginal person was said to live in limbo. Psychologically, marginal individuals were perceived to experience torment, to experience psychiatric and emotional problems, low self-esteem and identity confusion.

The related idea of self-hatred has also had more impact than warranted by research findings. It originated in the works of Kurt Lewin (1935, 1941), an influential psychological theoretician, who applied the notion to American Jewish people. Essentially the idea is that minority communities learn and accept the racist views of their self as imposed by the dominant society. Through these means, in the present context, Black people learn to hate themselves just as White racist society despises them. While the idea originated in attempts to explain the characteristics of the Jewish community in the USA, the notion of self-hatred has lasted longer in the form of 'Black negative self-identity' and has spawned a mass of academic writings, research and speculations. The most popular type of research in this area has been the 'doll studies'. Nevertheless, in spite of the long history of research and effort in this field, there is little to tell us, with any precision, what constitutes an identity problem in the Black child.

These ideas are ingrained into professionals' dealings with Black people, people of African descent. The issue is the routine nature with which we are prepared to see the roots of the problems of Black people as lying in their self-concept. For example, Babiker and Arnold (1997) have a number of arguments pertinent to race in relation to self-injury and self-mutilation. They suggest that individuals may be affected by racism, for example, as in the case of racist bullying.

*The trauma, fear, isolation and alienation which such experiences may lead to could clearly be expected to lead to self-hatred and thus to self-injury for some people. One significant way in which racist attitudes may affect people is in their perceptions of and feelings about themselves and their own bodies. Evidence that many black people are made to feel uncomfortable about certain characteristics of their bodies is provided by*

*practices such as hair straightening, skin-bleaching and facial surgery.*
                                    Babiker and Arnold, 1997, pp. 47–8

The lack of necessity of such claims draws attention to them. They are essentially conjectural and suffer from tunnel vision. They ignore the body enhancement which is characteristic of many White people. Tanning, fake and otherwise, make-up, plastic surgery, hair colouring, perming and all the rest would not be regarded as signs that White people are dissatisfied with their whiteness and Caucasian characteristics.

## Let's pretend

Few pieces of social research have achieved a political impact to match that of the doll studies by Clark and Clark (1939, 1947). Typically, in these studies, children are asked to choose whether a Black doll or a White doll is the most like themselves. In the Clarks' study, for example, many children chose their own race doll, but there were some Black children who chose a White doll rather than the Black doll. To simplify a little, these 'wrong' choices were regarded as demonstrating the lack of esteem blackness had for many Black children. Thus, the children were claimed to be identity-confused since they were Black but appeared to prefer whiteness, or they lacked self-esteem simply because they were Black. On the basis of this research, among other things, the USA anti-segregationist movement successfully argued to the US Supreme Court that school segregation (educational apartheid) was not only damaging to Black children. This contributed to the Supreme Court's 1954 decision that school segregation was detrimental to Black children and also unlawful. In the history of post-war race relations, this was an event of monumental importance. It has to be classed among psychology's major (vicarious) achievements, irrespective of the adequacy or inadequacy of the doll studies generally. Notice that the doll-play studies were politically used as a means of achieving integration out of separatism.

Helping achieve the end to school segregation or apartheid is commonly seen as one of the major achievements of psychology towards social equality. It is one of the showpieces of psychology and probably cannot be bettered as evidence of what psychology can achieve. The paradox is that this particular achievement was based much more on interpretation rather than indisputable evidence. So the spectacular success of psychology in this public domain needs to be assessed not only in terms of the positive nature of its outcome but also the damaging nature of some of its implications. The 'doll show' (or the 'let's pretend show') has opened in different locations and periods since the Supreme Court decision of 1954. These studies have been repeated, with variations, in many countries, but they have singularly failed to settle the basic worries about the procedures. It is worthwhile examining the British research of the 1970s in this area to illustrate some of the issues. During that period, Milner (1975) intellectually led research in this field. He examined the racial identity of Black children in Britain, using very similar procedures to those of the Clarks. In many ways the show was a big success, as the general findings of the original doll studies were replicated in apparently very dissimilar circumstances. Consequently, Milner's studies have been very influential on practitioners in various professions in Britain and elsewhere, notably teaching and social work. Very few pieces of psychological research or theory have found such an audience outside of the profession.

Milner (1975) showed three different dolls of different skin tones to children in the 5- to 8-year-old age band in two British cities. One of the dolls was Black, another South Asian and the third was White. The dolls were appropriately ethnically or 'racially' painted and dressed. They were apparently fairly accurate in facial features, skin colour, eye colour and other anatomical features. The children were asked: 'Which doll looks the most like you?' In this study, all the White children chose the White doll; 76 per cent of the South Asian children chose the South Asian doll; but only 52 per cent of the African-Caribbean children chose the Black doll. That is, while none of the White children racially misidentified, 24 per cent and 48 per cent of the South Asian children and African-Caribbean children respectively did. When asked which of the dolls they would rather be, all of the White children chose the White doll, but four-fifths of the African-Caribbean children and two-thirds of the South Asian children said that they would prefer to be the White doll. Milner (1975) interprets this as 'apparently signifying that they would prefer to be white than a member of their own group' (p. 122). When asked which was the 'bad doll', the 'ugliest doll' and the 'nicest doll', approximately two-thirds of the South Asian and African-Caribbean children described the White doll in more favourable terms: 'In other words, the majority of black children ideally *prefer* to have white friends and playmates, and *aspire* to have white neighbours and companions when they grow up' (Milner, 1975, p. 122).

Several years later, a replication of this study did *not* find the same trend for such misidentification in Black children (Milner, 1983). A similar study in Britain by Davey and Mullin (1982) also failed to support Milner's original findings. Something had happened to change the often reported doll choices made by Black children. Milner suggested:

> During the same period, Britain's black communities were subjected to ever more extreme racism via the propaganda and provocation of overtly fascist political groups, out and out physical intimidation through racist attacks on people and their homes, while continuing to endure the day-to-day

*individual and institutional racism which circumscribes their life-chances. On the positive side, black consciousness has grown, black social and polit- ical organisations have flourished and black culture has evolved a specifically 'British' variant, all of which has given black children and youth an alternative, acceptable image of their group with which to identify. Both the good and the bad developments over the period can have left black chil- dren with little doubt (and little alternative) as to their identification. And this is surely what the doll studies have reflected, the progression of 'black- ness' from the negative towards the positive pole.*

Milner, 1983, p. 161

## A caveat

These new studies might have instilled hope and comfort in concerned individuals and groups. The message is hopeful enough: once, Black people in racist society grew to dislike their race and consequently themselves, but as a consequence of Black consciousness activity they no longer do so. Of course, it does assume that Black people did dislike themselves. However, other research suggests that, on a world-wide scale, the same social forces did not produce parallel changes in the 'enhanced' identities of Black children. For example, in 1987, consider- able media controversy erupted in the USA, following the reports of further studies of doll choice. Powell-Hopson and Hopson (1988) studied the choices made by Black youngsters between Black and White cabbage-patch dolls. She found that about two-thirds of the Black children in the study preferred the White doll, just as in the orig- inal studies by the Clarks (1939, 1947). A comparative study carried out in Trinidad and the USA also reported a tendency for Black children to prefer White dolls (Gopaul-McNichol, 1988). Gopaul-McNichol's find- ings clearly show that the forces claimed by Milner to have been responsible for British Black children's enhanced self-identity were not felt elsewhere, not even in a predominantly Black country like Trinidad. Milner's (1983) explanation for his findings, therefore, leaves several questions unanswered. For example, it does not address the observed negative relationship between Black children living in a Black country and having a negative racial identity and those living in a White society and having a positive racial identity. Thus, we are still left with the question of why Black children living in predominantly Black Trinidad should experience racial identity problems, whereas those living in predominantly White Britain have positive racial identity as a result of a brief period of radical social and 'political' changes (Owusu-Bempah and Howitt, 1999a). One obvious answer to this question is that, basi- cally, the misidentification studies, including the Clarks, are seriously flawed (Rosenberg, 1989).

The age of the children involved in the doll-studies is one of their inherent flaws. For example, Alejandro-Wright (1985) has argued that children in the age group used in these studies are not capable of experiencing racial self-hatred because they do not adequately grasp the concept of race. Indeed, what they appear to do is to classify people in terms of their literal skin colour. For example, they would categorize as Black people only those who have a very dark skin. They would also put into the category of White people, South Asian people and light-skinned Black people. Alejandro-Wright claims, therefore, that not until about 8 to 10 years of age do children begin to construe race in ways similar to its social representation (Farr and Moscovici, 1984), the way it is construed by adults; until then, it has no social significance for them. Similarly, Rosenberg (1989) argues that in the doll choice studies the children report pretty accurately in terms of skin colour rather than in terms of adults' conception of race or racial groups. Historical support for this can be found in one of the original reports by Clark and Clark (1947). In this study, 20 per cent of light-skinned children, 73 per cent of medium-skinned children and 81 per cent of dark-skinned children said that they were like the Black doll. This suggests that a concept such as Black self-hatred is unnecessary to explain the doll choices. Perhaps we should add that the concept of race is extremely complex and socially variable. So, for example, in apartheid South Africa, the category 'coloured' was determined by racial history, and not by skin to one. Likewise, Roma people (Gypsies) in today's Central and Eastern European nations, e.g. Slovenia, are frequently categorized as Black, and describe themselves as Black.

The complexity of the social construction of race for both Black and White young children has been demonstrated in many studies. Greenwald and Oppenheim's (1968) study is a classic demonstration. They used three dolls of different skin-colour, white, medium brown, and black, to test the Black self-hatred thesis. In these circumstances, only 13 per cent of Black children claimed that they were like the White doll. These figures are almost in direct contradiction to other doll studies using just a White doll and a Black doll, or White, Black and South Asian dolls. It is fascinating to note Rosenberg's (1989) observations on Greenwald and Oppenheim's finding regarding the White children and their doll choices: '44% of the white children said that they looked like the mulatto or dark brown doll. In terms of this criterion, then, the white children exhibit much more racial misidentification than the black' (p. 361).

At face value, this suggests that there is an urgent need to do something about White racial identity problems or White self-hatred. However, such findings would not seriously be interpreted in these terms largely because they are counter-intuitive. All the same, it begs the question as to why the notion of Black self-hatred seems such a reasonable concept to us that it is accepted virtually without question. There are a number of possibilities, of course, but racist societies have little difficulty in assuming that to be Black is to be doomed. After all, racism is little other than a process by which White society keeps Black people and ethnic minorities disadvantaged.

Most research has a currency of just a few years. Doll studies, on the other hand, have defied repeated criticisms and questions about their meaning and value, and have continued to influence theory and practice for more than half of a century. Furthermore, they seem set to influence future generations of psychologists. Of course, we recognize that, occasionally, a piece of research assumes more significance than actually warranted. Such research tends to have political or policy implications stretching far beyond its scientific bounds or practical utility (Howitt, 1992). Research in the area of race provides a clear example of this. In particular, studies of racial differences in intelligence gained more publicity and notoriety than could ever be explained in terms of the consensus that researchers achieved in their interpretation (Howitt and Owusu-Bempah, 1994). Black self-hatred is another example: believing that Black people hate themselves is to believe that they are damaged people to be dealt with as damaged people. It also serves to justify, in a curious way, the ghettoization or 'inferiorization' of Black people which has been a dominant feature of Western thought about Black and aboriginal peoples.

## The 'feel good' factor

The notions of Black self-hatred and identity conflict inevitably imply that the feelings of self-worth experienced by Black children are poor. There is little historical and contemporary empirical support for this. It is a myth, and serves much the same functions as any other myth; like most myths, it is not particularly amenable to alteration and change. For example, for over twenty years now, researchers have collected evidence which shows that Black people's self-esteem is no different from that of White people (Baldwin, 1979; Cross, 1991; Heiss and Owen, 1972; Owusu-Bempah, 1994a; Rosenberg, 1989), but still the myth lives on. In a review of studies published in the 1960s and 1970s concerning self-esteem in Black people relative to White people, Cross (1985) reported the following: 51 studies found the self-esteem of Black and White people to be equal; 21 found that the self-esteem of Black people was higher; 16 found the self-esteem of White people to be higher than that of Black people; 13 found that there was no consistent trend in either direction. Given that research tends to yield somewhat unreliable and inconsistent findings in general, the studies, overall, do not support the claim that self-esteem in Black people is any lower than that of White people. In fact, Cross's findings suggest the opposite.

Clark (1992) broadly agrees with this interpretation. She describes the findings of studies of Black self-esteem as 'contradictory'. Her own study examined racial preferences (for their own race versus the White race), racial attitudes (positive or negative), and aspects of the self-esteem of Black children aged between 8 and 12 years. Each child's self-esteem was measured using items from standard psychological tests (the Coppersmith self-esteem inventory and the Piers-Harris Self-Concept Scale). Instead of regarding self-esteem as a very general or global aspect of a child's experience, specific aspects of the children's views of themselves as individuals were assessed. The following were measured:

1  General self-esteem – e.g. 'I feel good about myself'.
2  Physical appearance – e.g. 'I am good looking'.
3  Social – e.g. 'My family is disappointed in me'.
4  Personal – e.g. 'I worry a lot'.
5  Academic/school – e.g. 'I forget what I learn'.

Using a sophisticated statistical procedure (multiple regression), it was found that: satisfaction with personal appearance and social acceptance, especially by significant others, best predicted self-esteem; and race did not affect specific aspects of self-esteem. In addition, the children's feelings about race were assessed with regard to: *preferences for Black and White races* (for example, asking the children which of two men, one Black and the other White, they would like to work for at a bakery) and *racial attitudes* (for example, whether a Black boy or White boy was the most likely to pick on other children). Contrary to the predictions of doll studies, none of the children showed a preference for another racial group: they identified themselves as Black.

Other studies also show that Black children's conception of the 'Black race' has no significant influence on any measure of their self-concept (e.g. Rosenberg, 1979, 1989; McAdoo, 1978; Spencer, 1984). Rosenberg (1979), for example, found no relationship between Black children's attitude to their race and their personal sense of self-esteem. McAdoo (1978), likewise, has described how negative cognitions about one's own race and positive personal identity co-exist in some Black children: how some Black children harbour negative attitudes to their own race but still hold positive views about themselves. According to McAdoo, the children are able to achieve this because they develop an ability to separate their racial attitudes from their ideas of themselves. This does not seem to be as difficult a feat to perform as it sounds. White racists who make generally disparaging statements or comments about Black people as a whole often specifically except Black people with whom they are friendly or have an acquaintance (Howitt *et al.*, 1989). Some European studies support these American findings. For example, in a study of the impact of ethnic minority status on global self-esteem comparing Dutch and Turkish children in the Netherlands, Verkuyten (1989) found no support for the widely held assumption that ethnic minorities have lower over-all self-esteem. That is, their low social status, powerlessness and subjection to prejudice and discrimination did not dent their sense of personal worth. Similarly, in Eastern Europe, Costarelli (1993) has observed that rural gypsies in Poland and Romania do believe that they are superior to non-gypsies, however poor and oppressed they themselves are.

Bagley and Young (1988) report conflicting findings in a series of studies in which pre-school children in Britain, Jamaica, Canada, Ghana and the USA were tested on their racial attitudes and self-esteem. Although, in general, they found no over-all relationship between racial attitudes and self-esteem, this was not true for White English, British African-Caribbean and Jamaican children living in Toronto. The White English children who positively evaluated white-ness had greater self-esteem, whereas the British African-Caribbean children had lower self-esteem if they positively evaluated whiteness. African children living in both England and Canada actually had higher self-esteem than White children did, in contrast to African-Caribbean children in Canada who had lower self-esteem than their White peers did. Unfortunately, the authors failed to report the relative self-esteem levels for all of the eight groups of children they studied. What we can say with some confidence is that the self-esteem of Black children in general is not closely tied with their valuations of whiteness. Nevertheless, Baggley and Young interpreted their findings in terms of familiar shibboleths about Black children's cultural needs: 'a secure, deeply-rooted black culture fosters healthy identity development in black children... There is little doubt that support for a group's traditional culture indirectly fosters both the family stability of that group and the development of a healthy ethnic identity in children' (pp. 57-58).

This, to us, is a tortuous conclusion since the study concerned the relationship between racial attitude and self-esteem rather than culture or family stability and ethnic identity. It seems that the investigators were too timid to attribute or associate the problems experienced by some of the children to racism, the main culprit. Weinreich (1983) acknowledges this. He sampled the self-esteem of adolescent offspring of White English, African-Caribbean and South Asian parents using a relatively complex procedure. Although the South Asian and African-Caribbean adolescents tended to be some-what lower in self-esteem than their White counterparts, it was very clear that the White adolescents devalued people of Indian and African-Caribbean origins. However: 'discrimination against blacks does not result in a general across-the-board self-devaluation of them-selves. In individual cases, elements of self-rejection as a result of discrimination do occur, though even then this may not be global self-rejection' (Weinreich, 1979a, p. 183).

# Changing direction

In order to help Black children, professionals and all concerned must carefully distinguish between the children's personal identity and their feelings about the Black community generally. Racism may negatively affect their perception or beliefs about their own race, but this does not automatically, nor necessarily, affect their sense of self-worth. Rather, it is their life-chances which are restricted by racism, especially institutional racism, including professional racism. Institutional racism thwarts their efforts and aspirations, and very likely makes them embittered and angry. Our focus, therefore, must be on the racist system rather than the individual psychology of the children.

Various studies support this claim. These include research which has specifically examined the relationship between psychosocial development, cultural identity and self-esteem (e.g. Leung and Drasgow, 1986; Terrell *et al.*, 1980; Whaley, 1993). These are factors worthy of investigation since they play an important role in the over-all adjustment of all children, irrespective of race. Studies in this particular area tend to support our argument that, in our efforts to provide Black children with a professional service, we should pay particular attention to the system or environment in which they operate as a whole, rather than their self-identity or self-esteem. For example, Whaley (1993) has argued that, in terms of educational achievement, competence rather than self-esteem is the key factor. A supportive environment, which at the same time fosters competence, appears to be a more important factor in academic success than self-identity. In short, as Hughes and Demo (1989) have urged: 'It is time we turned away from the issue of self-esteem... and focused instead on personal efficacy, the social-psychological characteristics most affected by racial inequality'(p. 154).

Many of the claims made about identity problems in ethnic minority children are little more than stereotypes conflated with half-digested humanistic psychology.

> There is a stereotype of children who are ethnically Asian, but who have been brought up in this country: those who are, in the language of two popular images, 'between two cultures' and a 'half-way generation'. It is that they live in a tension between two conflicting systems of meaning and value, and therefore experience a problem of 'personal identity'. A superficial analogy can be made between their predicament and that of the offspring of racially mixed marriages, who might also be supposed liable to 'identity-confusion'.
>
> Kitwood, 1983, p. 129

Kitwood suggests that Erikson's (1968) ideas about adolescence have been generally adopted because of the notions of adolescent rebellion which dominated the thinking of sociologists, psychologists, the media and, consequently, the Western world in the 1960s. The resonance between the popular concerns over the then new phenomenon of the teenager, and the emphasis of theories on the problems of establishing a personal identity, ensured their survival when much of Erikson's writings have been long forgotten. The hue and cry about the rebellion of White adolescents may have subsided, but only to be replaced by another – that of Black adolescents. South Asian female adolescents have attracted special attention from professionals, especially teachers and social workers. In this case, however, efforts are directed towards encouraging them to reject, rather than conform to, their religious or cultural norms (see, for example, Ahmed, 1991; Ely and Denny, 1987, for critiques of the above).

Some researchers have considered the possibility that self-esteem can be separated into the 'public domain self-esteem' and the 'private domain self-esteem'. Essentially the idea is that self-esteem owing to intimate interactions with significant others in one's life need not be the same as self-esteem resulting from interaction with the dominant culture through, say, the educational system in which racist assumptions are very often communicated. Thus Martinez and Dukes (1991), for example, emphasize the concept of 'ethgender' to describe the process whereby race and gender combine to produce life experiences which are more than the separate influences of race or gender alone. The experience of being a Black woman, for instance, is more than that of being a woman or Black. They studied two groups of adolescents over a period of three years. The 'ethgender' categories included Native American males and American females, African-American males and females, and White males and females, among others. These students were asked to rate how they perceived themselves on the measure of intelligence compared to the average for their age – this essentially was the measure of public domain self-esteem. All of the groups, with the exception of the White males, rated themselves lower than the age average. Clearly, the White males were markedly different from the rest in that they, on average, saw themselves as more intelligent than the rest. When it came to the matter of private domain self-esteem, the youngsters were asked to rate their personal satisfaction with themselves. The pattern changed somewhat: many of the ethgender groups now rated themselves above the average. African-American males and females, Chicanos, Chicanas and White males all rated themselves above average; however, Native Americans, Asian males and females, and White females generally tended to rate themselves below average. (It should be added that the study made allowance for factors such as parental education, academic achievement and other factors which might have operated as confounding factors, or influenced the findings.) Quite clearly, professionals need to be aware that the machinations of self-esteem are subtle and differentiated markedly by the particularities of the individual's social situation.

Other evidence that lends support to these findings can be found in Phinney's (1992) study. Her intention was to find a measure of ethnic identity which was largely independent of any particular culture. Thus, she sought to find a measure applicable to both Black and White youngsters. The Multigroup Measure of Ethnic Identity included items designed to measure aspects of identification with one's own group (e.g. 'I have spent time trying to find out more about my own ethnic group, such as its history, traditions, and customs.' 'I am not very clear about the role of my ethnicity in my life.' 'I have a strong sense of belonging to my own ethnic group.'), as well as orientation to other groups (e.g. 'I like meeting and getting to know people from ethnic groups other than my own.' 'I am involved in activities with people from other ethnic groups.'). In general, for the youngsters from ethnic minority groups, self-esteem correlated with ethnic identity, although the trend was not very strong. In contrast, there was no relationship between ethnic identity and self-esteem for the White youngsters. At first sight, this seems to support the view that self-esteem in Black youngsters is tied in part to regarding their racial origins positively, whereas White youngsters do not need to achieve an ethnic identity as part of developing self-esteem. However, there was an important exception. A group of White students were an ethnic minority in their school, and for this group ethnic identity and self-esteem were fairly highly correlated. It may be the institutional setting which determines the relationship of self-esteem with ethnic identity (e.g. Weinreich, 1979). Another important feature of the data was that ethnic identity was not (or inconsistently) related to orientation to other groups. That is, orientation to other ethnic groups does not influence orientation to one's own group, despite what the Black self-hatred lobby suggest.

## Transracial adoption, fostering and identity

Black identity conflict is a politicized issue in the area of transracial adoption and fostering. In the early 1970s, the USA National Association of Black Social Workers initiated a Black-children-for-Black families policy. This has had ramifications world-wide, and own-race adoption or fostering has been held to be the ideal in some other countries, including Britain. In Britain, for example, the Children Act 1989 fully embraces this policy. None-the-less, arguments for and against Black-on-Black adoption policy and practice continue among professionals, as well as in the public domain. Gill and Jackson (1983) list the following among the many arguments commonly put forward against transracial adoption:

1  The adoptive family will see the Black child as different and not belonging; family members as a consequence will fail to achieve

'close and intimate' relationships with the child.

2 Black children will feel isolated because they are racially and physically very different from the rest of the family.

3 White families have social contact primarily and overwhelmingly with White families, hence while racial background may have no bearing within the family, the Black child may be forced to be overly dependent on the family because race will hamper their integration into the White family's broader social network.

4 Transracially placed children will have problems in identifying themselves as either Black or White, and this confusion will lead to their having negative feelings of self-worth.

5 White families cannot teach Black children effective strategies for dealing with White racism.

6 Being brought up in a White family may make it difficult for Black children to relate to the Black community – they may feel rejected by that community.

7 Transracial adoption entails the Black community's 'servicing' the White community by providing it with children, one of the Black community's most valuable resources.

8 Transracial adoption, not being an equal two-way traffic, tends to define social advantage as being reared by the White community.

Just what are the experiences of children in transracial adoption? In terms of self-identity, to what extent is these children's self-esteem damaged by transracial adoption *per se*? Studies addressing these and similar issues remain somehow inconclusive. In Britain, the most widely reported study of transracial adoption is probably Gill and Jackson's (1983). This study was largely based on interviews with adolescent and teenage children. Of the children in the study, those of 'mixed-race' parentage tended to be of Anglo-Asian parentage rather than Anglo-African-Caribbean parentage. In this sample, only about a third had ethnic minority friends. None of the youngsters claimed to be having any serious difficulties with their peers. This picture was supported by information supplied by their schoolteachers who generally claimed that the children were average or above average in popularity with their peers. Again, the overwhelming majority of the children were described as having no particular problems at school; in fact, none of them was described as having many difficulties. Furthermore, in terms of ability, most of the youngsters were described as above average in ability and a good proportion were described as being among the most able.

One common argument advanced to claim the uniqueness of the problems facing Black children in White families generally relates to skills or techniques for dealing with racism. The basic tenet is that Black children in a racist society require certain skills to ward off racism or to neutralize its emotional effects. The field of transracial adoption and fostering provides an arena for this argument. Protagonists of this argument claim that only Black families are capable of coaching Black children in these techniques. 'Coping skills' to mitigate the damaging impact of racism and the ability to equip the Black child with these skills are held to be the Black family's prerogative. Convincing evidence to support this claim is hard to come by. The majority of the children in Gill and Jackson's study reported no particular problems, educational, social, emotional or psychological, in spite of the fact that, according to Gill and Jackson, their families in general had no particular plans or strategies for teaching the children about their racial background, nor were they consciously bringing them up as White children. It seems that this practice is not peculiar to White families of adopted Black children. For example, Tizard and Phoenix (1993) found such practices among natural parents of families of 'mixed-race' parentage. These studies also suggest that the families' failure consciously to school the children in specific ways of dealing with racism did not affect the children's ability to recognize the physical differences between them and others. In both Gill and Jackson's and Tizard and Phoenix's studies, the majority of the children identified their skin tone accurately, just as minority children do. These studies also show that, over-all, the majority of children of 'mixed-race' parentage are satisfied with their physical characteristics or racial identity. In Gill and Jackson's study, for instance, only about one-fifth of the children expressed a preference for White, and nearly as many said that they were very satisfied with their skin colour. The vast majority said they did not mind what colour they were.

Miller and Miller differentiate between different ways in which Black parents cope with racism, and which their children often adopt. Importantly, the coping style of the parents is especially relevant to the ways in which the child perceives himself or herself in terms of self-esteem:

> *In order to establish a protected sense of personal worth and a unified identity, children must be able to model an active coping style for the racially defined incidents that the child will inevitably confront. For example, imagine that a biracial child has been called a 'nigger' by a peer in the school classroom. The parent who offers only sympathy is using a passive coping style, while the parent who calls the school and the offending child's parents has used an adaptive active approach to handling the incident. Active coping helps the child correctly perceive racism and teaches how to handle discrimination without feeling personally stigmatized.*

Miller and Miller, 1990, p. 172

Miller and Miller recognize that the family is a major source of personal self-esteem and self-worth which can serve to steel the child against the negative consequences of racism, that self-esteem for Black children is related to personal support and encouragement at home; achievement itself, on the other hand, is related to racial and institutional barriers outside of the family.

Very often, when coping strategies or survival techniques are mentioned, it is in a taken-for-granted manner which assumes a shared understanding of what they are. However, the suggested defensive strategies, presented as helping Black youngsters to deal with racial hurt, hardly seem specific to these experiences (Tizard and Phoenix, 1993). Tizard and Phoenix have identified four different categories of defence mechanisms that the youngsters actually employ.

1 Mental defusion of the threat: this includes the mechanisms by which we alter our perceptions and feelings about threatening situations. Examples would include deliberately ignoring racism, diverting our attention to something else, deciding that the threat actually degrades its perpetrator, or regarding it as a joke or in some way positive.
2 Avoidance or escape: this strategy basically involves not getting into threatening situations in the first place or getting out of them as quickly as possible.
3 Directly tackling: this might involve verbal or physical attack, negotiating, using humour or taking the matter to someone in authority.
4 Reducing the effects of the threat: in this context, enhancing one's own achievements or prestige is an important strategy.

These strategies imply that racist situations are actually threatening situations.

Of course, Tizard and Phoenix observed a slight association between the children's attitude to colour and the strategy employed by their families. However, this association seems to be political rather than psychological. Namely, most of the children who expressed a preference for White lived in families who had no specific approach to 'Black pride'. On the other hand, the families of those children who stated that they were 'proud to be Black' were politically aware, and actively sought to inculcate into the children the 'Black pride' ideology. It ought to be stressed that both types of approach have been observed in Black families in both the USA and the UK (e.g., Johnson *et al.*, 1987; Wilson, 1987). These investigators are therefore right to caution against the idea that Black and 'mixed-race' families are the best place for the healthy psychological or emotional development of Black children. Nor are Tizard and Phoenix's and Wilson's findings a new phenomenon. As far back as 1934, Beckham investigated whether, and to what extent, racism was a topic for discussion in African-American homes. The study involved the families of 250 non-delinquent boys, a hundred delinquent boys and a hundred men. Of the adults, 71 per cent reported that race prejudice or racial discrimination was frequently discussed while, in contrast, even more of the boys reported that the issue of racism was seldom or never discussed in their homes. According to more recent investigations (e.g. Katz, 1996; Tizard and Phoenix, 1993), it seems that not much has changed in this respect. Beckam also found that among all three groups, the most frequent situation that caused a first racial humiliation was a disagreeable personal experience rather than a group experience, such as being called offensive names.

Research evidence does not support the importance attached to identity confusion in transracially adopted children; nor is the significance attached to the idea of 'survival skills' for dealing with racism justified on empirical grounds. Their only function, therefore, seems to be to pathologize and marginalize these children from mainstream professional service provision. These arguments enable White practitioners and the institutions they represent not only to shun their responsibility for these children's well being, but also to provide them with inappropriate and potentially harmful services. For example, among many other things, it enables them to define Black children's emotional, educational, social and psychological needs solely in racial terms, irrespective of their true causes (Owusu-Bempah, 1994a; 1997). Since, as the argument goes, they are not equipped (or perhaps refuse) to deal with these problems, they feel that it is legitimate to hold Black adults (often Black professionals) responsible for solving these children's problems; hence the creation of Black 'experts' in many institutions, notably in social work departments and schools (Owusu-Bempah, 1997). For example, in Owusu-Bempah's (1994a) study involving social workers, a majority of the respondents defined the Black children's needs in racial terms, and prescribed race-based interventions to meet their needs. For example, a significant proportion recommended a Black social worker as the children's key worker. Of course, a few Black professionals – social workers, therapists, clinical child psychologists and teachers – may have benefited in one way or another out of the argument and practice. However, if our ultimate concern is about the interests or well-being of the children, then it is incumbent upon us to provide them with services which promote their well-being, even if doing so is at our own expense as providers. This requires, at the minimum, a critical analysis and evaluation of not only what we say and are told, but more importantly what we do and the ways in which we do what we do, and, above all, the effects of what we do.

Not withstanding the paucity of the evidence in support of negative racial identity and low self-esteem in Black children, over-generalized assertions are often made about them, especially with regard to transracial adoption and fostering. For example, Small (1991) asserts that transracial adoption leads to: 'failure to develop a sense of black identity; failure to develop survival skills; failure to develop cultural and linguistic attributes to function in the black community; development of negative self-image (self-esteem); the development of a white identity could cause profound difficulties in the real world'(p. 66). Assertions such as this, as we have seen, have no empirical foundation; they are only of political or ideological interest; they are not seriously intended as a basis for professional practice. Even ideologically or politically, it is more interesting to ponder over what the argument would be if the situation were reversed so that White children became predominantly placed with or adopted by Black families.

It is generally acknowledged that it is Black children in the childcare system who tend to exhibit many of the psychological problems associated with negative personal identity and low self-esteem. Black children living with their families generally are as psychologically healthy as their White counterparts (Coleman, 1994; Tizard and Phoenix, 1993; Wilson, 1987). We suggest, therefore, that professionals working with these children, especially social workers and therapists, should seek to identify and deal with those factors within the system which are likely to be responsible for their difficulties. Such an approach would seek to address as adequately as possible such questions as the following raised by Johnson *et al.* (1987) among others:

1 Why do African-Caribbean children and children of 'mixed-race' parentage in care appear to be emotionally different from those in the community; furthermore, why is it that some continue to have these or even greater problems once they have left the care system?
2 What are the expressed or felt cultural and psychological needs of African-Caribbean children and children of 'mixed-race' parentage in care, in terms of the development of a satisfactory self-identity?
3 Do some forms of care lead to more satisfactory self- and cultural identities such as those typical of children living with their natural families?
4 What forms of care would provide the most satisfactory experiences for these children and their over-all well being?

To address these issues satisfactorily, we need, first of all, to suspend our (racist) beliefs about Black children's negative personal identity and group rejection and practices based on these beliefs and assumptions. Dean (1993) points us in a useful direction in this endeavour: 'We should also question our own motivation for accepting such definitions, since there is now a need for progression away from a simplistic conceptualisation of ethnicity based on a crude black/white dualism towards a more comprehensive understanding of the complex factors that contribute to the establishment of a personal and group identity' (p. 33).

# Culture and identity

The seemingly paradoxical nature of findings about the resilience of Black self-identity needs some demystification. Why does the relentless onslaught on Blackness by White racist society not have the expected effects? We have learnt elsewhere in earlier chapters that the conception of self viewed from beyond Western perspectives is different and integral to a radically different cultural system. The proper place of the self is in relation to other people, the community and the environment, rather than as a separate, striving, achieving selfish being. But we in the West are socialized to see the latter as the ideal. Consequently, it is beyond our purview to recognize that other cultures may develop a sense of selfhood that in its own way may be superior in many ways to that of the West. Instead of this recognition, we tend to disparage not only that which we do not understand but also that which we do not know. The ingrained Western sense of superiority is not shaken by the knowledge of the profoundly problematic nature of Western culture with its multitudinous individual casualties that need vast armies of psychologists, psychiatrists and social workers to treat, help and service. Only if we assume that Black cultural institutions such as the family and community are inadequate to prepare their members for the world can we equally assume that the Black sense of self should be flawed.

Psychology needs to regard culture and knowledge of culture not as the repository of strange and peculiar artefacts, but as the basic unit of psychological understanding. Traditionally culture has been seen as that thing beyond the discipline of psychology – the subject matter of other disciplines. Psychology's fascination with biology as the bedrock from which psychological understanding is built needs little attention drawn to it. However, psychologists concerned with racial issues have too often ignored the insignificance of biology in creating the wide-ranging differences between peoples. The flaw is not in the interest in the biological, but in the lack of appreciation of the cultural. It would appear that psychologists and related practitioners frequently practise psychology with the sort of rudimentary and inadequate understanding of other cultures that would have existed before their psychological training.

# Chapter 7

# Normal development: beyond the Western model

*The concept of the self as a separate, atomistic, private, autonomous indi-
vidual has been constituted by specific, complex, social, economic,
historical, cultural and psychological relations. It is my opinion that such
modern, Western self-claim to a historic rationality and universal objectivity not only is philosophically inadequate, but also serves neocolonial and
imperial goals of domination.*

Allen, 1997, p. 9

Western psychology's models of human development, including
evolutionary, psychoanalytic and cognitive ones, have their roots in
Judeo-Christian religion and philosophy. Despite this, they are believed
to be applicable to all human groupings, irrespective of the obvious and
many differences among them in terms of culture, religion, and political and economic system. Developmental psychology, and its divergent
trends, can be understood only by examining or viewing it in an historical context. The major traditions in developmental psychology are
based on widely different historical, philosophical, economic, and
political orientations; they are the products of the different geographical locations and physical conditions of the Western countries in which
they originated. They are by no means universal. Each of these models
was developed in a particular culture (Western) with particular needs,
in a particular era and in particular political and economic circumstances. Thus, they are inadequate in providing a complete
understanding of the developmental process and needs of the diverse
groups within even Western societies. Their application in cultures
outside the Western world is even more inappropriate, and only serves
to portray those cultures and their members as 'not normal' *vis-à-vis*
Western Europeans and North Americans. For example, Riegel (1979)
comments on evolutionary models of human development.

*Darwin considered development a process of continuous competition and
selection, whose direction and goals are determined by the 'successful
survivors' here and now. When translated into the matrix of behavioral and
social sciences, the 'successful survivor' becomes the white, middle-class*

> *adult male most likely engaged in manufacturing or business enterprise. From this point of view, deviant persons or nonstandard groups attain negative attributes only: children are regarded as incomplete adults; old persons as deficient;... colonial subjects, and nonwhites as far below the rank of white middle-class male adults.*
>
> Riegel, 1979, p. 332

Models based upon Freud's psychoanalytic theory of personality development are equally biased. Psychoanalytic theory is explicit in its definition of what constitutes a normal or healthy human development, explicit about the process whereby a person becomes normal or afflicted by psychopathology. The psychoanalytic criteria of what constitutes a normal development are unsurprisingly based upon Western beliefs and values about human development. None-the-less, these are assumed not only to be universal but also, more importantly, superior to other beliefs concerning human nature. Hence, those from cultures significantly or radically different, who do not fit the Western model, are seen as incomplete, as exhibiting inferior psychological development or even psychopathology. Psychoanalytic theory and practice based upon it, therefore, present Africans, Asian and others as abnormal, as having an undeveloped ego, as lacking the independent, self-reliant, self-directing ego of Western individualism; as lacking rational, logical, secondary-process thinking, another hallmark value of individualism; as enmeshed or exhibiting vague emotional boundaries between self and other, with much less of the self–other demarcation that is also characteristic of individualism; and having a weak conscience or superego because they are context-orientated as opposed to individual-orientated (Howitt and Owusu-Bempah, 1994; Kakar, 1979; Landrine, 1992; Owusu-Bempah and Howitt, 1999a; Roland, 1997).

Roland (1988) sees much of the problem as lying in investigators' frequent use of psychological developmental models of Western personality as the measuring stick against which psychological development from a variety of non-Western societies is assessed. Child-rearing and development from these other societies unfortunately emerge as inferior. That is, investigators fail to recognize that there can be other kinds of psychological structures and cognitive abilities with their own developmental stages and schedules which may contrast with predominant Western ones but which are adaptive to the different social and cultural contexts in which development occurs.

Western perspectives differ on many dimensions of development from those of other world cultures: ranging from emotion, personality, health and so forth. While Western psychology is concerned with the personality growth of the individual, Asian and African psychologies are concerned with one's harmony with other human beings, society, nature and the cosmos (Holdstock, 2000; Sinha and Sinha, 1997). In terms of personality, Yang (1997), for example, has criticized empirical research using Western concepts and methods on Chinese personality as theoretically deficient since such research makes no, or very little attempt, to construct theories of Chinese personality from an indigenous perspective. Yang suggests that the methodological and theoretical flaws in the study of Chinese personality must be remedied, not only by undertaking relevant empirical research from a Chinese perspective but also by developing theories which better reflect the Chinese social, cultural and historical characteristics. Yang is convinced that by shifting methodological and theoretical horizons from a Western to Chinese perspective, Chinese psychologists will not only be laying to rest the conceptual hegemony of Western or Westernized psychology over psychological research in Chinese societies, but, more importantly, they will also be opening up new paths to a more adequate understanding of Chinese psychological processes and behavioural patterns, and thereby be able to make real, unique contributions to the development of a global psychology for all human beings in all cultures.

Yang is not alone in his concern about the inadequacy and potential dangers of transporting Western ideas of personality development into radically different cultures. Howitt and Owusu-Bempah (1990a, 1994) found this to be common, notably in Africa. Sinha (1993) summarizes this general concern: 'Being limited by its methodology, which was modeled on the physical sciences, Western psychology, with its behaviouristic, and materialistic orientation, and wholly mechanistic view of humankind, failed to answer pertinent questions concerning complex human phenomena of personality development, emotion, integration of the individual, and societal behaviour' (p. 34)

## Developmental psychology: individual-focused

Many have expressed grave misgivings about the universality of developmental psychology, particularly on the grounds of its exclusive focus on the individual as a unit of analysis. Concurring with Bronfenbrenner (1979), Furth (1995) describes this as a major stumbling block for developmental psychology. This is particularly true of Piaget's theory of cognitive development. Holdstock (2000), for example, has argued that the continued belief in the individual as the centre of meaning prevented Piaget and developmental psychology from determining how understanding could occur between children, and ultimately how meaning could be transmitted between people. According to Holdstock, in order to provide a fuller understanding of human nature, developmental psychology must shift its focus towards rational accounts of human development. That is, instead of viewing development either in terms of the unfolding of innate or genetic potential, or solely in terms of environmental impact, the focus must be on relational units and processes. This calls for an ecosystem approach to human development: the individual should be viewed not only in terms of family, friends and community but as 'fully enmeshed in economic, political, educational, technological and other practices of the culture' (1991, p. 25). Holdstock (2000), in agreement with Vandenberg (1991), laments the absence of our relationships with others, which are so crucial in moral development, in Piaget's cognitive model of development. Both writers point out that the innate abilities of looking, hearing, sucking, and grasping of the infant are not only geared towards the development of sensory and cognitive functions, as Piaget assumed, but are structured patterns geared towards enhancing social interactions between infants and their care-givers and surroundings.

Piaget assumed that a general theory of cognition is possible, and that his theory of cognitive development is a challenge to ideologies of biological racism. None-the-less, as Buck-Morss (1979) has pointed out, Piagetian tests cannot be applied in cultures outside the Western world without implying Eurocentrism, the cultural superiority of the West. For example, cross-cultural studies using Piagetian tests suggest that Western European children undergo a more rapid cognitive development than their African peers (Berry and Dasen, 1974), even though in the first two years of life, they lag significantly behind African infants of their age group (Geber, 1957; Werner, 1972). In his critique of the cross-cultural application of Piagetian tests, Buck-Morss raises the following pertinent questions: what happens when the familiar Piagetian landmarks toward cognitive maturity are viewed from another perspective? How can they be said to reflect not a particular culture but a particular socio-economic structure? Howitt and Owusu-Bempah (1990, 1994) have raised similar questions in relation to personality tests in Africa and other parts of the world.

The assumption that Piaget's grand theory is race- and culture-free and so poses a challenge to biological racism and ethnocentrism is illusory, if not false. First, as we have argued elsewhere (Howitt and Owusu-Bempah, 1994), such claims only help us to deny the culture specificity of psychology as a whole. Second, they remind us also of Chomsky's (1979) suggestion that 'Cartesian dualism raises... a conceptual barrier to racist doctrine' simply because it does not distinguish between 'black minds' and 'white minds' (pp. 92–3) Cartesian dualism may be conceptually benign but not in its policy and practical implications. Many have argued that it contains assumptions which enable those who accept it to believe that they have greater moral or intellectual worth than those whom they oppress or exploit. For example, the Cartesian dictum *cogito ergo sum* has been employed in the service of racism, classism and other social inequalities to mean 'some think more than others, therefore some are more worthy "beings" than others'. This is evident in almost every sector of Western society, especially in education and employment. (See Howitt and Owusu-Bempah [1994] for a detailed discussion.) Likewise, the reported difference in Piagetian test performance between African children and Western European children has been seen as evidence of the intellectual superiority of Europeans over Africans, 'evidence' that Europeans are 'all brains' and Africans 'all brawn' (or genitalia) (e.g., Eysenck, 1971; Jensen, 1969; Rushton, 1990, 1992).

Besides the conceptual problems, there are methodological difficulties involved in the cross-cultural application of Piaget's theory of cognitive development. For example, a number of researchers have reported difficulties in setting up experiments in a way which their participants found relevant. This problem is exceptionally highlighted in studies involving the concept of intelligence. Durojaiye (1993) encountered this methodological problem in a cross-cultural study of the notion of intelligence as conceived by two distinct African national groups, the Yoruba of West Africa and the Baganda of East Africa. He found a remarkable similarity in the concept of intelligence among the two African peoples studied: both the Baganda and the Yoruba associate many attributes with intelligence. Intelligence for them is a living concept that is manifested in the day-to-day performances of the people and in the ways they meet and solve everyday problems. He found that among each group intelligence is not conceived as a unitary entity, but rather a multi-faceted one, evidenced by his finding that in each group there are seperate words to indicate different components of intelligence. Among the Yoruba for instance there are different words for wisdom, understanding, planning, knowledge, attentiveness, brains and thoughtfulness; there are other words for ingenuity, creativity, originality and discretion. Finally, 'there is a distinction made between constructive intelligence (*ogbon ewe*) and destructive intelligence, or skill in deception or cunning, which the Yuroba refer to as *ogbon arekereke*. The former is admired, the latter despised' (p. 215). Durojaiye was struck also by the emphasis given to 'harmony' by the two groups as a solution to problems relating to interpersonal and intergroup disputes. In terms of development, both groups place greater importance on psychosocial development than on intellectual development. What kind of psychological instrument is required to measure these various components of intelligence as conceived by the Yoruba? Durojaiye is of the opinion that: 'Theories of intelligence [or cognitive development] are incomplete without reference to the centrality of affect and values that determine the directions that human abilities will follow in different societies' (p. 219).

## Moral development: diverse views

Controversy surrounds also the universal relevance of Kohlberg's

(1969, 1971, 1984) six-stage theory of moral development, with its obvious implications for identity development. Many have argued that the theory is hardly applicable not only to cultures outside the Western world but also to certain groups within Western society, such as women (Dien, 1982; Gilligan, 1982; Ma, 1997; Simpson, 1974). Regarding its relevance outside the Western world, Ma (1997), for instance, agrees with Dien (1982) that different cultures have different conceptions of morality, and that the Western conception of morality, based on Judeo-Christian religion and philosophy, cannot fit into the frameworks of other cultures. This is reinforced by Simpson's (1974) suggestion that Kohlberg's moral principles are Western-biased, and so are inadequate to explain the concept of morality, in that they try to do so without references to other values or philosophies.

The major tenet of Western morality, on which Kohlberg's higher stages – stages five and six – of moral development are based, is that people are autonomous beings, free to make personal choices and to determine their destiny. As a moral free agent, one has to take responsibility for one's actions. The major element in the conception of morality in African and Asian cultures, on the other hand, is interdependence or human relatedness. Dien (1982) points out that at the core of the Chinese Confucian conception of morality is *jen* which is variously translated as 'love', 'benevolence', 'human heartedness', 'man-to-man-ness', 'sympathy' and 'perfect virtue'. 'It is basically the deep affection for kin rooted in *filial piety* and extended through the family circle to all men' (p. 334). According to Amaladoss (1999), Asian traditions, irrespective of religion, see egoism as the source of all evil. Taoism, for example, sees Western individualism and competition as nothing but a manifestation of that very evil. Various traditions propose different ways of opposing egoism. In the Taoist tradition, to get rid of the ego is to become aware of one's dependence on others. Such an egoless attitude gives rise to an ethic of sharing and mutuality. The world's goods are for the whole of humanity and to be shared (Dien, 1982). It is in this context of community that Asian and African traditions speak of duties rather than of rights.

In Asian cultures, as in other cultures outside the Western world, this ethic is firmly located in the family; it is not consigned to secondary socialization agents, such as nurseries, schools, or youth clubs. The family is seen as the prototype for all relationships. The primary relationship is the parent–child relationship defined by filial piety. Parents, and in extended families grandparents, aunts and uncles, are perceived as vehicles through which a sense of human relatedness is transmitted to, and manifested in, their children. Comparative studies involving African, Indian, Chinese, Japanese and American mothers indicate that the non-Western mothers prepare their children for a cultural environment in which psychological interdependence plays an important role in social interactions, including teaching and learning. They direct children's attention to the feelings of others; they challenge children to guess what they are thinking, they more often invoke people to whom their children are attached, such as relatives and close friends, as models of desired kinds of behaviour, and expect them to develop pro-social conformity as opposed to independence and assertiveness (Azuma, 1984; Roland, 1988; Whiting and Edwards, 1988). Azuma (1984) [in response to Gilligan's (1982) call, presumably by default] reminds us that the world of Japanese folktales is the world of the 'Great Mother', and that femininity rather than masculinity symbolizes 'self'.

Hsu (1983) proposed a hypothesis about the basic nature of three ways of life or worlds: the Chinese world is situation centred, the American world is individual centred and the Hindu world is supernatural centred.

> *The situation-centred world is characterized by ties which permanently unite closely related human beings in the family and clan. Within this basic human constellation the individual is conditioned to seek mutual dependence... The individual-centred world is characterized by temporary ties among closely related human beings. Having no permanent base in family and clan, the individual's basic orientation toward life and the environment is self-reliance... The supernatural-centered orientation enjoins the Hindu society to seek intimacy with the Ultimate Reality and/or Its manifestations and is commensurate with the idea, interpersonal relations, of unilateral dependence.*
>
> Pp. 1–4; in Ho, 1993, p. 242

To these worlds must be added the African world (Howitt and Owusu-Bempah, 1994; Owusu-Bempah, 1999a). The African world is not just community centred but nature centred; it includes the animate, the inanimate and the spiritual. African traditions make a distinction between a 'person' and 'personality' (Holdstock, 2000; Mbiti, 1969; Owusu-Bempah and Howitt, 1995). The central focus of the African concept of person or the self is the place of the individual in a web of interpersonal relationships. In contrast, personality is an individualistic concept, with its central focus on the individual's deep core of complexes and anxieties. It is 'a matrix or framework within which every human individual seeks to maintain a satisfactory level of psychic and interpersonal equilibrium, a process which Hsu (1983) calls *psychosocial homeostasis*. It is what distinguishes person A from person B as unique individuals' (Owusu-Bempah, 1997).

The centrality of human connectedness in the African conception of morality is evident in many ways in which it is described – interdependence, connectedness, co-operativeness, communalism, mutual support, collectivism, respect for others (especially the older people), extended kinship. As in many other cultures, such as Indian, Chinese and Japanese, the 'highest value [in African cultures] is placed on positive interpersonal relationships'. (Myers, 1993, p. 13). In African traditions:

> *One's orientation is social rather than directed toward objects. There is over-riding importance attached to social bonds and social relationships. One acts in accordance with the notion that duty to one's social group is more important than individual rights and privileges. Hence one's identity is tied to group membership rather than to individual status and possessions. Sharing is promoted because it confirms the importance of social interconnectedness. Self-centredness and individual greed are frowned upon.*
>
> Jagers and Mock, 1993, p. 394.

Like other peoples, African other-centredness or social consciousness has important consequences for the way in which children are raised. A majority of infants in Africa are breast-fed on demand. They sleep with their mothers immediately after birth and are carried on the backs of their mother, other adults, brothers, sisters and cousins. This ensures close physical contact during the early years, in contrast to European babies who are placed in cots or transported in prams and isolated at night. Thus African infants and children experience the social environment as nurturant and supportive, an anchor; they do not need to manipulate it by, for example crying or throwing tantrums to have their needs met. Because they are fed on demand, instead of at specific schedule, they learn to monitor their bodily functions; they do not require external mechanistic devices, such as clocks, tell them to eat, play, sleep or rest. This experience extends to childhood. Even in the urban areas, African children are not made to keep to as structured a routine regarding play and going to bed as in the Western world (Whiting and Edwards, 1988).

The interrelatedness of the African concept of the self cannot be stressed enough. A person can only really be human when other people are there to complete his or her humaness; the individual cannot be human alone, in isolation. Personhood is dependent upon relationships with others. The Cartesain dictum 'I think therefore I am' becomes 'I am because we are'.

In Africa, being in communion with others is not just a sociological, philosophical or grandiloquent notion. It is a moral one (Owusu-Bempah, 1999a; Silavwe, 1995). It provides a foundation for an ethic that is infinitely human. Mbiti (1969) conceptualizes each individual as a community of selves emphasizing human interdependence. This does not imply a dependency on, but rather a respect for and responsibility towards, the other. The same respect is bestowed on the self, which is never regarded as being of lesser importance than the context to which it belongs.

# Respect for other views

It is unjust for one population forcibly or surreptitiously to impose its standards or will on other populations.

> *In relation to the Third World, cultural imperialism [including psychological imperialism] can be defined as the systematic penetration and domination of the cultural life of the popular classes by the ruling class of the west in order to reorder their values, behaviour, institutions and identity... to conform with the interests of the imperial classes.*
>
> Petras, 1994, quoted in Fernandes, 1999, p. 17

It has been argued that cultural invasion represents the most invidious form of imperialism (Fanon, 1967; Freire, 1972). We see psychological invasion or imperialism as equally insidious, if not even more so. In the rest of this chapter and in the following chapter, we examine some of the ways in which ignoring the psychologies of other peoples has led to misconceptions and misrepresentations of Black childhood in particular.

One of the primary functions of Western social research and theory is the maintenance and dominance of White European culture (Bulhan, 1981; Howitt and Owusu-Bempah, 1994; Owusu-Bempah and Howitt, 1995). Stated in this bald fashion, such a view tends to raise hackles. We are imbued with the idea of social research as a dispassionate scientific quest for objectivity, truth and revelation. Consequently, these objectives are assumed to be intrinsic to any famous research. Unfortunately, this doggedly naive view tends to be resistant to the repeated examples of an ideological bedrock underlying research. Such ideological features determine what is thought about, what is studied, what is reported and how it is reported, what is taught and how it is taught. Research on Black people has demonstrated the overwhelming role of racism in providing the interpretative framework for studies of Black people (Guthrie, 1980; Nobles, 1980; Williams, 1980). While virtually all aspects of the lives of people of African descent, especially, have been subject to racially motivated disparagement, the question of Black identity has tended to be seen as benign, even as sensitive to the situation of Black children in a racist world. We see the issue of human development and identity as being different and certainly not benign. Identity, like IQ, has been a weapon against Black children. Unfortunately, unlike IQ, it is difficult to see how something so social as identity can be used to reinforce dominant Western values and the associated disregard and dismissal of things beyond the Western perspective.

# Fuzzy concepts, fuzzy boundaries

We all assume that we know what self-identity is; it is a concept, which is all too easy to recognize in name. What it actually is, however, may be quite a different matter to many of us. For example, talk of 'identity problems', 'identity crises', 'identity conflict' and 'identity confusion' makes an awful lot of sense until we try to define a little more clearly what we mean by each of these things. The superficially commonsensical nature of the concept of identity means that these terms tend to go unchallenged, to take on a taken-for-granted aura. While this means that the concept is easily accepted, it also means that it can be used with the utmost flexibility to explain everything in general and nothing with precision. There is another problem. Given that identity is an everyday term, it seems somewhat unnecessary to ask: 'What do you mean by that?' We risk revealing our 'ignorance' by such questions. Actually, such a question might have the opposite effect; it might actually show wisdom or the possession of a critical or questioning mind. So we take the question a step further and ask:

1  What does identity mean to two Western individuals?
2  What does identity mean to a Western European, a Japanese, Chinese, an African?

Care needs to be taken to avoid giving concepts an unwarranted aura of tangibility. In other words, we should not push them beyond their proven applicability or usefulness. The notion of race itself is a good example of a flexible and ill-defined concept; it is assumed to refer to some absolute reality but it is far from the case. Classic examples of its misapplication include the classification of Jewish people as a distinct racial group. Jewish people, like Hindus, Catholics or Mormons are a religious group, and so do not constitute a biologically or racially distinct group from other human groups. Another example is the way in which race was used in the nineteenth century to refer to a nation rather than to a biologically defined human group – the British race, for example. Just as there is nothing in the biological make-up of these putative races which distinguishes them from other races, so there is nothing in the brains or minds of individuals which can be clearly defined as their 'self' or their 'identity'. None-the-less, most of us think we have a good idea of what it means if people speak of their own or another person's self or identity. We hardly consider what the self or self-identity actually is, how we develop it, or how it affects our relationship or interactions with those around us – other 'selves'. These are not mere philosophical questions; they are of practical significance.

What we have learnt already about self beyond Western boundaries should make us very uneasy about how we use the concept. What we have learnt so far suggests strongly that we may have great difficulty in disentangling the Western ideal self from our work as psychologists and other practitioners dealing with people of other cultural backgrounds. Nevertheless, we have found numerous instances of writings which describe practices and theories which fundamentally misconstrue the nature of identity in other cultures, but nevertheless include beliefs and recommendations which may profoundly affect the lives of ethnic minority children within Western geographical boundaries. In all of these cases there is not only a sense of the profound neglect of understanding cultures beyond the dominant Western boundaries which inform psychology but also profound naivety about the way that culture and the individual interact.

## Notions of the self

There are numerous overlapping terms describing the 'self': self-concept, self-identity, self-image, self-esteem and ego strength. Despite their somewhat different nuances, these terms essentially refer to how people see themselves and how they think others see them. This means that our social environment has a major impact on our conceptions of our self. As previously noted, one could not have a concept of self without having a concept of others. Hence the self has been deemed to involve all the things which may be used to distinguish people from one another – our thoughts, beliefs, values, attitudes, aspirations, behaviour, experiences, bodies, relationships and material possessions. This is just about the same range of characteristics on which we evaluate people, and are evaluated by others. In simple terms, our sense of self develops within a social or community context. In the Western European context, however, the centrality of the notion of 'self' has been emphasized, historically, in the belief that knowing one's self provides comprehension of one's future and place in the order of things, that people's conception of self guides their behaviour and expectations from life. In cultures outside the Western world, however, the notion of the self transcends one's future or aspirations. In these cultures, the issue of the self is fundamental not only to the question of who one is or what one is but also who and what one *was*. Furthermore, as we have already partially documented, one's sense of self derives from the corporate self of one's family group or community (Mbiti, 1969; Owusu-Bempah and Howitt, 1995). In many cultures outside the Western world, therefore, the answer to the question 'who am I?' must be sought in the question 'who are we?' (including the dead as well as the living). What all this means is that the issue of the self does not render itself readily to simple, stock answers, especially in today's 'global village' world.

The self concept emerges from different sources and *I* is expressed in different ways in different cultures (Damon and Hart, 1988; Kim and

Choi, 1994). Thus, even though Western cultures generally place a higher premium on individualism than collectivism, they still differ in the extent to which this is accepted or encouraged. For example, egotism or self-preoccupation has been found to prevail more in some Western cultures than in others. It is reported that in other cultures, outside the Western world, any overt emphasis on the self is viewed with suspicion. According to Stevenson (1991), Chinese people, for example, regard any expression of individualism as an unhealthy thing. Triandis (1994) supports this view, claiming that Chinese people tend to prefer self-effacement and endorse group-orientated self-concepts more than individualistic concepts. As far as Western cultures are concerned, Heuvel *et al.* (1992) provide an illuminating illustration of cultural differences in self-perception. They investigated the self-concepts of 11-year-old Dutch, Moroccan and Turkish children living in Amsterdam. The children lived in similar socio-economic environments. Yet, the investigators found intercultural differences in the ways in which the children looked at the self. For example, the indigenous Dutch children used many more psychological (or individualistic) statements than their Moroccan and Turkish counterparts. The latter used substantially more references to social (or group) aspects of the self.

## The self as a socio-cultural product

This section provides a brief summary of some of the most historically influential theorists of the self in social psychology, starting with William James. William James (1890), the philosopher–psychologist, was the first theorist to formulate a comprehensive psycho-social theory of the self. James saw the self as a social product rather than something innate; he saw it as developing out of a tapestry of social experiences. The main thrust of his argument is that social comparison is the key to the development of the self concept. That is, our sense of who we are is achieved by comparing what we know of ourselves with what we know from the information or feedback we receive from significant others. This argument concerning the social origins of the self concept is accepted by many modern Western theorists, including psychologists and sociologists who stress the importance of the social milieu in the development of the self. It is also generally accepted that other people influence our ideas about ourselves. We need other people for social comparison in order to determine what is distinctive about our own self. Also we are affected by other people's (especially those emotionally close to us) emphases on our social and psychological characteristics, as well as their expectations of us and what we should be or become.

Influenced by Cartesian dualism, James suggested two main aspects of the self: the *Me* (the objective self) and the *I* (the subjective self). The *Me*, or objective self, consists of the known aspects of a person (those aspects of a person known also to others). These include not only the individual's physical body but also their ancestors, reputation and material possessions (including animals, bank-accounts and credit cards): 'In its widest possible sense a man's Self is the sum total of all that he *can* call his' (James, 1950, p. 291, emphasis in the original). The *Me* is everything that a person can call his/hers. James distinguished further 'sub-selfs' of the *Me*. In descending order of importance, he identified these as:

1 The *Spiritual Self* – a person's inner or subjective aspect. James described it as the hub from which radiate all other aspects of the *Me* or the objective self. It is the source of a person's interests, efforts, attention, will and choice; it comprises one's intellectual, religious and moral aspirations.
2 The *Social Self* – James claimed that a person does not have only one social self, but many social 'selves', as many as there are individuals or groups whose opinions one cares about. The most important of these is the family or loved ones; each one of these is shown a different colour or hue of oneself.
3 The *Material Self*, as the term implies, comprises the material possessions or artefacts which one sees as part of oneself; for example, a child's computer games, posters, wallpaper, toys and so forth are all part of this aspect of the sense of self.
4 The *Bodily Self* is about our body image or physique; hairstyle, shape, weight, musculature, height and toiletries are all aspects of the creation of a favourable body image; perhaps vegetarianism, dieting, exercise videos and jogging are all modern manifestations which James could not have anticipated.

The discussion so far suggests that the first two elements characterize collective cultures, whereas Western cultures are characterized by the latter two.

In James' conceptualization, the *I* (or the phenomenological self) is the other major component of a person's self concept. He described the *I* as the active part of the self, as the initiator, organizer and interpreter of one's experiences. According to James, our experiences are central to our sense of personal identity in that they enable the development of self-awareness, and, hence, personal identity. He identified four types of experience essential to identity development:

1 *Agency*: The experience of agency, basically, relates to one's sense of autonomy or being in control. It provides one with a conviction that one actively structures and processes one's own experiences – that one's experiences are one's own and not those of others. The strong

resistance of many Western teenagers against pressures to live their parents' lives, as it were, is perhaps a good illustration. It demonstrates the importance of the sense of autonomy to them.

2 *Continuity*: The experience of continuity is to do with the stability of the self. That is, to develop or maintain a stable personal identity, a person needs a sense of security, of belonging. The implications of a disruption to this type of experience are obvious, particularly for transnationally adopted children children in the public childcare system, or those experiencing parental divorce or separation. It implies that to experience the sense of continuity or to maintain a stable self-identity, the child needs to be the same person, the child, for instance, of the same parents and not of these parents today and those parents tomorrow.

3 *Distinctness*: This refers to what sets us apart from others, what makes any two individuals, even identical twins, feel different from each other. The experience of distinctiveness is crucial for the development of a sense of individuality, of being distinct or different from others. In professional work with children this is an important aspect of the development of personal identity. Unfortunately, professionals often neglect it.

4 *Reflection*: James saw this more or less as the end product of the processes of identity development. He described this experience as a stock-taking process whereby a person derives self-consciousness; he saw this, in turn, as a means of shaping one's experiences or ideas about oneself in order to achieve a full sense of self.

James saw the sense of personal identity as precious to psychological well-being and disruptions to it as damaging. He emphasized that personal identity arises mainly by combining the experiences of *continuity* and *distinctness*. They were, for James, the most crucial experiences for a stable and healthy self-concept. He strongly believed that any difficulties arising from these types of experience had serious consequences for one's sense of self and, consequently, one's psychological integrity. Thus, he warned: 'The worst alterations of the self are associated with disruption in identity fostered by a loss of continuity and distinctness' (p. 207).

This loss has practical implications. Taking the above example of children in the care system, it means that in order to develop and maintain a stable sense of self-identity, it is necessary for the children to have experiences that facilitate their sense of continuity (Owusu-Bempah, 1995; Owusu-Bempah and Howitt, 1997) and distinctiveness. Research tends to support James's emphasis on the importance of these experiences to one's psychological well-being (Coppersmith, 1967; Materska *et al.*, 1987; Wooster and Harris, 1973). However, cross-cultural studies suggest that Western cultures and collectivist cultures emphasize different experiences. For example, the former places a high premium on personal autonomy; the latter places greater emphasis on continuity.

In collective cultures, the need for a sense of continuity is met by living in a community of selves, by having a sense of human connectedness, while experience of distinctness is fostered by interdependence, one's relationships with others (e.g. Brandt, 1979; Church and Katigbak, 1992; Ho, 1979, 1993; Sastry and Ross, 1998; Wallendorf and Anould, 1988; Yang, 1986). Individuals also require stable environments and relationships that provide them with a sense of agency, that is, the feeling that they partly determine what happens to them and their futures.

## Cooley's social mirror

William James's ideas of the self-concept were further developed by later influential theorists, especially Cooley (1902) and Mead (1934). These theorists also saw the social milieu as the locus of the self. However, they placed even greater emphasis on the role of social interaction in the process of the emergence of the self-concept. Cooley, for example, developed the idea of the *social looking-glass self* in which feedback from others is an essential feature of the development of the self. Thus, other people are analogous to an undistorted mirror through which we discover our selves. Since the reflection is what we believe others see or think about us, it includes both evaluative and descriptive aspects. The evaluative dimensions include the moral, spiritual and intellectual judgements that we believe others are making of us. In contrast, the illustrative dimensions are what we believe other people see when they look at us. So it is not just a matter of how people respond to our behaviour or actions, we also form an opinion of ourselves from how we think others see us. This is very close to James's notion of the 'social self'. Different people or groups perceive us differently and react to us differently. For instance, they have different expectations of us, and we view ourselves according to their perceptions or expectations. Goffman (1959) recognized and graphically described this process forty years ago.

## Internalized expectations

Mead (1934) extended this social aspect of the self further away from James' stress on the importance of subjective experience. To Mead, the self arises out of both social interactions and the individual's concern about these interactions – how others react to them. In the development of the self, however, Mead placed special emphasis on the role of the family (in collective cultures, including the extended family and the community); he claimed that we internalize the expectations that significant others have of us as a sort of conscience. That is, our internalized expectations provide a source of internal regulation that eventually guides and maintains our behaviour in itself. Put simply, Mead saw feedback from others as providing standards by which we evaluate and regulate our own behaviour, even in the absence of other people.

## Relevance to practice

This brief summary of the major psychological and sociological notions concerning the self-concept raises a number of important practical questions. For example, we may ask in what ways and to what extent do these notions of the self influence the thinking and practice of professionals (such as social workers, teachers and clinicians)? Which of these ideas are the most pertinent to professional work with Black children and adolescents in a multicultural setting?

The social science literature is replete with suggestions that Cooley's 'social looking-glass self' is especially pertinent to the self-concept of Black people, especially Black children. It is frequently argued that the White community represents Black people's 'social looking-glass' (i.e., their significant others) so that Black people, especially children, perceive themselves and behave according to the racist views held about them by the White community. Also, following Mead, but conveniently disregarding his (and James's) emphasis on the importance of the family, and the fact that different cultures have different conceptions of the self, as we saw earlier, ethnic minority people are held to internalize White racist attitudes and expectations. Consequently, Black people, particularly those of African descent, are believed to have negative perceptions not only of themselves but also about their 'racial' group. Many professionals, influenced by the Western conception of the self, accept these suggestions unquestioningly and act upon them. They believe that Black children have a tendency to prefer White to their own colour and treat them accordingly. This is in spite of the existence of a substantial body of contrary research evidence that we discuss in the following chapter. None-the-less, it is hardly surprising that this pernicious myth persists, given its long history and scientific aura. For example, writing in 1930, Jung asserted: 'The Negro... would give anything to change his colour; so too the white man hates to admit that he has been touched by the black' (Jung, 1930, p. 196). Other more modern authors routinely call up fundamentally similar ideas, but rather more subtly communicated: 'Ethnic self-misidentification represents a form of denial but it also comprises a form of psychological mobility. Actual social mobility is impossible: these young girls cannot exit from their race in reality. They take the next best option: they exit subjectively' (Breakwell, 1986, p. 85).

While Jung's racism is well-established (Dalal, 1988), it is more worrying that beliefs such as Breakwell's have become accepted and quoted by professionals working with Black children, and also applied to age groups rather older than Breakwell had intended (Maximé, 1991a). However, although theories concerning identity make a lot of sense, they can be dangerous when they are used in a universal and prescriptive rather than a specific or descriptive way. Furthermore, there is a risk that a social problem is actually articulated in terms that imply that the problem is rather psychological: that it is in the psychological make-up of the Black child rather than a result of broader social processes. So, for example, Breakwell provides us with a case study of a young girl who is portrayed as experiencing an identity crisis. The case study is of Qulsoom, an 11-year-old British girl of Pakistani parentage. Her parents immigrated to Britain a few years before her birth, but her father in particular had retained the religious and other cultural standards he had in Pakistan.

> *At home, Qulsoom has to comply with the requirements of the Muslim faith and must perform in the manner expected of a young woman now eligible for marriage. At school, until now, she has been able to pursue her education in the western manner, marked only by her skin and dress. She has imbibed two systems of values and expectations. Until recently she found no difficulty in reconciling the two within herself. Each set of values had quite separate domains of operation and she kept them apart, never looking at their mutual exclusiveness.*
>
> *The problem has now arisen that Qulsoom, being of a marriageable age, should be withdrawn from her school, which is coeducational, prepared for marriage and kept chaste. Qulsoom is now becoming aware of very different demands being made on her by her teachers and her father: they require incompatible behaviour from her. They break the continuity of her self-definition which previously derived sustenance from both of her cultural positions. Her father demands total conformity to the role of a Muslim woman.*
>
> Breakwell, 1986, pp. 6–7

Qulsoom's father, has made a plan for her to be sent back to his home village where she will receive better preparation for immediate marriage. For Breakwell, this is a situation in which Qulsoom's identity is in threat because she has no means of controlling her own future

> *The continuity of Qulsoom's identity is attacked by forces which she cannot control. Perception of this loss of control can itself engender a threat to identity by initiating a loss of self-esteem. Qulsoom, for instance, feeling totally frustrated in her attempts to determine her own future, turns her anger upon herself, castigating herself for her weakness and imperfection. She points out: 'Good Muslims do not have these problems but proper British girls would not accept this'.*
>
> Breakwell, 1986, p. 7

While this is certainly a complex social situation for an 11-year-old to face, it is far from obvious the degree to which it reflects a crisis of identity. Why not call it a role conflict or socio-cultural conflict, so locating it in the social world rather than in the mind of the child? Qulsoom appears to know exactly who she is and where she belongs. Her problem is the conflicting demands placed on her by her father's cultural/religious beliefs and those of her school's headteacher. So is this a situation in which the difficulties are created by her sense of identity, or is it one created by the twin demands on her? More importantly, could one provide counselling or therapy which would solve Qulsoom's problems? Would providing her with information about her Pakistani culture materially affect the difficult situation she is in? Qulsoom may be facing profound difficulties, but these are essentially not matters of her personal identity. They are rather variants on the family crises that may happen whenever there are apparently incompatible pressures on a young person. However, in their dealings with Black children, professionals disregard such important issues as these, because they have a readymade explanation for the children's difficulties – 'identity crisis'.

The problem with the example of Qulsoom lies essentially in the way in which a stereotypical case is chosen to illustrate problems faced by Black children – in this case Black Muslim young females. Worse, however, than the author's selection of such cases as examples of threatened identities is that this way of contextualizing the cases has encouraged others to the view that identity crises are characteristic of Black and ethnic minority childhood (e.g. Coward and Dattani, 1993). It is highly debatable whether cases like Qulsoom's reflect identity crises. Curiously, despite this example, Breakwell is well aware of the social rather than psychological nature of such difficulties. It is a pity that such stereotypical portrayals of Black childhood are presented.

## In the interest of the child?

It is a truism that Black and ethnic minority people in predominantly White societies are subject to all sorts of racist humiliation, but this does not automatically result in self-hatred or own group-rejection. All the same, professionals such as teachers, social workers, school psychologists and therapists, very often ignorant of other conceptions of personhood or the self besides the Western conception, obdurately hold on to the false belief that, because such groups are subject to racism daily, they must hate themselves.

Irrespective of whether the children's difficulties are attributed to racism, or whatever else, the solution generally accepted by teachers, social workers and therapists is to work with the children to improve their self-identity or self-esteem. In some cases, this also involves efforts to impose a 'Black identity' on children who perceive themselves differently.

## Black identity work

Programmes designed to improve Black children's putative negative self-concept take no account of other conceptions of the self than the Western individualistic notion of personhood. Instead, it is the 'self' as described by Mead and Cooley which forms the basis of these programmes and other practices with these children (Owusu-Bempah, 1997). Although neither Cooley nor Mead was specifically concerned about the self-concept of any group of people, these programmes assume their ideas of the self-concept to be particularly applicable to the self-identity of Black children, irrespective of their cultural backgrounds. They excuse aspects of the system or society at large which is largely responsible for the children's difficulties and, instead, problematize the children. This is particularly so in their dealing with the so-called 'mixed-race' children.

> *When people say that mixed race children have 'identity problems', what they usually mean is that mixed race children have problems fitting themselves into socially defined categories; more specifically, that the children have difficulty discovering where they belong in relation to the black and white groups. When 'identity' is used in this sense, it is being viewed from an interactionist, rather than a purely psychological, perspective.*
>
> Wilson, 1987, p. 21

Still, many continue to problematize African-Caribbean children and children of 'mixed-race' parentage by insisting on the 'need' for professional childcare workers to strive to improve their 'negative self-identity'. They do not see that this serves the needs of a racist society rather than those of the children. Ironically, some even advocate it as a necessary anti-racist/anti-discriminatory strategy. For example, Thompson (1993) suggests, as a necessary step towards anti-racism in social work, a recognition of the 'need to help develop a positive black identity. This applies particularly to areas such as fostering and adoption... and would apply... to work with black elders (p. 78).

Similarly, some social services departments have established special clinics, often staffed by Black therapists, to work on the self-identity of Black children in their care (Coleman, 1994). They believe that the children's 'damaged' self-identity is the result of White people's racism expressed verbally and behaviourally towards them. However, if the White community is the culprit, then it is not the children who need therapy. There is no denying that racism is damaging to the children. What is puzzling is why it is they who 'need' therapy and not the White community, whose racism causes the damage. It is obvious that eliminating the pathogen, racism, would be a more sensible and effective strategy. In short, some might suggest that attempts to repair damage to a person's identity caused by racism in a racist society are like saving someone from drowning by mouth-to-mouth resuscitation under water. The intention may be good, but the efforts are patently misguided, and even more harmful. Owusu-Bempah (1994) has suggested that helping children entails a recognition and adequate understanding of their situation, including their psychological, social and material circumstances. The helper should be prepared to investigate and consider objectively factors that may cause or contribute to their difficulties. The use of abstract and nebulous concepts such as self-identity and its associated stereotypes to explain and resolve a child's difficulties may only serve to distract attention and resources from those clients who may need them most. Overall, it may do more harm than good.

Haraway (1994) implicitly agrees with our view that professionals and institutions hold on to the idea of Black self-hatred, not because it enables them to understand Black children or their needs better, but rather to control them better. She argues that by disregarding the nature of Whiteness or White identity as problematic, it becomes easier to problematize Blackness and Black identity, and consequently to subjugate and control Black people. Indeed, the idea of multiple identities in relation to children of 'mixed-race' parentage, for example, is used to create an image of the difficult and pathological nature of their Blackness and identities, and also as an excuse for treating them as a problem. In the context of psychology, Haraway (1994) uses IQ (or intelligence) as an illustration of the ways in which unfounded ideas about Black people are given social reality and used by institutions to dominate and control them. She describes IQ as a way of making concrete or material something that is a social invention:

> ... a materialized fiction. It is an example of an apparatus for materializing the world, and these forms are themselves modes of domination. These apparatuses produce subjects with various adjectives attached them who can be measured, for example a student with a particular score or a pregnant teenager with a specific profile that puts her at risk for further surveillance... What we lose track of, institutionally, is that there is an apparatus for the producing and sorting of people, as distinct from a natural object which can be measured.

> Haraway, 1994, p. 31

We must not lose sight of how the Western concept of self-identity is similarly employed as an apparatus for coding and categorizing people, an excuse for treating them differently from other people. Barnes's comments are apposite.

*The history of this country is replete with instances of the creation of theo-
ries to demonstrate the inferiority of black people – theories that can provide
justification for the oppression of black people, self-serving theories directed
to maintaining the oppressor's convictions of his own superiority. Historically, biological or genetic factors have been evoked as explanatory modes to
account for the status of Black people; today the vogue is to call forth environmental factors. **However, it is of small benefit to black people
whether an environmental hypothesis is chosen over a genetic
hypothesis, if explanation remains at the level of the black individual or family and does not begin to deal with the forces in the larger
society responsible for creating these conditions.***

Barnes, 1980, p. 110; emphasis added

Unwary Black professionals follow this fashion. Many Black and ethnic
minority therapists, teachers and social workers subscribe to the belief
that Black children, especially those of 'mixed-race' parentage, have a
negative self-concept. They believe also that the children's putative
negative self-concepts result from their lack of awareness of their
'Black' cultural background. These practitioners' westernization seems
to preclude them from appreciating the inherent 'victim blame' of this
belief and the practices based upon it.

This makes the notion of 'Black perspectives' in social work, for
example, questionable. Black perspective usually means the views of
Black professionals rather than a clearly articulated community
perspective. So the question arises of whether one is talking of the
perspectives of Black service-users or the perspectives of Black practitioners (Owusu-Bempah, 1994b, 1999c). If it is the latter, then all that
one can say is that their professional or Westernized views do not seem
to be radically different from those of their White colleagues. Indeed,
there is very little reason to believe or expect them to be (Owusu-
Bempah, 1989, 1990; 1994a). In spite of their strong opposition to racial
discrimination in employment, training and promotion, they perpetuate racism in service provision (very often unwittingly) because of their
professional status that they owe to their Eurocentric professional training and the endemic institutional racism of their organizations or
agencies. They cannot, therefore, legitimately speak for Black people
generally, just as White professional or middle-class women cannot
claim to represent the views of all women irrespective of class, colour,
ethnicity or global location. In the context of feminism, for example,
Essed (1994) argues that it is not possible to speak of a Black women's
point of view on matters of their social position. She points out that
Black professional women may vigorously oppose racial oppression
because of their Blackness, but they may reproduce class oppression
because of their middle-class or professional status.

This process whereby the victim becomes a victimizer has been
recognized by a number of observers (e.g., Bulhan, 1985; Fanon, 1967;

Fernando, 1989; Howitt and Owusu-Bempah, 1994; Owusu-Bempah, 1990, 1994a). Fanon's notion of psychic alienation delineates this process (Bartky, 1990). This notion proposes that the prime purpose of psychological oppression is to ensure that people who are the benefi-ciaries of oppression do not appear to be oppressors. Black and ethnic minority professionals in White socio-economic structures *are* psycho-logically oppressed. At the same time they are beneficiaries of the racist social order, at least, *vis-à-vis* their Black and other disadvantaged clients. This is not to deny, ignore or belittle the alienation they may experience personally as Black people in a racist superstructure. It is an attempt, rather, to untangle this complex and emotive issue by address-ing some of the ways in which, and the extent to which, they participate in the subjugation and control of their Black clients. Compared to their oppressed clients, they are privileged. Being in a privileged position may make it difficult for them to appreciate the tightrope on which they are balancing. As Trepagnier (1994) has observed, privilege has a self-validating aspect which makes it difficult for the privileged to recognize as such.

> *I think whites are carefully taught not to recognize white privilege, just as males are taught not to recognize male privilege. I have come to see white privilege as an invisible package of unearned assets which I can count on cashing in each day, but which I was 'meant' to be oblivious.*
>
> Collins, 1990, p. 190

Many Black and ethnic minority professionals are taught likewise through their Euro-centric education, training and professionalization. But this is merely a variant on the argument that Western psychology dominates the indigenous psychologies of other cultures and contributes to the lack of development of culturally more appropriate approaches.

## Rejection as natural

Inherent in most of the ideas about identity discussed so far is a view that a child largely constructs an identity from the building blocks provided by the family or immediate community. The famous theories of identity provided by Erikson (1950, 1968) make no simplistic assumptions of this sort. He viewed identity formation as a process in which the young person takes an active role. The young person has a say, more or less, in the type of identity to foster, even if it means going against the wishes or expectations of significant others, parents or community. For example, Erikson identified a process whereby roles valued by the young person's parents or social milieu are actively disdained or rejected. Erikson termed this process *negative identification*.

Good examples include Western youngsters who outrightly reject the models held up to them by their parents or community: for instance, the middle-class youngsters who become dropouts. So, if father is a teacher, social worker or a brain surgeon, that is the last thing son or daughter will aspire to be. The term can also be used to describe the often related process by which a youngster identifies with things which are not valued by the family and other significant adults in the community. In the West, for example, this is illustrated by the succession of pop-music heroes abhorred by adults but adored by their children. Many of these 'heroes' have been considered by adults to be dangerous or, in some other way, unsuitable. Much the same process of identification can operate in relation to a person's cultural background, including religion or political beliefs. Some people aspire to moving outside of their socio-political class and, in doing so, reject everything that that class stands for. Similarly, many youngsters reject their religious upbringing and, sometimes, adopt one radically different in style from that of their family, or reject religion entirely.

Identity, in the Western European sense, is essentially relative in that it is only possible in relation to the identities of other people, including both the people whom we are like and those from whom we are definitely different. In this sense, in order to achieve a coherent identity, the individual needs to be able to both identify with as well as repudiate the identities of others. In this way it is possible to clarify what we no longer are and what we never will be. There is nothing in these processes which can be labelled pathological; there is nothing pathological about resisting an identity defined and evaluated in relation to another's or a group's values and aspirations. In fact, Erikson (1968) counselled resistance to self-definition by others.

## Constructing a Black identity?

Identity is not a static entity; it is a personal quality that develops and changes throughout one's life (Erikson, 1950, 1968). It is interesting, then, that the concern about Black self-identity has led to attempts to develop models to describe and explain the development and dynamics of self-identity in Black people (e.g. Cross, 1978, 1991; Thomas, 1971). Because these models are seen by some as developmental (in the sense of human development), they are often presented as applicable to all Black people, irrespective of age, education, social class or even geographical location (e.g. Maximé, 1991a, 1993a, b). A common assumption of these models is that the process of acquiring a Black self-identity begins with the abandonment of 'Negromancy' that Thomas (1971) has described as an internalized or interiorized view of oneself as defined by White racist society. Negromancy is obviously an undesirable psychological state to be in, since it is claimed to give rise to a feeling of self-worthlessness. Cross (1977) has equated it with mental illness.

The notion of Negromancy is essentially similar to symbolic interactionist explanations of Black self-hatred. None-the-less, Cross (1978) has proposed a five-stage model for abandoning Negromancy and developing a healthy Black self-concept. Cross terms the first of these the *Pre-encounter* stage. According to Cross, it is a period during which the individual mentally bypasses or avoids the 'stigma' of being Black. The Black person at this stage favours everything White and rejects all that is Black. Furthermore, there is a denial that racism exists in society. The next, the *Encounter* stage, involves a cataclysmic event that requires a fundamental reorientation and a new understanding of Blackness on the part of the individual. The events that cause this revision are racist encounters. At this stage, different ideas are sought and tested out and finally accepted by the individual as valid. However, this is not completely internalized by the individual and requires external reinforcement of its validity. The third is the *Immersion–Emersion* stage which is a period of almost exaggerated idealization (or idolization) of all things Black and a rejection of Negromancy, one's former self. During this period, interaction is directed towards Black people, and White people and Whiteness are despised. Overt displays of Blackness in styles of language, dress and culture are characteristic of a person at the Immersion–Emersion stage. Gradually, during this stage, the individual is more reflective about Blackness and less all-accepting. The fourth, *Internalization*, is a much more relaxed and comfortable stage that manifests itself in the acceptance of a Black identity; the sharp edges have worn away and a sense of personal at-ease begins to replace the extremity of the previous phases. It is a period during which individuals are more at one with their new Black identity and no longer need to be defensive about it, permiting less hostility about Whiteness. The final stage in Cross's model is *Internalization-commitment* which entails action and commitments which permanently and continually involve the expression of the new-found Black identity. At this final stage of becoming 'Black', the individual becomes an active and contributing member of the Black community.

These stages have been graphically described by Thomas. Although Thomas's description, as reported by Cross (1980), does not match exactly with Cross's five stages, it captures the flavour perfectly.

*When you find a brother who wastes all his time rapping on Whitey, you know he's at the first stage. As he moves on to the second stage he is testifying to all the pain he has endured because he has contributed to the process of denying the self. Another part of the second stage is learning to express his anxieties about becoming black; he gets confused as to whether this step has to include burning down the city or grabbing a gun. In the third stage we get into information processing on the cultural heritage, not only the*

*African background but the black contribution to our homeland, America. You go out of this stage into activity, working through a particular group to find linkage to the larger black experience. The fifth stage is transcendental through your unique blackness you lose your hangups about race, age, sex and social class and see yourself as a part of humanity in all its flavors.*

Cross, 1980, p. 83

Whether or not this is a realistic assessment of a common sequence is not completely clear. What is virtually self-evident is the message in Western societies, that the fulfilled Black identity, or any other identity that is not White, is a politicized identity. According to this model, to maintain their psychological integrity, the individual has to have a continued, active involvement in the Black (or ethnic minority) community which extends into the future: 'Here the individual advances on the previous stage by involving him or herself in black groups or community issues' (Maximé, 1991, p. 108). Or more clearly stated: 'in order for Black identity change to have lasting political significance, the "self" ("me" or "I") must become or continue to be involved in the resolution of problems shared by the "group" (we)'. (Cross, 1977, p. 86).

## Limitations of negromancy

In all its manifestations, as described by its proponents, the model is about the process of becoming 'Black' in a political sense. As such, it is best regarded as a conversion model. It describes the ways in which a person may come to acquire or hold a different world-view from the one they hold, and the conditions under which the new perspective may be maintained over time. Thus, it is not peculiar to Black people or Black identity formation. Rather, it is applicable to all groups who subscribe to particular ideologies – trade unionists, religious groups and so forth. The model has greater political than psychological significance. This is acknowledged by Cross (1980). Indeed, the process of 'negromancy' or 'negrescence' (becoming Black) is not fundamentally different from Freire's (1972) notion of 'conscientization', the process whereby the oppressed become politicized or take active interest in political, social, economic and cultural matters that affect their lives.

Notwithstanding, some insist that the model of psychological negrescence or 'negromancy' is of developmental significance and is therefore pertinent to understanding identity development in Black children. For example, Maximé (1991a) describes it as a developmental model which 'lends itself readily to understanding the problems of Black identity confusion' (p. 108). There appears to be nothing in Cross's writings to suggest this to be the case. On the contrary, *all* the evidence provided by Cross and Thomas (Cross, 1980) in support of their thesis is based upon studies involving adults; none of these studies included even adolescents. It is therefore difficult to accept the claim that the model is helpful to our understanding of the psychosocial development of Black children. It is equally difficult to see its contribution to methods of helping those children who may be experiencing emotional difficulties, as Maximé (1991a, 1993a, b) seems to claim.

Evidence also tends to question the claimed relationship between the various stages of the model and mental health or psychological wellbeing, and hence, the model's therapeutic value (e.g. Carter, 1991; Parham and Williams, 1993). For example, Carter (1991) correlated the different stages of psychological negrescence with various measures of mental health and psychopathology. Although the relationships were statistically significant, they were generally relatively few and largely indicative that individuals were in the pre-encounter stage during which they identified with White and rejected Black identity. Factors such as anxiety, memory impairment, paranoid thoughts, hallucinations and concerns about the use of alcohol were associated with being high on the measure of pre-encounter. Being concerned about drugs was associated with the Immersion–Emersion stage, but being in this phase was also associated with better memory. The evidence is not particularly convincing since paranoid thoughts were as high in the internalization phase as in the pre-encounter phase – quite the opposite of the theoretical expectations. Furthermore, the study appears not to have attempted to make allowances for various cultural, social and demographic factors which might be expected to be related to psychological functioning and attitudes.

One of the studies which are presented as supporting the model is that of Munford (1994). She examined the relationship between the stages (pre-encounter, encounter, immersion and internalization) of Black identity formation and depression. Of course, one would expect greater depression in those in the pre-encounter phase, and lower depression in the internalization phase. The data do provide some support for these expectations. However, a measure of self-esteem was the best independent predictor of depression, and the racial identity stages accounted for relatively little additional variation. Generally, the evidence supporting the 'negrescence' model of Black identity formation is not very strong. For example, when asked about changes in their racial identity, nearly half of Black adults mentioned positive changes. One in twenty reported negative changes, and about a quarter described how their racial identity oscillated between the positive and the negative. Another quarter reported no change at all (Parham and Williams, 1993). Change was not generally the result of negative experiences with White people. Over a half of the respondents mentioned personal insight rather than external influences or racist encounters as determinants of change. About one in ten mentioned positive experiences with White people as their reason for change. However, most significantly, only about one in eight of the Black adults mentioned negative experiences with White people as the source of their changed racial attitudes. In other words, most of the changes did not fit the 'negrescence' model that holds negative experiences with White people as a trigger for the process. None-the-less, race-related experiences do seem partly responsible for changes in identity in some cases. Thomas (1971), for example, found that Black adults who had many racist experiences tended to be the most at ease with the physical characteristics of African-Americans. Those who reported experiences of discrimination in housing and education tended to have the strongest sense of psychological concern and commitment to the problems of African-Americans.

We see psychological negrescence, the process of becoming ' politically Black', as a conversion model, as opposed to a developmental model. It simply does not involve the socialization processes which would occur to a Black child in Africa or anywhere else beyond Western boundaries. Psychological negrescence is about political or ideological conversion, and not the process by which children achieve a sense of identity. We also agree with Cross (1971) and Thomas(1971) that the process may be triggered in some cases by racist events or one's experiences of racism. However, it is incorrect to assume that such experiences are almost always negative in their long-term effects. Such experiences can be generative, or energizing when they serve as a stimulus or motivator for a reconstruction of the self-concept in a positive direction. Research to test this view requires a radically different approach from the conventional one that seeks to construe and portray Black and ethnic minority adults and children, using Western models of human development, as hapless and passive victims of racism (Howitt and Owusu-Bempah, 1994). The question posed by Barnes (1980), in the context of African-Americans, is relevant here: 'Is it possible that the black community can and does serve as a mediator between the black child and the pernicious impingement of the white society, such that the child can develop a self-concept that is enhancing of himself and of his group...?' (Barnes, 1980, p. 112).

The answer to this question is surprisingly easy once one goes beyond the rhetoric and misemphases of the academic and professional literature on Black identity. Black children can, and usually do, achieve positive views of themselves. Nevertheless, neither they nor their families and communities are credited with this. Instead the preference is to portray Black children as damaged characters with a damaging history, and from a damaging social environment. The next chapter turns to the evidence against this pernicious myth and an examination of what the Black self may be.

# Chapter 8

# Mixed-race and mixed cultures

*The presence of racially mixed persons defies the social order predicated upon race, blurs racial and ethnic group boundaries, and challenges generally accepted proscriptions and prescriptions regarding intergroup relations. Furthermore, and perhaps most threatening, the existence of racially mixed persons challenges long-held notions about the biological, moral, and social meaning of race.*

Root, 1992, p. 3

Second-guessing the thoughts and feelings of any group is a profoundly hazardous enterprise. This is as true of one's own group as it is of other groups. It would be a risky gamble for anyone to claim, for example, that they understood what the group or national psychology of Russia, China, Japan, Estonia or Britain was. Yet, with ease, many use skin-deep characteristics of Black and other ethnic minority children of equally or more diverse national, ethnic and social backgrounds as a basis for making what, in the circumstances, can only be described as wild conjectures regarding their psychology and what makes them tick. While diversity among some groups (White European groups) is publicly hailed, exalted and protected, it is regarded as a social problem among others. Paradoxically, it is treated as a bigger problem when the difference is not great. That is, ethnic minority groups who do not 'deviate' widely in physical or cultural characteristics or in other ways from White people are regarded as constituting an even greater problem by White society. This, indeed, may at least partly explain the British Home Office's (1981) statistics regarding the differential racial attacks against people of South Asian origins. These estimated that African-Caribbeans were 36 times more likely to be racially attacked than White people, while South Asians were 50 times more likely to be racially attacked. In terms of skin complexion and other anatomical features, people of South Asian origins are closer to White people than people of African descent are. In fact, according to physical anthropological classifications, people of the Indian sub-continent belong to the Caucasian group (Montagu, 1974, 1997). It is worth noting that there is also evidence of the differential treatment of South Asians and African-Caribbean's in the job market (Brown and Gray, 1985; Brennan and McGeevor, 1987; Modood *et al.*, 1997). As far as children are concerned, those of 'mixed-race' parentage, the offspring of Black and White unions, have been historically seen as a social problem by society as a whole. For example, Dummett (1984) quotes a right-wing national politician who claimed: 'the breeding of millions of half-caste children will merely produce a generation of misfits and increase social tension' (p. 177). It is not only right-wing politicians or bigots who target these children for surveillance. Members of even the 'helping' professions, as we have seen in preceding chapters, are also prone to making this type of conjecture. Again, Dummett (1984) describes a health visitor who summed up the cause of the 'problems posed by these children' (as perceived by the health visitor) thus: 'The problem lies in the mixtures' (p. 177).

These are not merely ageing and crude examples of a previous generation's offensiveness. Similar rhetoric underlies the pronouncements of modern professionals who may disguise their sentiment as a concern for the children (Connolly, 1998). The new spin is to be a little less forthright. Nevertheless, 'mixed-race' children continue to be portrayed as problems and alleged to be incapable of integrating their Blackness and Whiteness into a coherent racial identity by many professionals (Owusu-Bempah, 1994a; 1997). These professionals pay scant attention to the serious research on 'mixed-race' children which clearly indicates that they experience no more frequent or greater psychosocial developmental problems than other children do. Complacency is an unaffordable luxury to those who genuinely wish to provide a professional service to children, regardless of colour, ethnicity, religion and so forth. We must always guard against the groundless assumptions that dominate areas of professional thinking (Howitt, 1992; MacDonald, 1990; Owusu-Bempah, 1994a).

## Singled out: the ghost of the 'marginal man'

'Mixed-race' children are not immune to identity problems any more than they are to any of the many problems that potentially face children in Western societies. Nevertheless, the belief that identity crises are endemic to children of Black and White unions would appear to be no more than a racist assumption. Why professionals, as well as the policies and procedures of their institutions, so readily accept a view of 'mixed-race' childhood as pathological is important. It is a mistake to assume that issues become focused upon because they reflect real problems in society (Howitt, 1992). If notions of 'mixed-race' identity serve the needs of the practitioner better than they reflect the needs of youngsters in the community, then it is first and foremost a professional problem. If the interests of 'mixed-race' children are harmed by crass assumptions, then the solution must be in the training and education of the professionals and not in therapy for the children. Therapy is based on the assumption that there is a problem and that it is located within the children. Often, the problem is attributed to their skin tone, at least implicitly, rather than their inner characteristics. The following quotations from the case records of social services departments bear testimony to professionals' preoccupation with skin tone and the apparent crises that might occur over it:

> *X is the only mixed-race child in the family... his half-sister has been vindictive and vicious, refers to black animals and has suggested that they be sent back to the jungle...*

> *Of twenty-one cases of mixed-race children at a Classifying School, ten were reported as being 'colour sensitive', to the degree that it was regarded as worthy of report.*

Hitch, 1983, p. 109

Describing the offspring of Black and White unions, one therapist obscures the issues and illustrates the difficulties inherent in this area: 'The quest for self-identity has been more complex for African-Americans than for all other groups in American society' (Bowles, 1993, p. 417). Although, the context is that of material intended to inform social workers, no clear justification is made for such a claim which conflates self-identity and racial identity. Significantly, at first impression, such claims assume an aura of reasonableness and common sense. However, underlying the rhetoric, the words seem to work more towards reinforcing racist assumptions commonplace among clinicians, teachers, social workers and other professional groups. Echoing Park (1928) and Stonequist (1937), Bowles claims: 'Children from black/white unions have typically faced resistance from blacks, from whites and from society where tradition has been that "one drop of Black blood" has meant that one is identified as black' (p. 417).

Bowles describes working therapeutically with ten young adults from 'mixed-race' backgrounds. This was apparently the sum total of his experience with this group of clients over a thirty-year period. It would, therefore, be wrong to assume that racial identity problems were a central feature of this clinician's work. A careful examination of the case studies suggests that they overestimate the extent of such difficulties. Four of the ten cases involve women born to Black fathers and White mothers. In three of these, the mothers actively encouraged their daughters to regard themselves as White. In the fourth case, both parents agreed to bring up the child as 'biracial'. In practice, however, the girl had spent her youth in the Black community and felt closest to her paternal family. It is not surprising, then, that Bowles found that she was actually rather settled in her identity. The other six cases involved the offspring (two males and four females) of Black mothers and White fathers. Bowles claims, influenced by 'Black politics', that the parents had reared their offspring as Black. This led to their identity crises since the children were being forced to deny half of their racial identity. Bowles found the sons of the White fathers to be the most disturbed because they had 'dis-identified' from their Whiteness. Another explanation given by Bowles for the sons' disturbance is that realizing, for example, how limited their career opportunities were in comparison to those of a White son of the same father, caused them shame, anxiety and depression. Superficially, this complicates the issue: what was the root cause of their emotional problems, their self-identity or their limited life-chances? Bowles fails to consider the latter as a possible cause of his client's problems. However, these cases are in support of our argument that racism damages Black children's opportunities more than it does their self-worth (Owusu-Bempah, 1997; Owusu-Bempah and Howitt, 1999).

There is also something odd about a situation in which a father actively encourages his son to 'dis-identify' with him. Bowles describes this as a partial denial of self (on the part of the son). This may well appear to be the case from a therapist's (detached) perspective, but to the client it may mean something a great deal more serious than a simple denial of self. For a child, especially an adolescent, it is likely to be a very confusing and hurtful experience. He is likely to ask himself a lot of perplexing and uncomfortable questions such as: 'Who is denying or rejecting whom?' 'Why does dad not want me to be like him, is it because there is something wrong or bad about me?' 'Is he ashamed of me?' In his desperate efforts to find answers to such questions, one possible conclusion to be drawn by the child is that his father hates or dislikes him, for whatever reasons. Having such doubts or feelings about the relationship with one's natural father (or mother) cannot be a comfortable experience for any 'normal' child or adult (Owusu-Bempah, 1995; Owusu-Bempah and Howitt, 1997). In fact, it is likely to have lasting deleterious effects on the child, as attachment theory would predict. It is therefore not surprising that Bowles' most disturbed clients were those who had had such an experience. These clients' problems are therefore not characteristic of 'mixed-race' children, as Bowles seems to imply.

## Who is confused?

*There are cases which represent a more extreme degree of maladjustment than identity confusion. This is the situation where a person is socially assigned to a group, but does not wish to be a member. What is more, the members of that group also reject him and would not admit her to membership even if he wished to join. In addition, the group to which she feels she belongs is also denying him membership. She is rejected by both groups and belongs nowhere.*

Hitch, 1983, p. 107

So, the theme of the 'marginal man' is brought back to life to reinforce the assumption that children of 'mixed-race' parentage are inextricably driven to psychological turmoil as a consequence of attempting to internalize the very different realities of 'being Black and White' in a racist society. In symbolic interactionist terms, Hitch is suggesting that these children's self-definition and self-evaluation are inescapably formed in the image presented to them by the dominant White world. As we will see, the truth is, if anything, that feelings of self-worth are generally independent of social definitions of the worth of one's racial group (e.g. Beckham, 1934; Rosenberg, 1992).

Although different cultures perceive 'adolescence' differently, there seems to be little doubt that in Western capitalist, individualist societies, during certain stages of any child's development, especially in adolescence, the issue of identity can often loom large. Adolescence is a period of exploration, including identity and other things. Some of the seeds of a meaningful, stable and continuing identity are set at this stage, as others have been in earlier childhood. According to Huang (1994), the vastly increased capacity for abstract thinking that occurs at this time of transition from childhood into adulthood increases the individual's potential to explore roles and identities. We would stress that shifting identities or experimenting with different identities is an essential part of that exploration; it is part of a normal developmental process among Western young people. Thus a Black child, for instance, growing up in a Western socio-economic structure may identify with a White person as part of experimenting with the role of that person – a carer, teacher or a media personality – without being psychologically damaged by it. Similarly, a White child may identify with Black blues singers, neighbours, family friends or pop singers. Any ensuing damage, according to our conceptualization, is merely the result of the overreactions of adults who fail to recognize things for what they are. For example, psychological harm may follow as a direct or indirect consequence of a youngster being labelled as suffering from identity confusion.

Montagu (1974, 1997) is at pains to point out to us the fact that all human beings are so mixed with regard to origin that, between different groups of individuals, intergradation of 'overlapping' physical traits is the rule. It is for this reason, among others, that it is difficult to draw up more than a few hard and fast distinctions between even the most extreme types:

*The essential reality of the existing situation ... is not the hypothetical subspecies or race, but the mixed ethnic groups, which can never be genetically purified into their original components, or purged of the variability which they owe to past crossing. Most anthropological writings of the past and many of the present fail to take account of this fundamental fact.*

Haddon and Huxley, 1936, quoted in Montagu, 1977, p. 49

According to Montagu, the words 'genetically purified into their original components' do not refer to pre-existing 'pure races', but to the earlier states of the ancestral group entering into the formation of the mixed-race or mixed ethnic groups as we know them today.

Lamentably, it is not only anthropologists who fail to take this basic and obvious fact into account. Fundamental emotional panics arise when we are faced with meeting the needs of 'mixed-race' youngsters. It is anxiety brought about by the elements of racist thinking which are hard to escape in the Western world. Notice the relative lack of professional concern about the psychosocial developmental problems facing the children of other ethnic minorities in Britain, such as the Irish, the Spaniards and the Poles compared to Black children, including those of 'mixed-race' parentage. We do not consider it vital to define their psychological or cultural needs. For example, as a minority group in mainland Britain, anti-Irish feelings are commonly expressed through innumerable anti-Irish jokes that routinely circulate. Despite this, we know of no attempts to systematically teach, say, Irish culture to such children or to place them with Irish foster parents. Even if it is assumed that children of Irish descent are 'invisible' within White communities, they will still usually know their origins and of the hostility faced by their parents. Yet, it is extremely doubtful if professionals interpret the emphasis placed upon the importance of cultural awareness to Black and 'mixed-race' children in local authority care as applicable to other children of equally mixed descent and those from other ethnic minorities. In fact, we know of no reported evidence to suggest that they do. The contrast is marked.

When it comes to 'race', we seem unprepared to accept similarities, so much so that we tend to create them where they do not exist. However, we always ensure that these artificial differences are in our favour. Much of the belief and many of the assumptions about the 'psychopathology' of 'mixed-race' children stems from the works of Park (1928, 1931) and Stonequist (1937), reinforced by the Clarks' (1939, 1947) doll studies and subsequent studies based upon them. However, loath as we are to take the interpretation of the 'let's pretend' (doll and photograph choice) studies seriously, an exception should be made for one. This exceptional British study (Wilson, 1987) used coloured photographs in which skin tone, hair and facial features varied in sensitive ways which transcend many of the problems of the early and disputed research. The study involved 6- to 9-year-old children with one Black and one White natural parent. They all lived with their natural parents. Among other things, these youngsters were asked to say which of the photographs looked the most like themselves and which looked the most like their best friends. An important aspect of the research was that the children also sorted the photographs into racial groups, and explained to a 'spaceman' how this classification was done. Up to the age of about 8 years, fairly simple colour categorization procedures were employed. Above this age the first evidence of the use of racial categories as opposed to colour categories is found. This 'mixed-race' sample accurately selected photographs depicting either a 'mixed-race' child or an African-Caribbean child as being the most like them. Indeed, 80 per cent of them made such accurate choices. 'Misidentifications', by and large, involved picking a child of 'single-race' African-Caribbean (14 per cent), or a photograph of a child of Anglo-Asian parentage (4 per cent). Significantly, only one child picked a White photograph. Clearly this is not enough evidence upon which policy or practice should be based.

The relationship between the skin tone of the child and that of the child chosen from the photographs was also explored. About two-thirds of the children made a choice of photographs which accurately reflected their own skin shade. Furthermore, there was no bias towards Whiteness or misperception of being White, since precisely equal numbers of the children chose a photograph of a child with a lighter skin colour than their own as those who chose a photograph with a darker skin colour. The children were also asked to indicate which child in the photographs they would ideally like to be, if they could be 'magicked' into someone else. Similar trends emerged: about half of them chose a 'mixed-race' Anglo-African-Caribbean (49 per cent), about 18 per cent chose a single-race African-Caribbean, about 14 per cent chose an Anglo-Asian, and about 18 per cent chose a White child. When asked which child they would like to stay with them at their home overnight, the order of preference was for a 'mixed-race' African-Caribbean, followed by 'single-race' African-Caribbean, White, South Asian and Anglo-Asian.

Wilson's study demonstrates that children of Anglo-African-Caribbean parentage in Britain are not confused about their racial and cultural identities. It also supports the argument that evaluations of skin tone do not follow a simple Black–White continuum (Porter, 1991). A study by Porter, carried out in the USA, found that for Black children aged about 9 years, honey-brown was the most frequently preferred skin tone, followed by a very light yellow. Darker brown colours were preferred by relatively few of the children; dark brown tended to be low on the list of dislikes. None of this provides much support for the Black self-hatred thesis since, generally, the preferences were more for Black tones than for light tones. The Black self-hatred idea would require that the lightest of tones would be the most preferred.

Tizard and Phoenix (1993) carried out another important British study of 'mixed-race' children living with their natural families. Their findings explode most of the myths about these youngsters. The study concentrated upon the following aspects of 'mixed-race' children's' experiences: (1) how they regard themselves racially; (2) whether being of 'mixed-race' parentage creates identity confusion; (3) the centrality of racial identity in their lives; and (4) their affinity to different cultures and people of different races. The overwhelming majority (86 per cent) of the mixed-race sample claimed to not want to be another colour; neither did they feel that a White identity was ideal, even though sometimes they felt this way, especially when they were faced with racist abuse during their younger years. A few of the youngsters reported that they would have preferred to be either Black or White, although they had no strong preference for either of these racial groups; only three youngsters wanted to be White, and one wanted to be Black. Overwhelmingly, the children had a positive racial identity (usually 'mixed' or 'brown'). Contrary to popular claims, it was found that the presence of a Black parent at home did not seem to make any difference to the child's sense of identity. The following finding is important: 'there was a stronger tendency for those who had a problematic identity to say they had been told by their parents to be proud of being black, or of being of mixed parentage' (Tizard and Phoenix, 1993, p. 61).

Generally, 'mixed-race' youngsters in Tizard and Phoenix's study regarded themselves and others like themselves as 'brown', 'mixed' or 'coloured'. The term 'Black' tended not to be used to describe other 'mixed-race' people. Some youngsters knew of the argument that in a racist society they should regard themselves as Black, but chose to disregard this view: 'I wouldn't call myself black. I mean, lots of people have said if you are mixed race you might as well call yourself black, but I feel that is denying the fact that my mother is white, and I'm not going to do that' (interviewee; quoted by Tizard and Phoenix, 1993, p. 47).

Other findings from Tizard and Phoenix's study included the following: (1) none of the 'mixed-race' youngsters considered themselves White; a small percentage felt themselves to be somewhat lighter than Black; (2) living with a Black parent did not influence whether they classified themselves as Black; (3) Black identity was characteristically found in the youngsters with the most highly politicized views about racism; (4) wanting to be White was related to being affiliated with White people for friendship and culture; it was primarily determined by the racial composition of the school a child attended. On the basis of their findings, Tizard and Phoenix concluded:

*The question of whether someone is 'black enough in culture and attitude' ... seems to assume that there is a unitary black culture shared by all black people, irrespective of their gender, age, social class, occupation, or country of origin. We do not believe that there is such a culture; what unites black people is their experience of racism. In our sample, whilst all but two of the black parents had grown up in Africa or the Caribbean, most of the young people had been born in England. Only a third felt any loyalty to their black parent's country of origin, and their ties to it seemed very weak. They saw themselves very much as English, or British, and particularly as Londoners.*
Tizard and Phoenix, 1993, pp. 174–175

## Denying the other's self-definition

Given that the majority, if not all, of 'mixed-race' children in Britain see themselves as either English, Scottish, or Welsh or simply British, why do we insist that they are something else? Why do we insist that they belong to a different race and culture to that of their White parents? Is it because, as Root (1992) and Montagu (1974) have argued, they represent living and growing evidence that proscriptions and prescriptions governing intergroup or interracial relations, especially sexual relations, have been violated? If so, then, Chancellor Williams (1974) argues that, in terms of Black–White sexual relations, for example, the taboo surrounding interacial sexual relations applies only to Black male–White female liaisons. It has never, throughout history, applied to White men–Black female liaisons:

> The 'master race' always kept its own women 'sacred' and secluded behind the walls of their homes. They were not allowed to go outside except under guard. African women had no such restrictions or protection. They were fair game for men of all races, and for them it was always open season... The 'master race', then, while loudly proclaiming a strange doctrine of 'racial purity' for itself, has been the world's leader in bastardizing other peoples. And it has been done on a grand scale in the United States, in South Africa, in East and West Africa. And so it was in [Ancient] Egypt.
>
> Williams, 1974, pp. 73–77

Throughout history, the offspring of Black–White unions have usually been disparaged not only on ideological grounds but also (pseudo) scientific ones. Guthrie (1976) reports that the mulatto hypotheses, which involved Black children in continuous massive assessment studies between 1916 and the 1930s, were formulated from two perspectives. One held that persons of racially mixed ancestry were *inferior* to those of 'pure' (unmixed) backgrounds. The other view held that racially mixed individuals were *superior* to those of 'pure' backgrounds. According to Guthrie, 'scientific' data were collected and detailed in support of both views. For example, he relates one study which claimed that Black–White 'crosses' in Jamaica left the offspring with 'long legs of the Negro and the short arms of the white, thus putting them at a disadvantage in picking up objects from the ground' (p. 63).

Not everyone, even in those days, supported the 'racially mixed' inferiority hypothesis. The White psychologist Herskovits (1934) conducted the most extensive review of studies based on this hypothesis. His conclusion was that: 'no significant correlations have been made between the amount of Negro blood represented in individuals – whether estimated on the basis of inspection, by the use of genealogies, or by anthropometric measurements – and standing in tests' (in

Guthrie, 1976, pp. 63–4). Yet, in spite of these findings, the mulatto hypotheses continued, and still continue (under the guise of negative self-concept) to maintain widespread support among many researchers, therapists and practitioners.

Whatever our reasons or motives for our stubborn refusal to acknowledge their membership to their White parent's group or culture, the net effect is that we psychologically deny them citizenship of any Western nation, including Britain; we are instilling into them a sense of being strange or even alien, of not belonging. In short, by refusing to validate their self-definition, we are saying to them: 'You do not belong here, you belong somewhere else.' In Britain, for instance, it is noteworthy that we do not communicate such messages (not even covertly) to the offspring of White British–White American unions living in Britain.

Although a small minority of Tizard and Phoenix's 'mixed-race' respondents had problems associated with racial identity, these problems were not restricted to this group of children. Other children also exhibited such problems:

*Although only a minority of the mixed-parentage sample experienced problems with their racial identity, the proportion that did so was twice as large as it was in the case of those with two black parents. Their problems were those that have always been recognized for people of mixed parentage: a feeling of being 'different', a feeling of being torn between two sets of competing loyalties and in some cases the experience of hostility from black children, as well as white.*

p. 162

This, however, should not encourage anxiety that these children desperately need help, since balancing between competing loyalties is a common social experience which needs to be negotiated and managed in most instances. Alternatively, the feeling of being 'different' and the experience of split-loyalties are at least partly due to the hostility from both communities, rather than being an intrinsic aspect of the children's personality. That is, the problem lies with both Black and White communities, children and adults, including professionals who seem unwilling to accept similarities in matters of race, and not with the individual child

Many of Tizard and Phoenix's findings are also reflected in a US study of Black/White biracial children (Kerwin *et al.*, 1993). The participants included boys and girls aged 5 to 14. Although a self-selected sample, it is important that these children did not seem to have racial identity difficulties that might cause any concern. It is also notable that their parents seemed to have a 'secure' sense of their own racial identity. Moreover, the parents did not seem to seek to have their children identify more with one racial group than the other. This sense of a lack of conflict is emphasized by few difficulties the parents had with their extended families, although some grandparents had apparent concerns about 'mixed-race' children in terms of society's reactions to them (a common euphemism in a racist society). One of the major findings was that the 'mixed-race' children did not demonstrate the problems that historically have been attributed them: none regarded themselves as 'marginal' persons stuck between two cultures. Instead, a degree of enhanced sensitivity to the two sub-cultures was a feature of the children who tended to see that the cultures had much more in common than differences. Despite the small scale of this study, it does nothing to detract from Tizard and Phoenix's British findings.

The history of 'mixed-race' children has been somewhat complex in the Western world. For example, as recently as 1967 interracial marriage was constitutionally prohibited in most southern states of the USA. Until very recently, this was also the case in South Africa. Socially, it is still generally discouraged in Western societies, including Britain (Alhibai, 1987; Montagu, 1974, 1997). Some professionals have made a massive leap from this legal apartheid to psychological processes in 'mixed-race' children. Children of 'mixed-race' parentage have been historically regarded as mentally internalizing social apartheid such that they find it impossible to merge the Black and the White elements of themselves. On the contrary, it is abundantly clear from research that, generally, Black, White and 'mixed-race' children achieve identities for themselves which effectively integrate many pertinent aspects from their racial and/or cultural background. Thus it is grossly presumptuous to suggest that the minds of children of 'mixed-race' parentage are more conflict-ridden than their Black or White counterparts.

Of course, things sometimes go wrong with the identity development of some 'mixed-race' children. For example, Gibbs (1987) describes problem cases of youngsters who identified with the White parent and rejected minority status and characteristics. Sometimes the youngster might resort to highly stereotypical behaviours associated with the minority group. The question is whether these cases are at all representative of 'mixed-race' youngsters in general. Gibbs and Hines (1992) studied 'mixed-race' adolescents aged 12 to 18 in the San Franscisco Bay area of California. Their sample was rather informal and involved only twelve youngsters from ten different families. The findings of the study included the following: (1) half of the youngsters identified themselves as 'mixed-race'; (2) a quarter as Black or African-American; (3) only two were unsure about how to describe their racial identity; (4) the majority (80 per cent) were content with their dual heritage since they did not wish to belong to a particular race; (5) only one child wanted to be Black, and another White; (6) none had a preference for a White spouse; and (7) two-thirds had Black friends, while about the same number had White friends. In brief: 'the majority of this group appeared to be comfortable with their social identity as biracial persons and had established positive relations with Black, White, and other mixed-race and minority peers' (Gibbs and Hines, 1992, p. 232).

The small number of poorly adjusted children in Gibbs and Hines's sample tended to be from single-parent households. These children had little contact with their other parent and/or their family and friends. Gibbs and Hines found 'intact' families to be among the factors associated with positive psychological adjustment. Our own research (Owusu-Bempah, 1993, 1995; Owusu-Bempah and Howitt, 1997) suggests that the children's lack of contact with their non-custodial natural parents' extended kin at least contributed to their difficulties.

There is a tendency to regard 'mixed-race' issues as Black–White issues. However, a study by Hall (1992) firmly reminds us that this is not the case. Hall studied young men and women of African-American-Japanese parentage in the USA (mostly the fathers were African-Americans). These were, in a sense, people who could be regarded as representing the archetypal 'marginal man', in that despite looking Black and living in Black communities, they decided to find their racial identity outside of the Black community. About a third of the participants in the research said that they would not wish to be categorized as either Black or Japanese, as it was important to them to acknowledge the racial backgrounds of both parents. According to Hall, when the participants chose to identify themselves as anything other than Black, it was seen as a positive statement of something comfortable and viable to them; in no way was it seen as a statement of a feeling of being marginal or outcast. Also, their self-esteem was unrelated to their choice of racial identity label. This may be speculative, but imagine how such 'mixed-race' people might be thought of by British social workers, teachers, therapists and other professionals who casually accept the view that it is problematic to achieve a 'mixed-race' or 'dual heritage' identity. Here are socially defined Black people who believe that they are Japanese!

## Mixed-identity development

Stripped of our perverse desire to impose cultural and psychological anomalies on mixed-race individuals, the simple truth is that far too little is known about the processes by which 'mixed-race' identity is achieved, assuming there is such a thing. This is partly a consequence of the historic tendency for research on 'mixed-race' children to be firmly located within the psychiatric hospitals and clinics of North America or the British public childcare system. Without question, this has led to the dominance of unsustainable notions of pathology and maladjustment being attached to these children (Hall, 1992). Worse still, both researchers and practitioners ignore research concerning 'mixed-race' unless it corresponds to this pathological model. Too often writers revert to identifying conflict and even turmoil rather than the normalcy of the processes involved. There is an urgent need to move away from the former model if we are to understand better the psychosocial development of children of 'mixed-race' parentage.

'Mixed-race' identity can only be achieved in a social context in which certain definitions of race and cultural boundaries are dominant. Inevitably, the ways in which society categorizes children may reflect the world-view of dominant sectors of society (Johnson, 1992). So, although categories, such as 'mixed-race' and African-Caribbean are acknowledged by White communities, these distinct groupings are nevertheless treated as members of the broader classes, such as Black and African, by them (Wilson, 1987). As a consequence, all children with any Black ancestors are treated as if they were 'single-race' individuals with their origins in Africa. According to Jacobs (1992), the newer terminologies such as 'mixed-race', 'biracial' and 'dual heritage' encourage children to regard identity development as a struggle. Jacobs describes three stages in the development of biracial identity:

1  Pre-colour constancy (up to about 4 years): at this stage the child has not learnt to categorize evaluatively on the basis of skin colour; nevertheless the child will engage in exploring colour in appropriate circumstances.
2  Post-colour constancy (about 4.5 to 7 years): at stage two, the child has begun to appreciate that their skin colour will not change despite continuing to explore and experiment with both social roles and their sense of identity. It is a period of ambivalence over racial identification in which, usually, the initial stance is towards a White identity and a rejection of the Black identity although this can and does vary.
3  Biracial identity (8 to 12 years): the child understands that racial identity is determined by parentage, and skin colour is at best an uncertain indicator of race; the child understands the use of the social categories of Black and White and knows where its parents stand in relation to these categories.

These stages contain an important message for child-rearing. In particular, it is as valuable to help the children to label themselves as 'mixed-race' as it is to give support when they experience even ambivalent or uncertain feelings about race. Parents and childcare professionals need to understand that such racial ambivalence is not pathological but an important part of the mechanism by which a 'mixed-race' child explores issues of race and racial identity before finally achieving integration of the two aspects of its heritage. The danger lies not so much in episodes of racial ambivalence, but in undue parental and/or professional concern interfering with such exploration (Owusu-Bempah, 1997). 'Mixed-race' children should not be cornered into feeling that there is a problem about their identity. Much the same is true about pressures on children to choose a 'Black identity' rather than their preferred White, brown or 'mixed-race' choices, or vice versa. It is an irony that those professionals who try to foreclose the identity formation of these children are at the same time among the vociferous advocates for the acceptance of, and respect for, human diversity.

A slightly different version of Jacob's model also stresses that developing a 'mixed-race' identity involves three stages (Kich, 1992):

Stage 1:   This stage entails the painful experience of regarding oneself as different from other people.
Stage 2:   This is a process of trying to become understood and accepted by others in order to come to terms with oneself; not surprisingly, the response of parents to the child's efforts at this stage is crucial to the process of identity development.
Stage 3:   This is a long-term and continuous process reflecting the way in which personality develops and adjusts throughout life. Once a 'mixed-race' self-identity has been achieved, accepted and imposed in social interactions, there is still psychological work to be done. This 'mixed-race' identity will need to be reassessed, reincorporated and reaffirmed when important transitions are made, such as leaving the parental home, the birth of offspring or moving into a new community.

These stages indicate that the process of achieving a 'mixed-race' identity is personal as well as social. In fact, Kich emphasizes that 'mixed-race' identity formation is not a matter of increasing self-acceptance alone, since experiences discrepant with self-acceptance may facilitate a reconstruction process, which leads towards the sense of 'totality' characteristic of the 'mixed-race' identity. At the same time, the sense of being both 'races' and neither is maintained.

It is difficult to assess the depth of such processes, given the apparent ease with which many 'mixed-race' children achieve their identity. Any study that attempts to understand these processes is likely to overlook the fact that Western conceptions of adolescence do not reflect cultural universals. This may be one of the reasons for profoundly overestimating the extent of identity crises in children of other cultural backgrounds. In this context it is worth stressing the views of Huang (1994) who points out that Western concepts of adolescence may not have parallels in Asian cultures. Western concepts suggest that adolescence is a process of developing a sense of oneself as an individual with an individual identity. We saw in Chapter 6 that other cultures are more oriented towards the family, the group or community. In such cultures, one's sense of identity may be more dependent on one's place in the kinship scheme and the rules that govern family or group structure and continuity. Often, there is also active discouragement from seeking a sense of identity outside the family especially. While Huang writes of Asian families in the USA, the essential point applies equally to many African, African-Caribbean and South Asian communities in Britain and other parts of the Western world. Clearly it would be reckless to disregard this factor when considering the so-called identity problems of Black children generally; one might well be imposing a Western conception of identity on children who require a sense of family or group identity much more than individualized or egocentric identity.

It is clear from Huang's work on Asian-American children that the so-called identity problems in Black children in the Western world are merely aspects of something a little broader. For example, Huang suggests that Asian-American youngsters may face difficulties in handling simultaneously the Western and Asian values concerning identity. Hence they appear to employ four typical patterns of strategy to circumvent these problems, each with its own distinct mental health implications:

1  Alienation/marginalization: this strategy is characterized by nega- tive perceptions of one's own culture and of oneself based on the dominant society's attitudes; youngsters who use this strategy become 'estranged' from their minority culture but are also inca- pable of adjustment to the majority culture.
2  Assimilation: those who employ this strategy are seeking to inte- grate with the dominant culture, while neglecting or avoiding ties with their minority culture.
3  Separation: this is characterized by an exclusive emphasis on the minority culture alongside severing contact with the majority culture.
4  Integration/biculturalism: this strategy involves the retention of the minority culture while reaching out, at the same time, to adapt to the majority culture; it is regarded as the most psychologically positive strategy.

It is clear that, of these strategies, *integration/biculturalism* would be a more helpful one to be adopted by Black children in White dominant cultures. However, methods to help these children to adopt this strat- egy must be within the context of the family. Professional intervention must avoid working with them in isolation; excluding the family risks decontextualizing the children from their minority culture, amounting to the second strategy – *assimilation*: 'In general, clinicians working with children and adolescents agree that working with the family system and the school system facilitates effective psychological intervention' (Huang, 1994, p. 23).

The question that arises is just how one can differentiate between a fully integrated 'mixed-race' identity and psychopathology simply from surface appearances. A child with elements of two distinct cultures inevitably has to keep some of them separate and this may be mistaken for an identity conflict. The basic issue is the extent to which an identity needs to be smoothly integrated for it to function effectively. This is not something peculiar to 'mixed-race' individuals; 'monoracial' individuals might be faced with considerable difficulties if they had to demonstrate each and every facet of their identity. For example, their work identity may be considerably at variance with their other identities, such as those with a friend, parent, or even a grandchild. Every person's identity is negotiated and displayed as a subtle interplay between the individual and a given sociocultural context (James, 1890, 1950; Rosemont, 1997).

## Loss and separation: the social problem of identity

Identity formation in 'mixed-race' children is clearly not the problem that many have held it to be. Indeed, many of the assumptions about the psychological and cultural needs of 'mixed-race' children have proven to be false. The persistent claim that these children have psychological problems has only partially and unsatisfactorily been explained. What might be profitably explored, however, is the question of what the minimum requirements for satisfactory identity formation may be. In research on children brought up in single-parent families, we have found that children need a sense of socio-genealogical connectedness with both parents in order to prosper. A lack of information about one or both parents is damaging to one's sense of personal identity.

Owusu-Bempah (1995) and Owusu-Bempah and Howitt (1997) investigated knowledge concerning the absent parent as a factor influencing the general social and psychological adjustment of children living in single-parent and reconstituted families. Using an in-depth interviewing technique, the amount and quality of information possessed by a child about their absent parent was examined in relation to the child's behaviour, emotional adjustment and academic achievement. Regardless of the reasons for the absence of the parent, and regardless of their family's material circumstances, a child who possessed adequate and favourable information about the absent parent fared the best in general. Children who possessed no information, inadequate and/or damaging information about the absent parent tended to exhibit the worst behavioural, academic and emotional difficulties. Many of the problems associated with single-parent upbringing seemed to be concentrated among this group of children. Parental or socio-genealogical information was found to be an important factor in determining a child's general well-being. Many other studies have reported an association between damaging information about one's parent(s) and developmental problems, including self-identity problems (Epstein, 1976; Erickson, 1950). The literature suggests that this is one of the common factors involved in the problems of many of the children with whom social workers, therapists and other childcare professionals are involved (Banks, 1992; Barn, 1990; Bebbington and Miles, 1989; Coleman, 1994; Coward and Dattani, 1993; Maximé, 1991a, 1993b; Mullender, 1991). Unfortunately, these professionals seem to be so preoccupied with the children's 'race' or 'Blackness' that they tend to lose sight of this and such other important factors that affect the children's general well being. Banks illustrates this unfortunate oversight very clearly:

> *The social services client families that have been referred to me have usually been single parent white women with one or several children of mixed ethnicity and sometimes white children in the family from other unions. I have found that there is often some anger about the absence of the black father or his behaviour that caused the separation from the family. This may go beyond a dislike of the individual and spill over into a bitter grudge against black people as a group. This resentment may lead to a considerable amount of psychological aggression (and sometimes physical abuse) directed toward the child, often unconsciously, almost as a form of negative transference in the psychodynamic sense. As one mother repeatedly said in a session in the presence of her eight year old boy 'Every time I look at him (the child) he reminds me of that black bastard and what he did to me. If Nathan ever grows up to be like him I'll kill him'.*
>
> Banks, 1992, pp. 33–34

Remarkably, Bank's recommended 'therapeutic' intervention for dealing with putative identity problems like Nathan's includes teaching the children imaginative stories.

The literature clearly indicates that a disproportionately large number of children who enter the care system, including fostering and adoption, consequently come into contact with childcare professionals from such or similar backgrounds. Therefore we would hypothesize that one of the social factors associated with these children's socio-psychological developmental difficulties is their loss of a sense of connectedness or continuity, rather than being due to their genetic make-up or culture as the clinical literature seems to imply.

# Chapter 9

# Eurocentric assumptions, counselling and psychotherapy

*I have noted a steady increase over the past 15 years in the number of refer-*
*rals of biracial children and adolescents for psychological evaluation and*
*treatment from public and private agencies, in the number of case presenta-*
*tions by social work graduate students, and in the number of case*
*consultations requested by youth-serving agencies, all resulting from*
*emotional and behavioral problems in this particular group.*

Gibbs, 1987, p. 267

## Black children and mental health

It is well established that mental health services treat Black people
differently from White people (Fernando, 1989; Howitt and Owusu-
Bempah, 1994; Mercer, 1984; NAHA, 1988). This is not a simple matter
of differential psychiatric diagnoses being applied to Black and ethnic
minorities and White people, since it is perfectly possible that the
psychiatric disorders experienced by different ethnic groups are in fact
different (Flaskerud and Hu, 1992). However, evidence that the psychiatric labels given to Black and ethnic minorities and White people
reporting identical symptoms may be rather different is substantial
enough to cause concern about racism in psychiatric diagnosis and
treatment (e.g. Littlewood and Lipsedge, 1989; Shaikh, 1985). This is
further reinforced by evidence that Black, ethnic minorities and White
people reporting very much the same symptoms are actually processed
through the psychiatric system differentially (MIND, 1993; NAHA,
1988).

Almost all of the above is based on research involving adults in
which children do not figure to a significant extent. However, the
evidence we have about children directly supports the thrust of the
findings of research involving adults (e.g. Garland and Besinger, 1997).
Strong evidence comes from a study by Cohen *et al.* (1990) in which the
characteristics of youngsters in a psychiatric hospital and a correctional
unit were compared. The research took place in Richmond, Virginia,

and included all 12- to 15-year-olds entering either type of institution during a five-month period. Specifically, the researchers wanted to know whether children and adolescents in the two types of facilities differed in the degree or kind of their disturbances. Furthermore, they wished to know whether demographic characteristics (including race) were any different in the two types of setting. Over two-thirds of the children in the psychiatric hospital were placed there by courts, and all of them had been found guilty of offences which would be crimes if carried out by adults.

All the youngsters who agreed to take part completed a standardized psychological measure: *The Child Behavior Checklist* (Achenbach and Edelbrock, 1983). Scores were computed from this on: (1) social competence, (2) total behavioural problems, (3) internalization of problems (sadness, anxiety, somaticizing) and (4) externalization of problems (fighting, delinquency, swearing). There was evidence that the scores on the *Behavior Checklist* for both institutions were within the range expected of clinical patients for the measures of total behavioural problems. Internalization of problems was greater for the hospital setting than for the correctional setting. Using sophisticated analysis procedures, the researchers were able to hold constant any differences between Black and White children on *The Child Behavior Checklist*. Following this, the data showed that Black children were more likely to be put in the correctional unit rather than the psychiatric facility. Since the Black and White children were similar in terms of their psychiatric characteristics, the study shows a bias towards a more punitive stance in the disposal of Black delinquents.

None-the-less, some researchers are unwilling to accept the racially biased nature of the disposal of children. In a study, which bears some superficial resemblance to others, in that it looked for racial biases in the relative admissions of youngsters to either mental health or correctional units in New York (Kaplan and Busner, 1992), the conclusion was one of no racial bias. The researchers took court-directed admissions for 10- to 18-year-old Black, White and Hispanic youngsters. The main hypothesis guiding the research was that Black youngsters were more likely than White youngsters to be allocated to correctional facilities for punishment, whereas White youngsters were more likely to be sent to mental health units for therapeutic purposes. It turned out that, compared to their frequency in the general population, Black youngsters were much overrepresented in both types of establishment. Despite this, the relative overrepresentation of Black youngsters was substantially greater for the correctional units than for the mental health units: in correctional units the ratio of Black to White youngsters was 7 to 1 after adjustment was made for the proportions in the general population. On the basis of these findings, the authors dispute that there is racial bias in admissions. The logic of this is not clear since examination of their data very clearly suggests that, when corrected for population frequencies of Black and White children, precisely the trends predicted by their hypothesis were to be found. In the correctional facilities there tended to be more Black youngsters than White youngsters. In contrast, there were rather greater numbers of White children and relatively fewer Black children in the mental health facilities, compared with the correctional facilities. Law courts were more likely to send White youths for mental health treatment and less likely to send them for correction. The trend was the reverse for Black youngsters except that they were overrepresented over-all in both types of establishment. The absolute overrepresentation of Black youngsters in these institutions is not surprising given their overrepresentation in the juvenile justice system. So it would appear that Black youngsters suffer much the same fate as Black adults do in the mental health field.

Examination of the practices in other organizations may elucidate the issue. A USA study examined service provision to children with learning difficulties (Eyman, *et al.*, 1977). It was found that, irrespective of the degree of difficulty, White children were much more likely to be in the care of institutions, whereas ethnic minority children were left with their families. Longres and Torrecilha (1992), however, disagree that there is racism in the placements of Black children in the USA. They studied the placements of children who had been classified or diagnosed as having a drug or alcohol disorder, mentally retarded or mentally ill (including emotional disorders and behavioural disorders, or having some other developmental difficulties). Race remained a significant predictor of certain diagnoses, taking into account such demographic characteristics as age, sex and economic status. Black youngsters were found to be less likely to be diagnosed as needing treatment for drug or alcohol problems, but they were more likely to be in need of services for 'mental retardation' or developmental disorders. There was also some evidence that Black children were left in their homes when they were actually in need of professional services.

## Creating identity crises

Despite the generally problem-free nature of Black childhood which creates psychologically healthy, self-satisfied people, the attack on Black childhood has been maintained by therapists working with Black children and families. Indeed, those with seemingly the greatest concern for the welfare of Black children are at the front-line of this. A major risk with any therapeutic or clinical work is that it extends its concepts and findings into non-clinical settings. In the case of Black self-hatred, clinical workers provide seemingly dramatic examples of its dynamics and encourage the view that it is a general phenomenon, and also that it is a core explanatory principle of any behavioural or emotional problems exhibited by Black children (Foster-Carter, 1986;

Howitt and Owusu-Bempah, 1994, 1999a; Owusu-Bempah, 1997; Owusu-Bempah and Howitt, 1999a). In their dealings with Black children, there is a tendency to present the exception as the general rule. The question, however, is how the view that Black children hate themselves and want to be White has been maintained against the backdrop of research which identifies no evidence to support it. A cursory glance at the clinical literature on identity conflict in Black children demonstrates considerable cause for concern. Take, for example, the vignette used by Banks (1992) to illustrate Black identity difficulties:

> *Michael was a six-year-old boy of African-Caribbean origin who had been transracially adopted by white parents since the age of two-and-a-half years. He had been referred for psychological help due to his frequent insistence that he wanted to be white, his rejection of the view that he was a black or brown boy, his active avoidance of books and stories where black children were depicted and most disturbing of all – he had been caught on three occasions by his adoptive parents trying to scrub himself white using a toilet cleaner and bleach.*
>
> p. 43

Alarming as it might be to imagine a small child scrubbing himself with bleach, caution is needed for two reasons. First, it is not at all clear that the above vignette actually refers to a real child as opposed to a composite illustration of an extreme case. Second, if it describes a real child then we need to assess its relevance to Black children in general. The vignette is remarkably close to the unusual cases of Black children who have ostensibly damaged themselves by scrubbing or amputation (e.g. Alhibai, 1987). There are major problems in presenting extreme cases in order to illustrate the general. For example, it may be that the processes involved in racial identity formation in the average child are radically different from those involved in the pathological cases. After all, self-mutilation of the body in White psychiatric cases would not be seen as particularly helpful in understanding the way in which most White people form their somatic identity. Furthermore, it is unlikely that we would use these extreme cases to argue that all White people require psychiatric help whether or not they recognize the problem. In this case, many people would argue that these frequently cited case studies or scenarios about Black children are an exaggeration to make a point, but exaggerating to make a point does not necessarily or always make one.

Superficially, the case studies briefly described below by Maximé (1991a; 1993a,b) are more illuminating to our understanding of the thinking of professionals involved in identity work. These are dramatic cases. They are not much less gory than Banks's vignette, for example, nevertheless, they present an extremely disturbing picture.

*'I hate me! I am ugly! I am like them ... Black People ... all ugly!' Mary shouts as she wraps her arms with healing radiator-induced sores around her body and folds herself into a ball. Her attempts at removing her skin colour on the radiator were not successful and she is thoroughly disappointed.*

From the case of 10-year-old Mary, 1991a, p. 94

*'I attempted suicide' she offered untruthfully as I looked at her arms. Sue has laceration marks from her elbow down to her wrists; from afar one would mistake her arms to be adorned with bracelets, on approach however, you realise that they are all healed marks from razor cuts. Sue lacerated herself and tried to destroy the skin she carries.*

From the case of Sue, a teenager, October 1991a, p. 94

Assuming that these children's sores and lacerations were intended by them to obliterate their Blackness, we ought to know more about the origins of such self-destructive behaviours. Since we would not normally interpret such acts of self-mutilation to be the result of racial identity problems in a White child, the question becomes one of what could have caused such extreme reactions in these children. Unfortunately, Maximé gives us no further insight into the background of either of these children that might help us to decide whether these actions are a result of general problems in the lives of Black children or problems specific to Mary and Sue as individuals.

In other places, Maximé gives more substantial case studies of children who, she suggests, are experiencing difficulties due to racial identity problems, although they do not involve this sort of self-mutilation. These are worthwhile examining in detail since they do get closer to the roots of the problem:

*Charles was a boy of mixed parentage whose mother was a white business woman, and father an African who had long departed to West Africa. Charles enjoyed the first 14 years of his life in Suffolk. He was loved and protected by his mother who made it her duty as far as possible to see that he did not come into contact with black people lest he began worrying over his unknown father. Charles was happy and saw himself 'like other boys', this being assessed in material terms (pre-encounter stage).*

Maximé, 1991, p. 109

Maximé then goes on to describe how Charles and his mother moved to London after her promotion. Living in inner-city London, Charles was 'shattered' when asked by a group of White boys, 'whose side are you on?' This was apparently the first time that he had to categorize himself racially:

*Charles tormented himself for a week with this problem, never mentioning it to his mother whom he anticipated would be very grieved. Quietly, as Charles examined himself, he started asking himself questions and becoming frightened by the answers. Charles said that during this period he became terrified of interacting as he felt he was not sure who he was. He explained that a part of him viewed himself as 'white with a bit of black', while another part of him was predominantly black and responded painfully to negative images in the news media and in some books about black people... Eventually, Charles felt he could not face people outside the home as they all knew he was pretending and were watching him. Consequently, he became housebound for the next two and a half years and was diagnosed agoraphobic by various psychiatrists.*

Maximé, 1991, p. 109

This experience, putatively, led to a period of hostile relations with his White mother who was construed as symbolic of the White establishment. Although there is no physical self-damage in this case apparently, agoraphobic reactions are debilitating. This does not seem to be a simple case of racial identity confusion in a child of 'mixed-race' parentage. Maximé explains that the boy spent most of his childhood and well into adolescence without information about his father – his mother actually precluded this by going as far as preventing contact with Black people, lest questions were raised in his mind about his absent father. Undoubtedly, the mother was actively undermining Charles' genealogy or sense of continuity. While the racist question might have precipitated his psychological reaction, the seed had long been carefully sown by his mother in a fertile soil of problems.

It is fairly well established that the absence or denial of information about one's parent(s) is detrimental to one's general well-being. In our own research involving single-parent families (Owusu-Bempah, 1995; Owusu-Bempah and Howitt, 1997, 2000), we have encountered very similar cases to Maximé's Charles. One such case was Martin, a 15-year-old boy who lived with his mother and 17-year-old sister. Martin was 5 years old when his parents divorced. The children had had no contact with their father since then, for some ten years. The father lived abroad, and the mother disallowed them to maintain even telephone contact with him. The relationship between the parents was so hostile that, during the interview, the mother found it emotionally difficult even to mention the father's name: 'I just call him "ex"; I don't give him any name... I refer to him to the children as "your ex-father"'. Martin was reported by his mother to be acting out more severe emotional problems than his sister. She described him as a very angry youth that vented his anger specifically on her: 'Martin expresses his anger only at home; and he does so in violent ways – foot through the bedroom door, breaking windows and furniture and throwing things about by the week. At other times, he is sullen and withdrawn – locks himself up in his room.'

Martin's mother seemed to be in no doubt about why he was angry: 'I suspect that Martin's anger towards me may have something to do with cutting them off from their father... They have nothing to remind them of their father;... there are no momentoes of their father in the house... not even a photograph.' Like many of the parents involved in the study, Martin's mother was aware that her son's anger and behaviour was a reaction to her disconfirmation of his father, her denial of him and suppression of information about him. She acknowledged that Martin could benefit from help, but: 'I am reluctant to seek professional help for him, lest I be labelled an inadequate parent, for fear of having them taken away from me. I couldn't cope with that'. Had Martin's mother sought professional help for him (from a Black or White professional), it is very doubtful if, being White, he would have been diagnosed as experiencing self-hatred or racial identity problems.

Maximé's case studies are replete with examples of African, African-Caribbean and 'mixed-race' children whose responses were reflections of insensitive and racist handling by important professionals in their lives. For example, she mentions the case of a 6-year-old boy, Leroy, who tended to wet himself. When faced with imagery of Black people, he rejected the material and what he called 'jungle people'. His explanation for his attitude was: 'My key worker always says "Yuk" to them, they are jungle people, I don't want to be like them' (Maximé, 1991, p. 104).

However, the problem is not simply one created by professional workers alone: foster parents might engage in similar activities. In the case of Mary, Maximé (1993a) suggests that race was not talked about in her foster home. When Mary described her self as Black and ugly, the foster mother had said to her: 'You are *my* daughter and not ugly' which stimulated Mary to shout at Maximé: '*See! I'm not Black, I'm White! Tell her Mummy.*' (p. 177, original emphasis). The indications are that Mary's flare-up was the product of 'race' being a taboo topic in the foster family and the professional intervention which broke that taboo.

In the same article, Maximé describes another case, which raises further concern about the notion of Black children's self-hatred as the ultimate explanation for their problems, whatever they may be, and identity work as a panacea to those problems. This case concerns a 6-year-old boy, Henry, who lived with 'very middle class' White foster parents. According to Maximé, he viewed Black people very negatively and said of himself: 'I see myself as a spastic in a wheelchair, you expect people to watch at you, to laugh at you, to call you names. The only difference is that one day a doctor might come along, find a cure, and the spastic could get better. But I can't; I'm trapped in my skin, it just stays' (1993a; p. 176).

This may seem plausible to those who believe that Black children, especially those being cared for by White families, hate themselves and other Black people. The sceptic, on the other hand, may consider it too much of a feat for a 6-year-old boy to employ metaphors and the subjunctive mood!

## A conspiracy of the helping professions?

Much of the Black identity conflict casework involves psychologists and psychotherapists working alongside social workers. Social workers and teachers refer children to psychologists or therapists because they believe that the children are experiencing identity crises or racial/cultural conflict. Coleman (1994) claims that this is particularly the case with children of 'mixed-race' parentage. However, the few illustrative examples she provides describe children who have suffered abuse at the hands of one or both of their parents.

> *Consider Nisa, a black girl, sexually abused by her father, who as a result hates all back people and hates her own blackness; or Josephine, a girl of mixed parentage, physically abused by her African mother, who has grown to have a very negative attitude towards all things African. She identifies with the white parts of her mixed ethnicity. It is a very difficult psychological task to get such children to internalise their blackness and make them feel good about it.*
>
> Coleman, 1994, p. 4

Interestingly, Coleman's examples seem to have a rather different aetiology from those that Maximé describes. Nevertheless, there seems to be nothing profoundly complex about the cases of Nisa and Josephine. They are introductory psychology textbook examples of generalization. Abuse, physical or sexual, can be profoundly damaging to relationships and result in long-term conflicts with persons who demonstrate similar characteristics to the abuser. For example, Graham-Davies (1995) has shown that it is possible to predict problematic relationships simply on the basis of the extent to which a significant person in one's life is similar to one's abuser. In the light of this, abused children might be expected to reject major characteristics of their abuser, including their skin colour.

Despite the availability of rather obvious explanations for Nisa and Josephine's apparent ambivalence regarding their Blackness, Coleman prefers to regard the problem as one directly related to their identity, rather than to their specific and unfortunate experiences. Indeed, she suggests that all Black children in local authority care referred to her Child Psychology Service have four features in common: (1) developmental delay; (2) social/behavioural difficulties; (3) cognitive difficulties such as poor attention and impulsivity and (4) play disorder or uncooperativeness. Although Coleman claims that her clinic is specifically there to 'repair the children's identity damaged by racism', she does not say whether these are recognized symptoms of identity crisis. She acknowledges that the care system aggravates the children's difficulties, yet she considers the characteristics of the children's mothers to be the most important factor. Typically the children are 'mixed-race' and their mothers White. Some rather damning claims are made about the mothers. For example, Coleman portrays them as being ostracized by their families such that remarriage to a White man and giving birth to a White child provides a means of becoming reaccepted. To this is added the claim that 'mixed-race' children internalize their mother's racism as well as that of the wider community. This comment is revealing:

> *Many of the children of African parentage referred to the psychological service show clear signs of self-rejection of their ethnic identity. Many reject their 'Africaness' and wish to be identified as West Indian or Caribbean, especially Jamaican. They will adopt Jamaican language styles and pretend to others that their parents are Jamaican and not African.*
>
> Coleman, 1984, p. 5

If this is the case, then, it carries with it the very clear implication that Blackness itself is not what is being rejected but an African identity in favour of a Caribbean identity. Coleman fails to explain why African culture is rejected. These children's behaviour could merely be a reflection of the more streetwise and fashionable aspects of Caribbean culture, just as a lot of young people all over the world have identified in a varying degree with Bob Marley and his music. There is no implication that these children of African origins do want to be White. In a multicultural society it would be curious if the only alternative to being regarded as suffering from Black identity conflict is to accept the identity or culture of one's parents unquestioningly, without experimenting with other identities.

Members of the Roots Identity Group provide a further illustration of the pervasiveness of the notion of Black children's self-hatred and racial group rejection among professionals:

> *There were many incidents of Black children and young people being subjected to racial abuse, harassment and intimidation in neighbourhoods. There were some Black children who identified themselves as anything else but Black (i.e. Italian, Spanish, and so on). Some Black children and young people were known to be in fear of Black people or became extremely distressed when anything about Black people was mentioned or at any suggestion that the child had Black parentage. Some social workers related examples where there were tears and distress among Black children and young people when they were asked to define their ethnic origin through formal procedures. Moreover, in some instances the child or young person was encountering racism within his or her own family (i.e., where there*

*were White carers, parents, grandparents, uncles or aunts). Most of these experiences, attitudes and behaviours were in addition to behavioural difficulties and other concerns within the home or school.*

Coward and Dattani, 1993, p. 250

The bulk of this description directly supports the view that identity problems are not the problems these children have to contend with. Instead, what is being described is children trying to survive in racially hostile, racially violent and racially abusive environments. This racism might be community-based, but sometimes it is family-based too. Having to cope with racist assault from all quarters on their integrity, it is not surprising that some children resort to practical or pragmatic devices, such as denying their 'race', to get by. Thus we cannot take such instances as demonstrating identity conflict rather than fear. If a child in care fears abuse because of his or her 'race', colour or ethnicity, we should not be surprised that they are reduced to tears and show distress when asked to identify themselves ethnically or racially by representatives of social services. Social services is the very organization responsible for exposing them to such racial assaults.

Inevitably, those who present case studies of identity problems in Black adolescents provide details which are most relevant to their understanding of the processes involved, and may consequently omit or understate other aspects. Gibbs (1987) presents a number of brief case studies which, she claims, demonstrate identity problems. Take the following example:

*Laura, a 15-year-old born to a black mother and white father, was reared for seven years by her maternal grandmother after her parents divorced when she was six years old. She reported that she had been 'treated like a stepchild' and sexually assaulted by two maternal uncles, and that her maternal aunts were very ambivalent toward her, often teasing her about her light skin. At age 13 she was reunited with her mother and black stepfather because her grandmother couldn't manage her any longer.... In discussing her sexual activities, she said she really didn't like boys because they only wanted to get girls pregnant, but sometimes she felt strongly attracted to girls and couldn't handle the thought of being a lesbian. Laura's aversion to males apparently stemmed from the sexual victimisation she had experienced in relationships with her uncles (and her stepfather), all of whom were black.*

Gibbs, 1987, pp. 270–271

Whatever problems Laura has seem clearly to be the results of her appalling experiences. The literature on sexual abuse is replete with examples of children who were damaged psychologically and sexually by their abuse (Alexander and Lupfer, 1987; Howitt, 1992, 1995; Olson, 1991; Sandfort, 1988, 1989; Shearer *et al.*, 1990; Urquiza and Capra, 1991). Gibbs does not describe Laura as having a biracial identity problem but having 'a confused sexual identity'. Her ethnicity seems not to be the problem. None-the-less she presents her case study in a paper describing identity problems in biracial adolescents, thus giving the unwary reader the impression that Black children's identity plays a part in all their psychosocial problems. Indeed, Gibbs demonstrates the reality of this danger in her interpretation of another case study. She reports the case of Maria, a biracial 18-year-old, who was very much a model child, but had problems when she went away to college.

> *When she was encouraged to talk about her feelings, she explained that she had felt 'special' at home and didn't have much social life outside her family, so she was unprepared for the freedom of college and couldn't seem to fit in with either the whites or the blacks. She said, "When I'm with the white students, I think like a black person and when I'm with the black students' I think like a white person.*
>
> Gibbs, 1987, p. 271.

Maria, putting it in other words, was an over-protected child who could not cope with independence at college and was not able to relate to people of any 'race' effectively. It is to over-interpret her case to suggest that her problems were created by an identity crisis, although she artic-ulates them in terms redolent of identity difficulties. We should not unquestioningly take Maria's inability to relate to her Black and White peers as evidence of an identity crisis, even though a person in her situ-ation may interpret it as such. In fact, Black children may interpret their problems in terms of identity crises to professionals not necessarily because they believe that they have identity problems but because it is a fashionable terminology for describing their feelings and experiences. Alternatively, they may believe that that is the only explanation accept-able to the professionals they have (or have had) dealings with (Owusu-Bempah, 1994a). Durkin (1995) has observed the same phenomenon in relation to the so-called 'midlife crisis'. 'As the "midlife crisis" found its way from Levinson's pages to *The New York Times*, *Paris Match*, and the *Daily Mirror*, everyone began to feel entitled or obligated to have one. It is easy enough to contract: any or all symptoms of personal dissatisfaction or discomfort experienced by a middle-aged person can be categorised as due to "midlife crisis"' (p. 633).

We tend to underestimate the ease with which professional jargon enters common parlance and is used often with different meanings or connotations, and for different purposes. Following Durkin's line of argument, the issue can be construed as whether the occasional feeling of depression, self-doubt, uncertainty about the future and so forth is more prevalent or more intense in these children? It is important to go beyond the skin in order to provide effective intervention programmes to Black children and families who may need them. That is, profession-als need to look for and consider more seriously beyond-the-skin factors that may be associated with their Black clients' problems or needs. Our preoccupation with our Black clients' skin tone very often obscures our vision, blunts our assessment or diagnostic techniques and results in misinterpretations of their needs and the provision of inappropriate services to them.

None of this means that Black (or any other) youngsters always have a clear sense of their identity; there are circumstances in which a Black child may become thoroughly confused. However, based on what is known about the development of Black children, it should be stressed that we do not regard such circumstances as anything other than unusual. If significant people in a child's life give confusing messages, then we should not regard this as a healthy situation, irrespective of their point of focus. Consider, for example, the case of 7-year-old Kevin, reported by academic social workers (McRoy and Freeman, 1986). Kevin's parents had just divorced; he lived with his White mother and was not seen by his Black father. He was referred to school social workers because he fought a lot with other children during routine activities, but kept himself to himself in the playground:

> *The school social worker met with Kevin at school and also saw him and his mother at home... She learned that the family lived in a nearly all-white suburban neighborhood and that Kevin attended a school in which there was only one other black child. Although [Kevin's mother] identified Kevin as white, the teacher and other school staff and his peers identified him as black. Kevin's racial perceptions were confused. He was not sure what his race was, but he wanted to be seen as being like his white peers... Kevin had a light tan complexion with very curly hair and hazel eyes. He had been repeatedly called 'nigger' by his classmates.*
>
> McRoy and Freeman, 1986, pp. 169–170.

It is not difficult to recognize that Kevin had problems. Indeed one can only sympathize with him just as we would if his mother had told him that he was a boy, but his teachers and peers insisted that he was a girl. Kevin's confusion is due to his peculiar circumstances; it is not an inherent characteristic of 'mixed-race' heritage. It is interesting to note how the key social worker began to deal with Kevin's problems as essentially a problem of the racism of his peers: 'Initially, the social worker planned to do group counselling with Kevin and several other students who were having problems, but after explorations, she thought it was more useful to do a series of classroom sessions focused on differences among children and values related to these differences' (McRoy and Freeman, 1986, p. 171).

The social worker also helped make contact with Kevin's paternal family in order to establish 'positive Black role models' although no success was achieved in relation to Kevin's father. The key worker's efforts to provide Kevin with 'positive Black role models' superficially appear the appropriate approach. A closer examination of Kevin's circumstances, as described here, reveals something else. This approach is likely to aggravate his anxieties about his identity and compound its associated problems. The approach negates Kevin and his mother's definition of reality – his identity but at the same time confirms his peers' definition of reality – that he is a 'Nigger'. As we have indicated in the preceding chapter, to be helpful, intervention should have sought to contextualize the issue by working with both Kevin and his mother to firmly establish his identity or redefine it, if necessary. It seems that Kevin's immediate need is to know exactly what he is – Black, White or 'in-between'. The provision of 'Black role models' does not seem to be his immediate concern.

Curiously, however, many professionals seem to see 'Black role models' as a panacea for the problems of Black and 'mixed-race' children (Owusu-Bempah, 1994a; 1997). Besides, the importance of 'Black role models' to these children is dubious on empirical grounds. Once a child's core identity has been established, confirmed and reinforced by significant others, it seems to matter little the colour or sex of the role models available to them. In reality, children or adolescents have more than one type of role model, depending on their age, abilities and interests at any given period. For example, one of us is an African Black man with White and Indian family friends, some of which he has known for over twenty years. Many of these friends have very often presented him to their children (particularly during adolescence) as a model to be emulated academically. Is this to be interpreted as a form of child abuse on the part of the parents, as attempting to alienate their children against themselves and their racial group, including the parents themselves? Many successful White artists, singers and jazz players admit the influence of Black artists on them. Would one say that these artists have racial identity problems? Similarly, what White boxer has never dreamt of 'floating like a butterfly and stinging like a bee'? What young White male disco-goer would not like to dance like Michael Jackson? Equally, what are we to say or do about White men and women who spend time and money on having their straight hair curled? According to Cross (1991), Horowitz and Erikson, the forefathers of the notion of 'negative self-identity', became particularly interested in the self-concept of minority groups after changing their own identities – their Jewish names – in order to pass in American society. A psychodynamically orientated observer might, therefore, see our over-concern regarding Black children's 'negative self-concept' or self-hatred and Black role models as a projection of our own failures or anxieties onto the children. The therapist's (mis)interpretation of Maria's reasons for her choice of a White family placement (earlier in this chapter) may be regarded as providing tentative support for this view.

## Politicizing Black identities

Professionals within the childcare system seem to operate on the assumption that there is a 'natural' environment for Black and 'mixed-race' children in which their identity may flourish. Yet they fail to define clearly what this environment might be. In trying to describe such an environment, Cheetham (1991), for example, suggests, *inter alia*, that the following should be explored when reaching decisions about Black children:

1  The child's views about their racial or cultural background, and whether they have had opportunities to know, experience and discuss these while in care or not;
2  The child's particular dietary, language, medical, physical, educational or other needs;
3  Whether staff have undergone training which fits them for the task of dealing with Black children, and whether there are opportunities to involve outside organizations which might be more advantageous to the child.

Obviously, these requirements should apply to all children in the child-care system regardless of race, colour, ethnicity and so forth.

Given the predominantly very young age of children described as having identity crises, pictorial workbooks dealing with some of the issues have been produced. For example, Maximé (1991b) has provided a workbook *Black Like Me: Black Identity* which is claimed to help a child develop a 'positive and secure Black identity'. There is no evaluative research on this; however, examining the workbook in some detail suggests that some of its contents are highly stereotypical in nature: they reinforce existing stereotypes about Black children. For example, a Black child is portrayed waving to another Black person above a corner shop; several of the pictures and questions are about sports: 'I play net ball for my school and I am tall and strong' (p. 13) and 'What sports do you play?' (p. 14). Two pages of the book feature Black children playing leapfrog; another series of three pictures stresses physical appearance, especially hairstyle. In contrast, just two pictures are counterstereotypical in the sense that they show Black children enjoying schoolwork together. The workbook also stresses Black children's national origins outside of the United Kingdom as their identity: 'Do you know that even if your parents or you were born in Africa, St. Lucia, Grenada, Barbados, England or elsewhere that you are AFRICAN (AFRIKAN)?' (p. 27). In a sense, this diverts the children away from their citizenship (British) towards a view of themselves which stresses their ancestry. These children, like their parents, are often rejected by the wider British society and are not made to feel at home. Consequently, stressing Africa as their national origin is only likely to reinforce their induced feeling of alienation, of being 'immigrants'. Many of them have no allegiance to the countries of their parents' origin and see themselves as British, Londoners and so forth (Tizard and Phoenix, 1993). The book presents a politicized view of Blackness and pan-national identity instead of developing a healthy sense of personal identity.

Banks (1993) argues that there is little published work describing how to carry out therapeutic work with Black children. This is a little curious in the light of the existence of a substantial number of papers describing the special requirements of counselling and therapy with Black people in general (e.g. Boyd-Franklin, 1989; D'Ardenne and Mahtani, 1989). Perhaps the difficulty is that Banks takes identity problems in Black children as his point of focus. He describes 'Cognitive Ebonization' as his method of making Black children aware of their Black identity. However, it seems not particularly aimed at identity problems *per se*; rather it appears to be a training programme for dealing with the effects of racism: 'It aims to provide children with some sophistication about racism without disabling them with paranoia, to support their development of strong self-worth without being dismissive of others and to love their colour without denigrating other groups' (p. 43)

His methods are partially designed to reverse the negative connotations of the word 'Black' which tend to be a metaphor for bad and evil (e.g. blackmail, blackleg). Thus he recommends telling the children stories which present Black positively, for example, the story of *Basil: the handsome black beetle*. He recommends also that care should be taken when using ethnically related labels such as kinky hair, fuzzy hair, thick lips and flat nose. Since these tend to be somewhat negative in tone, Banks recommends that they be replaced by phrases such as full lips and broad nose. Furthermore, he suggests that the child's ethnicity should be clarified through a process of labelling. According to Banks, this is best done by a Black therapist who can make statements such as 'we are Africans' rather than 'you are an African'. In other words, the therapist should be of the same ethnicity or nationality as the child in therapy: 'adaptive reactions, coping styles and adjustment techniques cannot be adequately learned by white "teachers" in a white environment and passed on to Black children' (pp. 44–45)

Many of the goals of Bank's techniques are similar to those of others. These generally include Blackness as a positive goal, discovery of Black people's role in history, media presentations of Black people, use of multicultural materials and dealing with issues such as racism and oppression as they arise. They also stress and clarify that it is not the child's own fault and they are not responsible for the way in which they are treated.

Although descriptions such as identity conflict, identity crises and identity confusion quickly gain attention, they seem to be dealt with by using methods which scarcely warrant the drama that they engender.

Much of the problem is created by a confusion between what we can expect of a child subject to racist abuse and how that child will respond in a family of different ethnicity from their own. A good example comes from an account of the Ebony Project (Mullender, 1991) that is perhaps typical of the loose thinking surrounding the entire debate. The Ebony Project was designed to cope with a problem that was essentially manufactured. The project was a group set up specifically to work with the parents and children of transracial fostering families. Its main aim was:

> to meet the needs of those children and young people who are already **settled in white homes** and who, **as a consequence**, may be feeling confused about their identity, **flattened** by the racially motivated name-calling and other abuse which a white background has not given them the skills or the composure to handle, and generally lacking in self-confidence.
> Mullender, 1991, p. 25, emphasis added

This is a classic example of the assumptions underlying identity work. The passage clearly encourages the view that being in a White home or White neighbourhood automatically spells 'identity confusion' for Black children. It further assumes that there are defined skills that they need in order to protect their self-concept, self-confidence and emotional integrity. There is also something illogical about the project's rationale: How can a child having all these serious problems as a result of being in a White family be described as 'settled in that family?

In typical fashion, it is held to be the lot of Black workers to sort out the 'problem'. The project emerged from the work of a Black student social worker, on placement with a social services department, who was given the task of counselling a Black child in long-term foster care with a White father. The child 'seemed rather depressed'. Suspecting that the problem was extensive in such children, it was decided to run groups for children and families in similar circumstances. The main objectives of the groups were to:

1 provide positive Black adult role models;
2 network the Black children with each other;
3 educate the children about the positive contributions that Black people have made to Britain;
4 develop self-esteem through this education; and
5 make Black children aware of racism, discrimination and other aspects of being Black while developing their skills in dealing with such issues.

Group sessions included history of the Caribbean, hair and skin care, Black people in history, Caribbean food, language and dialect and Black music. During these sessions, the White foster parents were also instructed in cultural awareness, parenting styles, and 'survival skills' which their Black foster children would need in a racist society. These sessions used videotaped materials on racial prejudice, brainstorming ideas on the words 'black' and 'white' in everyday language and sessions on the geography, history and cuisine of the Caribbean. How this programme could achieve its principal aim, the enhancement of the children's identity, without tackling the cause of the children's 'confusion' and what 'flattened' them is open to conjecture.

## Confusing the agenda

Coward and Dattani (1993) describe a very similar set of procedures. They used groups led by South Asian facilitators, and the procedures and materials were very much the sort of approach which is the foundation of racism awareness training, the big difference being that Black children were in focus rather than the racism of White adults. Like the other approaches, they provide little by way of evaluation of their success other than confidence that the approach worked. Indeed, Coward and Dattani specifically reject the need for any formal objective assessment of the value of their work. Although virtually identical ideas underlie all of the identity programmes for Black children, it is worthwhile examining Coward and Dattani's work in some detail in order to extricate the philosophy of the enterprise. For example, they indicate that racism dominates the lives of Black children:

> *experience of racism begins from a very early age and is likely to continue to gain momentum as the child progresses in age. It is within this background and context that... Black children should be empowered to take control of their own lives. They should be given help to sustain self-worth, positive racial and cultural identities and the confidence to live rich and fulfilled lives.*
>
> Coward and Dattani, 1993, p. 267.

There is something very patronizing about this. The somewhat flowery language – 'empowered', 'self-worth', 'rich and fulfilled lives' – disguises an unacceptable rhetoric. As usual, it is useful to take parallels with sexism in order to reveal inherent problems in Coward and Dattani's sentiments. Experiences of sexism begin from an equally early age, if not earlier, and continue to gain momentum as the female child progresses in age, but what would the authors suggest be done about that? Would they provide sexual identity therapy to girls, but ignore the problem in males – the traditional holders of power? For Black children: 'The Roots Identity group work we felt would, for some Black children, be the beginning of a process in the development of a positive Black identity. That is, it would instil a deeper sense of confidence and pride and provide some of the skills and tools for Black children and young people to live and survive in a racist society'(Coward and Dattani, 1993, p. 249).

The phrase 'to survive in a racist society' is revealing. The programme's objective was essentially to leave our own racism and that of society intact. Instead, it was designed to equip the children to learn to float, mouth just above water, in a sea of racism. In short, however such programmes are packaged, they seem to be in the best interests of anyone but the Black child that they purport to help. In particular, much of the identity work with Black children takes place within the context of social services departments where, very often, the employees carry out the 'treatment'.

*In a period of 12–15 months, our attendance at Child Protection Case Conferences and Statutory Child Care Reviews where black children and young people were involved revealed a pattern where specific work was being requested, or was recommended by ourselves, on developing positive self images for black children and young people ... Almost without exception, we were required to offer advice, support, suggestions of dealing with and resolving the effects of racism on black children and young people.*

Coward and Dattani, 1993, p. 250

These programmes agree unanimously that racism in the institution and individuals within it is at the core of the children's difficulties. It is, therefore, mind-boggling that they expend so much effort and scarce resources on the individual psychology (self-identity) of the victims instead of tackling racism itself. We recognize that others may see these programmes as a form of counselling, none-the-less, in other settings counselling is provided along with curative measures. Providing counselling alone carries the implication that the strengthening of the Black child is the appropriate course of action – the child becomes both the source of the problem and its solution. The following analogy may help put the issue into perspective. If someone stole the engine out of your car would you contact social workers, or therapists or the Samaritans to help you? Very likely, you would contact the police first and foremost; but if the police arrived and blamed you for not expecting this sort of thing since there are a lot of thieves about, would you regard this as an appropriate response from the police? In other words, advice on coping with racism is short measure compared to the appropriate course of action, which would be to offer advice, support and suggestions for getting rid of racism in the institution and its agents.

In their conclusion and recommendations, Coward and Dattani indirectly concede that identity work on Black children is misguided. For example, they recommend the following for delivering 'good quality services' to Black and White children and young people: 'For policy and practices of voluntary and statutory agencies to take account of the realities of this society and hence the specific needs of Black children and young people' (p. 260).

The realities of this society include racism, and the specific problems facing Black children and young people include racism. It is ironic that the authors wasted scarce resources on trying to change the children instead of trying to change the system. In short, none of the intervention programmes discussed so far seeks to address any of the important issues raised by Richardson (1990).

## What culture?

It is ironic that despite the emphasis on cultural restitution as a solution to children's difficulties, what passes for and is recommended as culture might best be described as a pastiche of a culture. Perhaps this is inevitable when psychology is understood solely from a Western perspective. Teaching African history, for example, is almost radical from this viewpoint. The simple truth is that the culture which practitioners see as a lifeline for troubled children has little or nothing to do with any indigenous culture. We have indicated some of the features of this earlier and elsewhere; however, we should now turn to the issue in more detail. In doing this, we are indebted to Holdstock (2000), a Dutch clinical psychologist with many years' experience in teaching and researching in the African context. In contrast with those who see culture as largely consisting of the history of peoples, if their therapeutic recommendations are to be considered, Holdstock regards culture as much more complex. In particular, he recommends that people's beliefs should be regarded as more real by psychologists than anything in the material world. Not to appreciate this is a fundamental error. Consequently, beliefs that the human soul is immortal or that there is a supernatural are as important to understanding people as any other influence. The multiplicity of terms which are used to describe unverifiable realities indicate their importance – mind, spirit, belief, dreams and myths, for instance. To understand the psychology of Africans these must be incorporated, irrespective of their irrelevance for understanding Westerners, according to Holdstock. To Holdstock, childraising reveals the basic value system of the African. Generally abhorred practices in the West are integral to African life: breast-feeding on demand, sharing a bed with parents, and so forth. The child is in continual physical contact with others rather than physically isolated in nurseries and playpens. Holdstock sees feeding on demand as part of the mechanism by which dependency on biological clocks is developed. As previously discussed, quartz clock child-rearing is for Westerners and not Africans.

Psychology, as colonialists visited it on Africa, contributed to the domination and control of that continent (Howitt and Owusu-Bempah, 1994). By way of redress, it might be regarded that psychology has a responsibility to help Africans become critically aware of the traditional strengths of African society – the centrality and importance of the community. This would involve offering warnings about the ways that psychology may perpetuate imperialistic inequalities when physical colonialism has been replaced. For Holdstock, the consequences of this formulation should be a drive to explore and utilize elements of African culture including religion, philosophy, history and far more. Primary among this enterprise is the need to understand the spiritual dimension that characterizes the continent and African life. Sub-Saharan Africa is spiritual or religious in that it 'honours' a power which transcends humanity, but which at the same time is integrated with all aspects of life and which shapes living. The spiritual is not a separate institution as it is in much of the West. It is part of every moment. Furthermore, it is part of the unity of all things.

The individuocentricism of psychology is wrong for Africans. The growth of people is not an individual thing but part of a nexus of changes involving family, friends, economics and other wider aspects of society. Individualistic concepts of the self or identity are largely mean-ingless in traditional African culture except in so far as they recognize that there are individuals and individuality. However, it is a mistake to see the African self or identity as consisting of separate autonomous individuals who play out their existence against the backdrop of community and society. The aim of the development of self is the achievement of harmonious relations and interdependence with others to achieve a truly social self. Africans, as a consequence, need an active interest in the lives of others and accept being regulated as well as regu-lating others as unproblematic. From this African perspective the Western cut-off self with its dissociation from the community as well as the physical environment is merely a recipe for loneliness and isolation.

The individual in African culture is in a state of flux or fluidity with regard to others and the community as well as the physical and meta-physical universe beyond. The individual is regarded as being at one with all of these in a sense of oneness and intimacy. So the natural world – animate and inanimate – is part of this oneness, as is the spiritual world of coexistence with one's ancestors. To Holdstock (2000), this is different from other cultures. He mentions Hindu cultures in which there is fluidity for the self but it lies in relation to the metaphysical. The individual self is illusory and the self is only really found when an understanding of the immutable self is achieved.

In African cultures, ancestors are important and ongoing relation-ships. They link the living with the dead, and consequently show how that life and death are not quite the dualism of Western thought. Ancestors may be involved, like deity, in all aspects of living. Since they are people rather than gods or other spiritual beings, they are to be spoken with as with any other person. Ancestors are made manifest primarily in dreams, through a medium, or visions and voices. They are to be honoured ceremonially, and failure to do so brings misery. They are holders of the culture of the past. Similarly, harmony with nature is important because people are the beneficiaries rather than the masters/mistresses of nature. Nature belongs to both the heavens and earth. It may take the form of the rivers, sun, moon, stars, winds, mountains, rivers and trees. These are believed to be the residences of ancestors.

There is a separation between ego and the world in the African world-view, but the way in which this is expressed is communal. The self acts in relation to others and the self becomes known through this. The self does not become known through introspection, as Westerners believe. It is to be found through one's general behaviour, particularly in relation to others. Holdstock revises Descartes' dictum 'I think therefore I am' for Africa. There it would become 'I belong therefore I am'. Since a person is only a person through other persons, relationships with others involve both moral and ethical obligations. The concept of *ubuntu* provides the underlying guide. *Ubuntu* is described as the overriding important virtue in the African ethic. Holdstock suggests that it is hard to define *ubuntu*, that it is better understood by experiencing it. It is a sort of ultra-humanity. If it is lacking then this, in itself, is not sinful, bad or evil. It is more about achievement in the present life, which is not preparation, as such, for a life after physical death. It is one's present actions that form the basis of judgement. Seen this way, a person is never insignificant but a crucial player who has the gravest of responsibilities – relating to the community and others to the highest possible standards. This would be in conflict with the purpose of much Western counselling and therapy: that is, the freeing of the individual from the binds of guilt, responsibility and the family. With *ubuntu* as their guide, a person would heighten their awareness of the outcomes of their actions for the well-being or otherwise of others. But the depth of this is difficult for Westerners to comprehend. The spiritual world or the ancestors are part of this. Respect for the world in general including the inanimate and the animate is crucially involved in *ubuntu*. However, respect extends as much to the self as other aspects of the world engaged with – the self is not an inferior aspect of this psychological sense of interdependency. This is different from the humanism known in the West. The major distinguishing features are the commitment in *ubuntu* to communalism and the lack of value given to individualistic conceptions of the self. Western psychology has drawn to itself some of the Western ideas that are close to *ubuntu* and then charged clients a fee for their expression. For example, empathy, compassion and unconditional positive regard may be sympathetic with *ubuntu* ideals but regarded as marketable commodities rather than obligations.

Respect for others, interdependency, sharing and collectivism are matters about which much, if not all, Western psychology is silent if not antagonistic. Holdstock (2000), like others (e.g. Owusu-Bempah and Howitt, 1995), views Western psychology as being much more about self-centredness and private greed rather than any of these values. In African psychology good relationships with other people are a duty. In contrast, Western psychology sees good relationships with other people as vital for selfish reasons: that is, they provide Westerners with a positive self-regard, a sense that we are valuable. Western psychologists consider society as a network of relationships to be understood in rational terms with almost total exclusion of the spiritual. Holism, in Africa, is about experiencing life as wholeness with the different aspects forming part of the spiritual reality.

Of course, putting forward the concept of *ubuntu* as the key feature of African culture is deliberately provocative. However, that surely is the point. It is only provocative in that its reveals that cultural sensitivity is not what psychology's treatment of Black and ethnic minority children is about, despite superficial claims to the contrary. We do not suggest for one minute that *ubuntu* is what children of African origins in Western nations such as Britain need to deal with their psychological problems anymore than feeding them African menus is. What advocating *ubuntu* does is to show the impossibility of giving lessons in culture as opposed to learning within a culture. No wonder professionals working with Black children are willing to adopt quick-fix recommendations. That they may be counterproductive is not their problem.

# Chapter 10

# Intergrating perspectives: meeting wider neeeds

*In what ways are your programmes going to benefit the oppressed... black pupils in white societies;... ethnic and cultural minorities the world over? In what ways, that is to say, are your programmes going to close gaps, reduce inequalities, remove discriminations, in particular discriminations which are covertly, indeed invisibly institutionalised? And how are you going to win the trust of the oppressed? Which is to say, what risks – real risks to your material well-being, your career prospects, your reputation, your livelihood – are you taking? What boundaries of convention and courtesy are you prepared to transgress,... what comforts and friends are you prepared to lose?*

Richardson, 1990, p. 53

This final chapter reviews ways in which progress can be made when working with Black and ethnic minority clients. A degree of recapitulation is necessary in order to stress central facts about world cultures that are different from those of the West. The changing nature of one's clientele is a difficulty for any profession. We can all easily learn about other cultures, but what we learn is inevitably inadequate given their complex and changing nature. Psychologists need to be responsive and dynamic in their dealings with cultural issues and merely learning key facts about other cultures is not, in itself, the solution. Static knowledge tends to be formulaic and may, as a consequence, be harmful. Numerous examples of this were described in earlier chapters. In particular, we have seen how professionals try to deal with second and third generations from immigrant stock much as if they were in a sort of cultural time prison. Similarly, the way in which children of mixed parentage develop their own sense of identity is disregarded in favour of finding ways to make problems of these children. While racism or ethnocentrism plays its part, the sheer complexity of the task is likely to defeat any psychologist dealing with a multitude of cultures and cultural backgrounds. Another solution might appear to lie in specialization, but this avenue is simply not practicable in many areas of practice. Similarly, the answer does not lie in the deployment of professionals from the ethnic and cultural groups in question, since, as we have demonstrated, this does not ensure any greater sensitivity to the needs of client groups. Furthermore, it does little or nothing to help children to develop within the cultural mixes or new cultures and new senses of identity, which are both necessary and adaptive in the new environment.

## Applying concepts across cultures

The greatest care is needed when applying, cross-culturally, concepts originating in any culture, Western or otherwise. Advocates of the indigenous psychology approaches warn of the inevitable problems that arise when transferring psychological ideas from one culture to another. Enriquez (1997) encourages us to question the validity of all such concepts, taking none of them for granted irrespective of their origins. This critical stance should apply equally to 'native' psychologies as well as Western ones. As yet, we are unable to speculate effectively on how far ideas can be extracted from one culture and applied in others. What may be true for more traditionally orientated communities may be ludicrously inappropriate for these same communities following modernization or industrialization. Similarly, to use Western psychology's measures of personality, motivation and attitudes may miss the mark entirely when applied in traditional indigenous communities beyond the West. This is well illustrated by Shwendler's (1984) argument that psychological research has largely ignored many non-Western countries and their problems. Beyond the West, a country's priorities may lie in development and social change which psychological research and practice have generally ignored.

One question arising concerns the extent to which the micro interactions, which constitute psychologists' routine focus, simply reproduce macro-level issues. While most psychologists are familiar with claims of cultural bias in the psychological tests and measures used in the West, such critiques can be seen as merely the micro-level manifestation of a broader macro-level problem. Psychologists from other cultures extend the list of unacceptable consequences of tests and measures developed in and designed for the West when applied beyond their cultural ambit. Yang (1997) recounts attempts to use Western measures of personality in China without even systematic attempts to develop theories based on indigenous perspectives. Durojaiye (1984) explains how Western-constructed tests have been the predominant tests for educational and personnel selection in Africa. They are misplaced since they tend to exclude from education young people whose backgrounds were not conducive to school learning – that is, those with the most to gain. The cultural biases of the tests simply ensure that those who do well are those who are acculturated to Western thought. They are also irrelevant to the motivation systems of much of Africa.

Despite the difficulties inherent in adopting culturally relevant psychologies, certain broad patterns differentiate Western psychology from those in other parts of the world. We discussed this earlier, but the issue is so important that it warrants underlining. Page and Berkow (1991), among many others, suggest that the East–West difference is best illustrated by conceptions of self. For example, in Buddhism, personal growth and self-examination are not separate, whereas in the West we tend to self-exaimine at crisis rather than growth points in our lives. When the individual reaches a view of self that incorporates the totality of reality in so far as it can be experienced, then identity development is not over but has changed from the previous delusional state, which failed to encapsulate reality. From this and other perspectives, the Western conception of self reflects a state of inadequacy. In Buddhism, the concept of a separate self is illusory, encouraging ignorance and suffering. The 'selfish self', with its emphasis on 'me' and 'what is mine', is characteristic of the West and Western psychology and traits such as pride, conceit and egoism. This immature perspective is at the root of the troubles of the world when seen from the Buddhist world-view.

One should not overestimate the power of Western views and Western psychological views to dominate other peoples. Often Western psychology has been ignored as irrelevant because it fails to address the issues that are crucial to economically developing countries. For example, an indigenous psychology may be developed which meets the needs of national development better, so that the influence of Western psychology declines (Ching, 1984). There are parallels at the macro level with the micro level in the extent to which minority people reject or fail to take up Western psychological services in the West. Rosemont (1997) suggests that attempts to convince most of the world's population of the value of the West's individualistic view of humankind would generally fail. Community remains essential to most peoples' views of humankind. In this context, the observation that unless there are two human beings there are no human beings becomes important. Humanness is defined in relations with other people and not in terms of autonomy. For Rosemont, the multiplicity of social roles defines the unique self rather than what remains when each of these have been removed. People change with changes in any of their roles.

## Health and disease: cultural variations

Among the ideas and practices that vary across cultural contexts are beliefs about health and responses to disease. These cultural variations include those of mental health and psychological well-being. Even the World Health Organization's 'universal' definition of health is problematic in this context since the WHO defines health as 'a state of complete physical, mental and social well-being and not merely the absence of disease or infirmity'. Spiritual well-being is missing from this definition despite its centrality and importance to conceptions of general well-being in most world cultures. For example, traditional Chinese medicine regards mental disorder as a mixture of organic illness and mystical possessions, of hallucinations or depression, many of which are missing from the systems of Western psychiatry. Belief in mystical phenomena is far from being peculiarly Chinese. Possession by spirits is the commonest explanation of psychological problems throughout the world (Richeport-Haley, 1998). Consequently, Richeport-Haley advises, clinicians practising in multiethnic settings must be mindful that beliefs in spirit possession will be involved in some of the presenting problems of ethnic minority clients.

Despite the sharp distinction between psychology and religion in the West, the sundering of religion, philosophy and psychology is largely missing from Eastern thought – especially that reflecting Indian systems of philosophy. In rural areas of India, traditional indigenous healing practices are still prevalent (Kakar, 1982) and may involve 'rituals' with religious elements. This practice contrasts markedly with Western therapeutic procedures where the 'sacred' and the 'profane' have separated, where the profane dominates the realm of medicine and psychotherapy. In the West, psychology grew out of the scientific and medical traditions, and its development was largely independent of religion and philosophy. We may study the psychology of religion but 'the religion of psychology' is a curious, empty phrase. In the East, as in Africa, psychology, religion and philosophy remain united. As long ago as 1954, Parrinder noted that in African thought, the material (or the organic) and the spiritual are almost indistinguishable. For traditional Africans, there is no separation of issues of religion and magic from those of disease, whether physical or mental.

Even in the West, many have expressed reservations about the universal validity of the assumptions underlying the World Health Organization's conception of health on the grounds that it is Eurocentric. For instance, Littlewood and Lipsedge (1989) argue that diagnostic categories of mental illness reflect this Eurocentric conception, and ask: 'How applicable are European categories of mental illness to other societies' (p. 117)? Fernando (1989) adds that current systems of classification, apart from over-emphasizing pathology in thinking and behaviour, ignore the social, political and economic factors that may cause, or at least contribute to, 'illness'. We would add that the Euro-American systems of classification overlook the very dimensions crucial to mental disorders at the cultural level. Wijsen (1999) regards culture as the meaning system learned and shared by the members of a group, which is used by them to interpret experiences and to organize behaviour. Each of these learned, shared and generationally transmitted meaning systems includes ideas about health: mental, emotional, spiritual and psychological well-being. Knappert (1995) expands further on this way of understanding culture: 'it is a people's cosmology, their world-view, their beliefs in gods and spirits, their convictions regarding dream and reality, their relations toward the world of nature surrounding them, and their own place and function in that world, a description of the world we live in, not from a physico-scientific point of view, but as a spiritual world' (p. 11). van Beek and Blakely (1994) lend support to this view when they state: 'The things (humans have) created with (their minds) and worshipped in the spirit are as real to [them] as the material things [they have] made with [their] hands. The belief in the supernatural and in the immortality of the soul must be accepted as real facts that have led to action and results' (p. 19).

Every culture (or even sub-culture) is a different world with unique beliefs and psychology, so there are at least as many different worlds as there are religions and psychologies. Every religion has its own cosmology, its own cosmos, including psychology – that is, its own universe of reality. Lomov *et al.* (1993) appear to agree with this view when they argue, from a Russian perspective, that psychological knowledge, the ideas, concepts and theories of psychological realities, constitute important components of a culture. For them, myths, songs, proverbs, literature, political and medical treatises, philosophical and religious texts from the past have added to, and elaborated upon, the vast store of psychological knowledge. Further, the psychological picture of the world, reflected in all spheres of spiritual life, has, and continues to play, an important role in shaping and directing cultures. Lomov *et al.* are convinced that every culture is characterized by a unique set of concepts, images, a system of values and a specific type of the perception of the world (p. 104).

As a set of concepts and theories developed in the West, modern psychology and psychotherapy lack means of describing and understanding the mind in radically different cultures. Western conceptions of psychology may even distort perception and hinder a proper understanding of other cultures and their view regarding health and disease. Azuma (1984) is perceptive in noting how when Western-trained psychologists look at other cultures through Western lenses, they are very likely to overlook key aspects of those cultures since the schemata for recognizing them are absent from their education and training. None-the-less, he does not believe that Western psychology is useless for solving the problems of other cultures. He envisages that Western psychology needs modification to be relevant to a new cultural environment. Otherwise, Western theories and interpretations may distort features of other cultures and force them into the Western value system. In a somewhat similar manner, Ching (1984) suggested that shifting the focus from the 'impact of psychology upon Third World peoples' onto the 'impact of Third World peoples (especially their representatives in the West) upon psychology' may indeed enrich psychology and psychological services.

Beliefs are material facts, as real as any thing in the physical world (Holdstock, 2000). Consequently, the belief that the human soul is immortal or that there are supernatural beings is as important to understanding people as any other influence. To understand the psychology of Africans, for example, beliefs of this sort need attention despite their irrelevance to understanding Westerners. Psychologies beyond the Western perspective are primarily concerned about respect for other human beings but also for the physical and spiritual environments. In African psychology, for example, good relationships with other people are a duty. Thus, if an African client complains of someone, be they a family member, a relative, a close friend, a stranger, or even a dead relative (a 'living dead'), casting an evil spell on him/her, in many instances, this must not be taken literally. It is likely that the client is expressing guilt, concern, or anxiety about his/her having bad thoughts about that person, about not having positive thoughts about or the relationship with that other person which is demanded by the traditional African ethic governing interpersonal relationships. Traditional Africans are generally more concerned with persons than with things; as in other societies of the majority world, being separated from other people implies for the African a personal, cultural sense of hell.

In the fields of counselling and psychotherapy, Peavy (1996) demands a radical, new approach. They should be looked upon as forms of cultural practice rather than scientific undertakings. Defined instead as 'cultural healing', mental health services need to be constructed more out of (1) 'folk wisdom', (2) culturally sensible ways of communicating, (3) local, rather than decontextualized, knowledge and (4) aspects of the knowledge developed through both scientific and humanistic research. In a similar vein, Bohart *et al.* (1998) challenge the Division 12 of the American Psychological Association's task force's view regarding the nature or scientific status of psychotherapy. Empirically validated treatments, as required by the association, are restrictive and unjustified, and this requirement only serves to stifle psychological research. They contend that humanistic methodology should be placed on a par with natural science methodology: that is, humanistic or cultural assumptions should be equally valued.

The central themes of psychology beyond Western perspectives are conveniently summarized by Ho (1993): 'The principles guiding social action are as follows: (a) collective or group interests take precedence over those of individual, (b) the fulfilment of external social obligations takes precedence over the fulfilment of internal individual needs, and (c) securing a place in the social order takes precedence over self-expression' (p. 250).

Cross-cultural psychologists have given some attention to the issue of adapting research methodology to meet the requirements of different cultural contexts. Nevertheless, there is a need for further exploration of the limits to extending modern psychology to traditional societies and, but less obviously, modernizing cultures beyond the West. For example, as Owusu-Bempah (1999a) has argued in the context of social work theory and practice, we need seriously to examine whether it is feasible or even useful to extend Western psychological services beyond Western boundaries. There already exist 'traditional-supportive' psychologies, mainly based upon religious beliefs and cultural value systems, so why the need for outsiders? Page and Berkow (1991) see the answer, in part, in learning from such traditional supportive psychologies. They believe that psychotherapy, which often aims to increase self-esteem and self-efficacy, necessitates an understanding of the self. This can be enhanced by learning how other cultures perceive the self and its implications for mental health or ill-health, for example.

## Clinical practice with interdependent clients

Specifically, the Western notion of the differentiated, autonomous self, of the individual as independent of his or her environment and free from external control, is alien to most cultures outside the West. Markus and Kitayama (1991), Miller (1997) and Roland (1997) inform us that, within the context of world cultures, an actualized person is one who is most deeply connected to others and society as a whole. There are Pacific Island groups who view themselves not as bounded, distinct entities but as integral pieces of an eternal life scheme (Lesser, 1996). In some African cultures where the individual is less than human without 'us', the individual seeks the answer to the question: 'Who am I?' not only in the question 'Who are we?' but also in the question 'Who *were* we?' In the extreme, there is the Innu culture that does not even have a word for self-reference (Page and Berkow, 1991).

One of Foster's cases illustrates poignantly the futility of any attempt to generalise Western theoretical assumptions and psychotherapeutic interventions:

> *And how do we figure out the deep self-experience of a Middle Eastern man from a religious sect, who feels that without the tribe he was trained to lead, his self-esteem is unformed, non-existent? Do we view this client through the American self-psychological terms of a narcissistically derailed self, through the Ego Psychology lens of a poorly differentiated self? Or rather, as a person centred in the ensembled self-experience of his Eastern culture; where bonding to family and group kinship renders individuals who throughout life are deeply identified with others?*
>
> Foster, 1998, pp. 259–260

Foster is right in emphasizing how the hard clinical questions posed by these clients force us to take a look at both our theory and practice. A good start would be an acknowledgement that we can understand people only by respecting and studying how they understand themselves. People of every nationality seek self-understanding: their own character, their ways and peculiarities that differentiate them from other peoples (Lagmay, 1984). At the same time, they avoid being told by other peoples how they do, or should, understand themselves.

Abundant evidence suggests that, in Western societies, the Eurocentric assumptions regarding health, mental health in particular, have resulted in misdiagnoses and mistreatment of Black and ethnic minority clients (Fernando, 1989, 1995; Flaskerud and Hu, 1992; Howitt and Owusu-Bempah, 1994; Littlewood and Lipsedge, 1989; Mercer, 1984; Shaikh, 1985; MIND, 1993; NAHA, 1988). The Western ideal self is portrayed as a free agent out to gratify its whims; its efforts towards gratification must not be thwarted or the outcome may be parlous; it must have rights, privacy and autonomy to pursue its hedonistic ends or disaster looms. It must, therefore, be protected from all obstacles, including intrusions or encroachments from others. Thus the failure of a family to protect the privacy and autonomy of its individual members is seen in Western eyes as a type of family pathology, and family members construed variously as enmeshed, oppressed, victimized, and others as domineering, smothering and so forth. Much as we have seen earlier, investigators have documented how this 'sacred self' is unknown among cultures outside the Western world: in Asian (Bharati, 1981; Marsella *et al.*, 1985; Landrine, 1992; Shweder and Bourne, 1982); African (Mbiti, 1969; Owusu-Bempah, 1999; Owusu-Bempah and Howitt, 1995). Claims are also made of its rarity even among Western White women (Gilligan, 1982; Lykes, 1985). To members of collectivist cultures, the concept of autonomous individuals free to choose and make up their mind, or mind their own business, is alien. It is a bizarre idea that cuts the self off from the interdependent whole and dooms it to a life of isolation and loneliness (Fogel, 1993; Landrine, 1992; Shweder and Bourne, 1982).

If we perceive development as the 'development of people', the impact of psychology could be measured in terms of how much it helps people satisfy their needs; how it helps exploit their potential to the fullest; and what it contributes to helping individuals develop into well-adjusted, fully rounded human beings. When psychology fails to meet these objectives with respect to ethnic minority groups, should we question the amenability of the clients? Or, rather, is it the appropriateness and efficacy of psychological assumptions and methods that is at fault? Sue and Sue (1990) claims that the Western mental health literature eschews such important questions and plays down the formidable critiques of the Eurocentric assumptions of theories of normal human development and psychopathology.

Western rationality has its own peculiar parameters. Cognitive psychologists have studied the explanations that people give for our good and bad fortune. Nisbett and Ross (1980), found a 'self-serving bias' whereby people credit their own skills and abilities for their successes (dispositional factors), whereas they blame their failures on situational factors. Such tendencies, common in the West's individualist communities, are not so evident in collectivist cultures. For example, it has been shown that in situations where Americans used their ability to explain their successes but not their lack of ability to explain their failures, Japanese people showed the reverse pattern (Kashima and Triandis, 1986). In the Japanese case, there seems to be a 'self-effacement bias' (Nisbett and Ross, 1988; Stevenson, 1991; Triandis, 1994).

These attribution styles are not observed uniformly across cultures. Boski (1983) compared responses of students belonging to the three main ethnic groups in Nigeria – Igbo, Yoruba and Hausa. He found effort and ability frequently used to explain success, and situational factors more frequently given as reasons for failure. Within these overall effects, he hypothesized that each cultural group would show a different pattern based upon its prevailing cultural values. The predominantly Christian Igbos are more frequently found to endorse independent values, whereas the Islamic and traditional Hausa are thought to hold more interdependent values. Compared with the Igbos, Hausa respondents explained their success more in terms of contextual factors such as the nature of the task and luck but less in terms of ability. Therapists and counsellors, therefore, need to look at how often people of interdependent cultures use dispositional explanations for their presenting problems.

In therapy, there is an interesting variation on the theme. When ethnic minority clients make situational attributions, they may sometimes involve spirits: :

> *A young Central American couple presented the problem of violence by the husband. The couple accepted the idea that the husband had an **espiritu burlon**, a mischievous spirit that causes him to act violently. Juan and Rosa, in their late 30s, had been in Washington, D.C., for 8 years. They were sent to therapy by the court... Privately, Rosa reported that Juan threatened to hurt her and 'to take her eyes out.' Rosa is made even more fearful by the three dots that Juan has on his forearm, which, for her, reinforces his alliance with malevolent forces.*

Richeport-Haley, 1998, p. 81

As Westerners and those trained in Western psychology, it is almost automatic for us to regard such a spiritual attribution as primitive or irrational. We may well try to convince the client of a Western ('rational') interpretation. But the greatest care needs to be taken since imposing Western world-views, Western (positivist) psychological principles and practices may well be harmful to the mental health of peoples with a different world-view. Consequently, Gergen *et al.* (1996) argue that the practice of psychology is irrelevant to the Maori of New Zealand and a tool for their suppression. Furthermore, it contributed to the abnormalization of the indigenous population. Gantous (1994) claims that the use of interventionist strategies, based on the traditional scientific paradigm, contributed more to the problems experienced by the Canadian Innu than to illuminating pathways to the solution of their problems.

## Alienation through therapy

Psychotherapy is virtually unknown and unnecessary in a majority of cultures of the world. Even in today's Western world, there are audible questions about the relevance of psychotherapy based on Western views of 'normal' development, experience and behaviour to diverse populations. Encapsulated in human diversity are different shades of skin tone, culture or ethnicity, age, gender, as well as socio-economic background. Indeed, some have warned that psychology must seek to reflect the diversity of the populations it wishes to serve or perish. Otherwise, they say, psychology will not only remain irrelevant to clients' needs, but it will cease to be a viable professional resource to the majority of them (e.g., Hall, 1997; Huang, 1994; Landrine, 1992; Moncayo, 1998; Sue, 1988, 1998). In order to avoid this state of affairs, others (e.g., Richeport-Haley, 1998; Shiang *et al.*, 1998) have suggested incorporating specific cultural beliefs and behaviours into standard clinical treatments in order to make more relevant services to people from diverse backgrounds.

Many African and African-American psychologists and others view mainstream psychology as part of the mental health problem that it tries to combat (e.g., Akbar, 1984, Bulhan, 1981, 1985; Durojaiye, 1993, Masson, 1989; Owusu-Bempah and Howitt, 1994). Akbar (1984), for instance, argues that the Eurocentric preoccupation with deviancy and excessive involvement with victim analysis has become conceptually incarcerated in the approach to peoples outside the West. On a more general level, Sarason (1981) and Holdstock (2000) blame the nature of social psychology for contributing to the psychiatric course followed by clinical practice. Sarason contends that if social psychology had been more social it would have formed the basis for a clinical psychology that emphasized primary prevention and the social determinants of maladjustment. If this had been the case, clinical psychology would have been better able to work effectively within the political environment to formulate public policies to aid these efforts. Sarason describes the advent of clinical psychology during the post-Second World War period as 'the beginning of a disaster because it failed to prepare psychology for the public arena' (p. 827). In like manner, Albee (1982) and other writers (e.g., Fernando,1989; Paniagua, 1994; Richeport-Haley, 1998) have pleaded for recognition of the role of poverty, meaningless work, unemployment, racism and sexism in producing psychopathology. It is a futile hope that psychology and psychotherapy with the poor and powerless will alleviate suffering and despair. These will only yield to social and political solutions that tackle the incidence of problems, not bandage the wound. We have repeatedly conveyed this message in relation to identity work with Black children in British society (Owusu-Bempah, 1994a, 1997; Owusu-Bempah and Howitt, 1999a, b). The message is worth emphasizing further. We must recognize that the relationship of Western psychology to the rest of society is a power relationship and that psychologists carry out the mandate of the powerful; they serve those in power frequently at the expense of the powerless.

Although she was primarily concerned with ideas about the education of disadvantaged children in general, Pollard's (1989) distinction between 'static variables' and 'alterable variables' (discussed in Chapter 4) remains, for us, a key conceptual distinction which should be understood and acted upon by all professionals. Pollard's 'alterable variables' approach may be advocated as a practical and more helpful way of providing liberating services to Black and ethnic minority (and other socially disadvantaged) people. This involves, among other things, identifying those aspects of the institution that we represent which have a deleterious effect on Black people, and how we may change them. We need also to identify those aspects of the institution that may enhance Black people's psychological well-being and help in unfolding their potential.

## Cultural competence

The evidence is that ethnic minorities in Western societies relatively often choose not to take up mental health services and, if they do enter treatment, drop out at a far higher rate than others (Shiang *et al.*, 1998). One common view is that therapy ought to be provided by multilingual and multicultural practitioners in order to prevent such problems. The underlying assumption is that most therapists simply lack knowledge about the cultural and social backgrounds and lifestyles of minority groups although similar recommendations are not made for the working class, the elderly or children. There is an alternative possibility. A study carried out on behalf of the Joseph Rowntree Foundation suggested that ethnic minority families in Britain who upheld collectivist values were the best able to cope with many social and personal problems (Hylton, 1997). Furthermore, ethnic minority families actually preferred solving problems for themselves to seeking the help of voluntary or statutory organizations. The majority of the ethnic minority women interviewed had adapted to life in the United Kingdom yet preferred to say within their own cultural traditions. So it might be that the lack of involvement of ethnic minorities in therapy and their speedier exit from therapy is a consequence of different cultural beliefs about normal experience or behaviour, or that their communities provide alternative services through family and community support. Exploring such possibilities would be more illuminating and fruitful than speculation.

In collectivist cultures, the individual seeks to advance the family rather than the self. The individual is changed, adjusted and acted upon until he or she fits more harmoniously within the family, relationship or community, or the entire group is changed to improve the quality of life of all of its members. Therapy based on these values is appropriate in this setting. Unfortunately, this sort of family is wrongly perceived by some professionals, including therapists and counsellors, who see some members of these families as submissive or passive. It might be unhelpful to offer assertiveness training to members of collectivist families seen in this way since this would be inimical to therapeutic success, given that the family and its individual members function more as single, integral unit (Miatra, 1995): 'practice, if based on Western (professional) views of "normal" family function or child-rearing, can and does result in serious errors in assessment... and make "therapeutic" interventions useless if not abusive in themselves' (Miatra, 1996, p. 288).

This is a signal that we must suspend our claims regarding the universality of Western definitions of 'normal family', if by 'universal' is meant 'for all human beings'. It highlights the need for a wider knowledge-base about how families function and how children develop, as well as what experiences may be detrimental to them in the long term. Psychotherapy, like Western psychology and psychiatry, is predicated on the assumption that normal persons experience the self in an individualist framework. The challenge is that psychotherapy, from which family therapy derives, and which often aims to increase self-esteem and self-efficacy, necessitates an understanding of the self in a broader cultural context (Page and Berkow, 1991).

Issues of race and ethnicity cause anxiety both in everyday social exchanges and in the activities of clinicians and other therapists (Leary, 1995). This is unhelpful especially given the formidable task facing professionals in Western societies. Modern migratory patterns have ensured that almost every culture in the world is at least represented in any given country in the West (just as has happened in reverse). The excessive demands that would be placed on any practitioner wishing to be competent to know something of the cultures of all sectors of the community can be illustrated by briefly examining language – one of the key aspects of any culture. Knappert (1995) estimates that more than a thousand different languages are spoken in Africa. In Zaire, 326 different languages (not counting dialects) are in active use. Some African languages (such as Yoruba in Nigeria) are spoken by millions of people, whereas others are spoken by just a few. Quite clearly, no therapist could be expected to understand even just the beliefs and practices relating to health and illness of so many different cultures.

One common way of looking at the situation is to highlight therapists' poor knowledge and understanding of the cultures of their ethnic clients (e.g., Sue, 1988, Sue and Sue, 1990). This presents us with the obvious solution of instigating initiatives designed to improve the *cultural competence* of practitioners. According to Sue (1998), a competent cross-cultural/ethnic therapist possesses the cultural knowledge and skills to deliver effective interventions to members of that culture. However, is cultural competence really an essential requirement or condition in the therapeutic relationship, vital to an effective therapeutic outcome? Although a therapist may be knowledgeable about language and culture, factors such as social class and status differential may also militate against therapeutic effectiveness (Hall, 1997 and see also e.g., Fernando, 1989; O'Brian, 1990; Owusu-Bempah, 1997; Owusu-Bempah and Howitt, 1999a). Even though cultural and language barriers can hamper cross-cultural/ethnic therapy, ethnic and cultural matching, their removal does not ensure effective outcomes. The therapist's professional background and training based on Western values and assumptions, such as those regarding the 'normal' individual or 'healthy' family, may offset any gains from ethnic matching and cultural competence. Furthermore, the sharing of ethnicity by professionals and their clients does not always exclude the intrusion of crass stereotypes. For example, Hall (1997) recounts being approached by a Black therapist who was treating a 5-year-old racially mixed-parentage (African-American and Japanese) boy who was showing inappropriate sexual behaviour at school. According to Hall, the therapist initially attributed the child's sexual misconduct to the stereotypical 'heightened sexuality' of African-American males. The Black therapist was advised to investigate more extensively and it emerged that the boy's mother was sexually abusing the child. Such abuse is a well-established precursor to inappropriate sexual behaviours in children, so Hall asks: 'Why then did the therapist assume a genetic cause in this case?' Hall's answer is that 'not all the perpetrators of these cultural errors [racism] are White' (p. 645).

## Indigenous therapies

While professionals nowadays readily acknowledge that their client groups are culturally, ethnically and socio-economically diverse, less frequently do they recognize this factor as challenging the generaliz-

ability of therapeutic methods to beyond the Western European populations for which they were originally devised. Of course, there are
training models designed to remedy this sort of situation and to
prepare therapists, counsellors and others for effective work with
ethnic minority clients. Characteristically, such training has been dominated by issues of 'race', ethnicity and culture. This can easily lead to
feelings of insecurity among practitioners. Practitioners' sense of a lack
of competence in matters of 'race', ethnicity and culture can make them
feel de-skilled. Additionally, training programmes and practice which
over-emphasize ethnic/cultural issues can be criticized for lacking a
clear conceptual framework, for using simplistic and formulaic
methods to solve complex structural problems (Cacas, 1984; Fernando,
1989; Owusu-Bempah, 1997).

Among the solutions to some of these difficulties would be the
development of interventions that are culturally diverse enough to be
relevant to a wide variety of groups, regardless of racial,
cultural/ethnic backgrounds. Another route to cultural competence
would lie in the development of indigenous therapies. Following
Azuma's (1984) requirement that psychology needs to develop *in* a
particular culture before it can be applied to that culture, indigenous
therapies would involve distinctive theories and practices for each
cultural context. Western theories and research methods would only be
retained if they were relevant to that particular cultural context.

## Eco-systems approach

*If one finger is sore, the whole hand will hurt.*
             Chinese proverb; quoted in Smith and Bond, 1993, p. 119

The 'indigenous therapies' approach within mainstream psychotherapy is less than completely practical. There is a monumental amount of
work to be done given the institutional patterns of training professionals in psychological work and the limited resources devoted so far to
developing indigenous therapies. A somewhat more practical approach
for the meantime is the eco-systems perspective that manages to avoid
some of the inherent difficulties of current approaches to cross-
cultural/ethnic psychotherapy. The key feature of the eco-systems
perspective is the individual's 'goodness-of-fit' with their environment:
there should be an intimate interaction between individuals and their
environment (Wakefield, 1996). People form a symbiotic relationship
with their environment in which both are mutually influencing. In
Wakefield's view, a therapeutic intervention based on the eco-systems
perspective begins with a question: Is it more fruitful to study social
behaviour by focusing on an individual's motivations and cognitions,
or by examining the way social structures mould a person's behaviour

and thought? So in the context of family therapy, the issue might be expressed as whether intervention should focus on an individual member, the whole family, or adopt a broader perspective to understanding and supporting the family.

Interaction at any point in the eco-system affects the entire system. One implication is that intervention might be effective for indirect parts of the system. So for some ethnic minority families, the therapist might prefer to commence intervention with the neighbouring parts of the system in which, for example, the parent–child relationship is nested or embedded, such as grandparents or some other part of the extended family. We have already shown how, in Asian communities, the kinship system or the extended family is the social and psychological locus throughout life for the majority of members of the community. Social, personal, economic and status needs of the person are traditionally played out and fulfilled overwhelmingly within the extended family (Kakar, 1978). Treating some ethnic minority clients in isolation is, perhaps, the commonest cross-cultural, psychotherapeutic or professional error (Landrine, 1992; Miatra, 1996). All of this follows from the repeated observation that the self in collectivist cultures is usually defined in terms of social roles which exist for the good of people and not individuals. An eco-systems approach to cross-cultural/ethnic family therapy would minimize ethnic issues as much as possible and deal with cases in terms of the social context and family structure.

Some of the major advantages of the eco-systems approach (Wakefield, 1996) are:

1  It helps practitioners see the interconnectedness between the individual and their environment which is involved in that individual's problem. The focus is removed from the individual onto the transaction between the individual and their environment. Thus there is a dual concern in intervention which includes the individual but goes beyond the individual.
2  It is a method of assessment that is both useful and comprehensive.
3  It allows practitioners to employ appropriate domain-specific theories intervention.
4  The bias of practitioners towards person-centred therapy becomes difficult to maintain.

Richeport-Haley provides a case study that illustrates the benefits of using a client's family and extended family as a resource.

*A young man in his 20s was court ordered to therapy for possession and dealing of marijuana. He would be imprisoned if this happened one more time. His mother, who spoke only Spanish, and the oldest son, who translated for her, came to therapy. The goal was to get the boy off marijuana. The intervention was to have the family come up with a strong consequence if the youth relapsed. They decided that the consequence would be to ostracise the son from the family for three months and to shun him if he took drugs again. The son has not gone back to drugs.*

Richeport-Haley, 1998, p. 86

In this case, according to Richeport-Haley, the therapist did not need to understand the strong bond of a Latin American family and the difficulty it has in banning a member. The goal of therapy, regardless of ethnic group, was for the family to take charge of its member and formulate a serious consequence rather than have the community do so.

Thus, unlike some other approaches to identity work with Black children, for instance, (e.g. Banks, 1992; Coleman 1994; Coward and Dattani, 1993; Mullender 1991; Maximé, 1993a,b), the eco-systems approach is not intended to help people become aware of anything cultural, not even their cultural roots. In spite of this lack of focus on cultural or ethnic issues, paradoxically it can be seen as more culturally congruent than approaches that concentrate on ethnicity issues. As Richeport-Haley (1998) explains: (a) the family and/or social network are included in the therapy; (b) therapy does not stress exploration or insight; (c) it is action orientated rather than discussion orientated; (d) the therapist maintains a position of expertise and authority; and (e) the client receives concrete advice. The therapy's goal becomes one of enabling the family to operate effectively within the framework of today's reality, in preparation for tomorrow. This is a view that shares a lot in common with Fernando's argument:

*A cultural analysis which renders the personal distress of a Bengali woman in East London understandable in terms of her culture is hardly much use to a social worker or psychiatrist trying to help her if, and a likely 'if' in the present day, she is fearful of racist attacks and the local hospital services regard her as a nuisance. In such a case... an understanding of her culture must be integrated with an understanding of the social conditions that disable her in the society that she lives in with a sensitivity to the realities of life and ways of coping from her angle, in order to appreciate something of what it feels like to be that person.*

Fernando, 1989, p. 10

Elsewhere Fernando (1995) makes the following recommendations:

1  for Black and Asian people to be listened to and heard;
2  for Black and Asian people not to be treated as members of an homogeneous social group;
3  for individual practitioners, disciplines, professions and institutions to critically evaluate their structures and procedures for racialized and gendered practices and assumptions;

4   for research to move towards undertaking process-orientated work to illuminate how structures and procedures may operate to disadvantage particular social groups; and
5   to recognize the role of power relations in research and therapeutic settings.

The eco-system approach to cross-cultural therapy takes all of these recommendations into account.

## Confidentiality: a case in point

Have such cherished values as confidentiality, self-determination, autonomy, privacy and other professional principles a place in the eco-systems approach to therapy? Certainly such concepts have different meanings in cultures beyond the West. Some argue that values such as confidentiality and privacy are inconsistent with the use of family support systems and social networks (e.g. Owusu-Bempah, 1999a; Silavwe, 1995). Western values may harm ethnic minority clients because their individualist focus undermines traditional support systems based on the family and community which provide the resources for problem solving. This claim is supported by Hylton's (1997) study of ethnic minority families in Britain in which it was demonstrated how important collectivist values are to the well-being of Asian communities.

Confidentiality in professional practice takes for granted a dichotomy between the individual and the community. It assumes that the individual is autonomous from his or her family and community. In other cultures beyond of the West, however, the individual is so embedded in the community that the sense of selfhood, psychological and spiritual sustenance is through the corporate being of one's family, group or community. Personal problems are inevitably group problems, and so are collectively resolved by the community. In traditional collectivist societies, whatever happens to the individual is also felt by the community, and *vice versa*. There exists a community of fate. In Western professional practice, confidentiality requires secrecy and concealment. In contrast, in collectivist cultures 'personal' problems warrant the attention and concern of the extended family or group.

This deep sense of community should not be ignored when working with families from such backgrounds, or one might well impose an alien conception of individuality via confidentiality on those clients requiring a sense of kinship or group solidarity. For 'confidentiality' to be appropriate for professional work with collectivist communities, it needs to be seen more broadly as information to be confined to or held within the family and community; that is, confidentiality is information or knowledge not to be shared with out-groups (Owusu-Bempah,

1999a). The significance of confidentiality is its provision of safeguards for the group or community as opposed to its individual members (for detailed discussions see Owusu-Bempah, 1999a or Silavwe, 1995). However, 'community' implies a group of people with whom the client or family has close relationships, people who are interested in the client's well-being. This involves a *gemeinschaft* relationship with others rather than individuals living in close physical proximity with the client. Western confidentiality principles should not be seen as invariably inappropriate for work involving ethnic minority clients. We are merely highlighting that the application of Western principles is risky and fraught, warranting an ethic of sensitivity and caring when dealing with radically different cultures.

In this way, Western psychology is freed to address the needs it addresses best, unburdened by a duty to explain the universal human condition. We should accept that we do not know members of our own culture well and that we know members of other cultures even less. Our ideas and assertions about human nature should be revised and reshaped through reciprocal interaction with clients, increasingly so the more their worlds differ from ours. It is an excruciating process to attempt to liberate oneself from one's ethnocentric bias, especially the Western one that has so effectively exported itself to other parts of the world. None-the-less, the provision of relevant services to diverse client groups necessitates a thorough re-examination of the role of Western values and principles in all forms of counselling and therapy with ethnic minorities. This raises the need to be prepared to relinquish some of the power we wield by virtue of or professional and social status.

## Focusing on institutions

We have made our argument. That is, peoples outside the Western world and their cultures continue to be, at best, neglected by Western psychologists and related professionals. At worst, they are systematically disadvantaged by the practices of many practitioners. This applies to the very sort of people whom practitioners might be expected to protect most of all: young, vulnerable Black people and ethnic minority children and youths. That Black families, for example, are inadequate families that fail their children frequently and dramatically is a dominant theme in much of the work of Western trained professionals. The commonly held assumption that Black youngsters manifest 'behavioural difficulties' and 'intellectual deficits' (e.g., Brian and Martin 1983, 1989; Dwivedi and Varma, 1996; Eysenck, 1971; Jensen, 1969) has meant that public provision for these children has been tailored accordingly (but inadequately) for their welfare. We have shown that, for all of the professions we have considered, insidiously, myths and assumptions have led to inadequate and potentially harmful service provision.

Racial and cultural perspectives need constant revision and challenge when addressing the needs of Black and ethnic minority groups and their families. Race should not be regarded as the key feature of service provision for these groups.

We have seen how Black and ethnic minority children, from the nursery onwards, have different experiences from those of White children, even within the same classroom (e.g. Ogilvy *et al.*, 1990). This is also true of Black children in care. The reasons are complex and interacting, beyond the capabilities of individual professionals to alleviate completely. Bad decisions by our colleagues in other professions may have profound effects on our own work with ethnic minority people (Howitt and Owusu-Bempah, 1999). To understand what happens in the classroom may be crucial to understanding a child's response to social workers, for example. A change in a child's situation does not mean that he or she will slough off memories of past experiences with professionals. Later interactions with another group of professionals may compound the difficulties or the extent of a child's problems.

It is incumbent upon professionals to monitor critically, and where necessary rectify, those aspects of their practice that may jeopardize the futures of ethnic minority people. Professionals should not make problems of people who do not (or are unwilling to) achieve 'success' defined solely in European, middle-class terms. In these circumstances, the professional role should be to challenge the European definition of success on their behalf. After all, it is a fundamental right of each group 'to participate in the creation of meaning for [itself] and for the social world of which [it is] a part' (Gilkey, 1976, p. 57. Quoted by Willie, 1993, p. 455). Definitions of success and reality may need particular attention. As Willie (1993) insists: 'None is totally without power; all groups have power derived from their uniqueness and, therefore, the capacity to veto business as usual'(p. 454).

It is insufficient and, possibly, counter-productive to dwell solely on the activities of individual practitioners. The role of the institutions employing these professionals may be more profound and more amenable to coherent and rapid revision. Failures to provide adequate and appropriate services for all client groups by institutions may be more damaging than those of individuals within the organizations. As many have argued, institutional racism and its attendant failures in terms of service provision involves or implicates everyone within the institution (Bulhan, 1985; Dummett, 1984; Fanon, 1967; Howitt and Owusu-Bempah, 1994; Owusu-Bempah, 1985, 1990). Dummett (1984) described how, in a racist society, institutions can perpetrate racism without any overt expression of that racism. Similarly, racist institutions frequently perpetrate racism and contribute to racial disadvantage even when their personnel reject racist beliefs (Macpherson, 1999). Institutions can be structured in ways which disadvantage Black people (Richardson, 1990). At school, to reiterate a now familiar example, the children may not be expected to do well or succeed. If being Black or a member of an ethnic minority is associated with being unmotivated, or uneducable or simply a nit-wit prone to behavioural difficulties, then to steer the child into sports, woodwork or metal work, as Dwivedi and Varma (1996) recommend, may be seen as the best thing. In this case, boxing gyms or athletics tracks may be considered better for African-African or African-Caribbean children than a life of drug-pushing, petty crime or prostitution.

Having the right policies, the right racial or ethnic mix of personnel, an equal opportunities unit within the organization may be excellent for a personal or institutional image, but none of these translates itself into 'good practice'. 'Posturing' is probably too strong a word since it may offend those who wish to do more; nevertheless it is important to be firm about whether non-discrimination or anti-discrimination practice is the objective. Despite the absence of legal compulsion, many organizations self-proclaim their non-discrimination or anti-discrimination status. This is often on the basis of adopting an equal opportunities policy. In a large number of cases, this amounts to no more than a paper exercise, having little or no practical consequence because no further measures are taken to implement it or make it effective. Public relations are best served rather than a genuine desire for change (Owusu-Bempah, 1989a). It is only when an organization makes a genuine attempt to translate its equal opportunities statement into effective policies and procedures that steps towards reducing racial inequalities are effectively being made. Anti-discrimination practice is more than claiming to provide a fair service and highlighting discriminatory institutional policies and procedures. It is also about not carrying out such policies or procedures. True anti-discrimination professional practice does not distract clients from the real causes of their problems and from concrete solutions of those problems (Freire, 1972).

Of course, we may reiterate, to enable practitioners to practise thus, their education and training should be empowering. As Spring (1994) has argued, students should be equipped with: 'the means to critically appropriate knowledge existing outside their immediate experience in order to broaden their understanding of themselves, the world, and the possibilities for transforming the taken-for-granted assumptions about the way we live' (p. 27).

This view is further reinforced by Buck-Morss's (1979) observation of Piaget's insistence that the principle goal of education is to create individuals who are capable of doing new things, not simply repeating what other generations have done. The second goal of education is to form and shape minds that can be critical, can verify and do not accept everything.

# Recommendations

It has to be every practitioner's responsibility as well as that of their employers to articulate more precisely just where that practitioner stands in relation to 'race' and racism. Assumptions which go unsaid and unexamined are the most dangerous since they guide decisions with the least likelihood of revelation. Strategies for supplying adequate care for all clients by professionals have to begin by developing awareness and recognition of the potential difficulties at all levels of the organization. The following would be a minimal list of considerations (Richardson, 1990; Bushell, 1992; Hall, 1992; Howitt and Owusu-Bempah, 1994):

1  Professional bodies involved in any sense with the care of Black and ethnic minority communities need an effective anti-racist and anti-discrimination policy. This should cover all sectors of the organization's activities. It is unrealistic to expect that the needs of these communties can be met by an organization that fails, for example, their children and families. One critical feature is the need to recognize and acknowledge that traditional practices in relation to these communities have been profoundly damaging. Any assumptions about the deficiencies of Black families need to be exposed and rejected. All of this boils down to the recognition and acknowledgement that ethnic minority children and their families may be subject to the most adverse of circumstances partly because of their experience of both covert and manifest structural discrimination.
2  Any attempts at tokenistic solutions should be resisted. Having a few Black professionals to deal with Black people, for example, should be seen as a rejection of responsibility rather than its acceptance. Infinitely more valuable is the genuine political and personal desire that the same services, resources and opportunities be made available to all families regardless of 'race', ethnicity, religion and so forth.
3  The implementation of the policy needs continual monitoring for effectiveness and penetration throughout the workforce and workplace. This requires allocation of responsibility to a group within the organization supplemented, as appropriate, with community representation.
4  It needs to be recognized that anti-racism or anti-discrimination is a process that may change and develop as the needs of communities change and develop. Furthermore, emphases continually change over the course of time and what may seem to be a state-of-the-art practice at one point in time may become rather inadequate and old-fashioned in a few years. It has to be accepted that the issues and ways of dealing with them may change rapidly and unpredictably

over time. The task includes being aware of the changes and prepared to accommodate them.

5 Agencies and professions have tended to be rather slow in recognizing the extent to which they are a part of the problem and not just a part of the solution. The welfare of Black people requires the recognition of the extent to which institutional racism as well as personal racism within institutions remains a problem. The best interests of Black and ethnic minority communities cannot be met in these circumstances. It is akin to removing a sexually abused child from their home only to be abused in a children's home or foster care.

6 Agencies and professions must clarify to professional workers that racist beliefs, hidden and manifest, in so far as they affect and influence the delivery of services to clients, reflect professional incompetence and cannot be tolerated in a highly trained and skilled workforce sensitive to social inequalities.

7 It is incumbent upon those responsible for the training of the workforce of caring professionals to insist upon a level of training that teaches the nature and dynamics of racism in the broader society. The importance of such training to the welfare of all people, including Black people, must be emphasised to students at all levels.

8 Every organization, agency or professional body responsible for the welfare of children should have an anti-racist policy that reflects a commitment to addressing the needs of Black families. Outside consultants may be required in many cases.

9 The inadequacy of professional training regarding work with Black and ethnic minority clients has been noted by many investigators and observers (e.g. Bushel, 1992; Dominelli, 1989; Howitt and Owusu-Bempah, 1994; Owusu-Bempah, 1989a, 1990). Training therefore needs to be altered to approach practice from an anti-racism/anti-discrimination perspective; training must pay particular attention to literature, which challenges or questions orthodox theory and practice. (Owusu-Bempah, 1999c)

Regarding psychology, and psychological practice specifically, Hall (1997) has pointed out that the future of psychology lies in our accepting that human behaviour is determined and measured in a socio-cultural context. This context is in a state of flux. Psychology must adapt to changes in the society in which it is practised, including demographic changes, or lose its relevance as a profession, Hall warns. She identifies these areas as needing urgent attention:

1 Education and training: we must ensure that the psychology curriculum is culturally inclusive. For example, approved psychology courses might be required to diversify their curricula or lose their accreditation.

2 Practice: accrediting bodies, the professional bodies of psychology,

should ensure minimum competency of all practising psychologists through undergraduate and postgraduate education and training. Practising psychologists must understand the impact of culture, family structure, oppression and political issues, stigma or status, and socio-economic differences within groups.

The aim of the endeavour is to find ways of helping others more effectively. Nevertheless, in tandem with this is the possibility of a two-way process in which the Western psychologist learns not only to do psychology better with people of other cultures, but also to learn more about their Western selves in their search for personal development. Allen concludes:

> *For those of us in the modern, technological, industrialised West, complex non-oppressive encounters with other concepts of self can reveal new worlds of meaning: new ways of freeing our imaginations and of being more in touch with our emotions; of experiencing nature and the cosmos; of relating to death, time, and history; of understanding and creating our own selves and our relations to others*

Allen, 1997, p. 21

This statement reflects what our call for a psychology beyond the Western perspective is all about.

# References

Achenbach, T.M., and Edelbrock, C.S. (1981). Behavior problems and competencies reported by parents of normal and disturbed children. *Monographs of the Society for Research in Child Development*, 46 (1), 1–82.

Ahmad, D. (1990). *Black Perspectives in Social Work*. Birmingham: Venture Press.

Ahmed, S. (1991). Cultural racism in work with Asian women and girls. In S. Ahmed and J. Small (Eds) *Social Work with Black Children and their Families*. London: Balford/BAAF, 140–154.

Akbar, N. (1984). *Chains and Images of Psychological Slavery*. Jersey City, New Jersey: New Mind Productions.

Albee, G.W. (1982). Preventing psychopathology and human potential. *American Psychologist*, 37, 1043–1050.

Alejandro-Wright, M. (1985). The child's conceptions of racial classification: a socio-cognitive developmental model. In M.B. Spencer, G.K. Brookins, W.R. Allen (Eds) *Beginnings: The Social and Affective Development of Black Children*. Hillsdale, New Jersey: Erlbaum, 185–200.

Alexander, P.C. and Lupfer, S.L. (1987). Family characteristics and long-term consequences associated with sexual abuse. *Archives of Sexual Behavior*, 16, 235–245.

Alhibai, Y. (1987). The racist child. *New Society*, 4 December, 13–15.

Allen, D. (1997). Social construction of self: Some Asian, Marxist, and feminist critiques of dominant Western views of self. In D. Allen (Ed.) *Culture and the Self: Philosophical and Religious Perspectives, East and West*. Boulder, Colorado: Westview. pp. 3–26.

Amaladoss, M. (1999). Globalization and counter-culture: Liberation movements in Asia. In M. Alamadoss (Ed.) *Globalization and its Victims*. Delhi: Vidyajyoti and Welfare, 132–158.

Amin, K. and Oppenheim, C. (1992). *Poverty in Black and White: Deprivation and Ethnic Minorities*. London: CPAG.

Appiah, K.A. (1985). The uncompleted argument: Du Bois and the illusion of race. In H.L. Gates, Jr. (Ed.) *'Race', Writing and Difference*. Chicago: University of Chicago Press, 21–37.

Asante, M. (1980). *Afrocentricity: Theory of Social Change*. New York: Amulefi Publishing.

Asante, M. (1987). *The Africentric Idea*. Philadelphia: Temple University Press.

Azuma, H. (1984). Psychology in a non-Western country. *International Journal of Psychology*, 19, 145–155.

Babiker, G., and Arnold, L. (1997). *The Language of Injury: Comprehending Self-Mutilation*. Leicester: BPS Books.

Bache, R. (1895). Reaction time with reference to race. *The Psychological Review*, 2, 475–986.

Bagley, C., and Young, L. (1988). Evaluation of color and ethnicity in young children in Jamaica, Ghana, England, and Canada. *International Journal of*

*Intercultural Relations* 12, 45–60.

Baldwin, J.A. (1979). Theory and research concerning the notion of black self-hatred: A review and reinterpretation. *Journal of Black Psychology*, 5, 51–77.

Banks, N. (1992). Some considerations of 'racial' identification and self esteem when working with mixed ethnicity children and their mothers as social services clients. *Social Services Research*, 3, 32–41.

Banks, N. (1993). Identity work with Black children. *Educational and Child Psychology*, 10, 43–46.

Barker, M. (1981). *The New Racism: Conservatives and the Ideology of the Tribe.* London: Junction Books.

Barn, R. (1990). Black children in local authority care: Admissions pattern. *New Community*, 16, 229–246.

Barn, R. (1993). *Black Children in the Public Care System: Child Care Policy and Practice.* London: Batford.

Barnes, E.J. (1980). The Black community as the source of positive self-concept for Black children: A theoretical perspective. In R.L. Jones (Ed.), *Black Psychology*, 2nd Edn. New York: Harper and Row, 106–130.

Barth, R.P. (1997). Effects of age and race on the odds of adoption versus remaining in long-term out-of-home care. *Child Welfare*, 76 (2), 285–308.

Bartky, S.L. (1990). *Femininity and Domination.* New York: Routledge.

Basu, A (1997). Reducing concern with self: Parfitt and the ancient Buddhist schools. In D. Allen (Ed.) *Culture and the Self: Philosophical and Religious Perspectives, East and West.* Boulder, Colorado: Westview.

Batta, I., McCulloch, J. and Smith, N. (1975). A study of juvenile delinquency amongst Asians and half-Asians. *British Journal of Criminology*, 15, 32–42.

Batta, I. and Mawby, R. (1981). Children in local authority care: A monitoring of racial differences in Bradford. *Policy and Politics*, 9, 137–149.

Bebbington, A. and Miles, J. (1989). The background of children who enter local authority care. *British Journal of Social Work*, 19, 349–368.

Beckham, A.S. (1934). A study of race attitudes in negro children of adolescent age. *Journal of Abnormal and Social Psychology*, 39, 18 –29.

Beiser, H.R. (1988). "I ain't nobody": A study of Black male identity formation. *Psychoanalytic Study of the Child*, 42, 307–318.

Bennett, L. (1990). The 10 biggest myths about the Black family. *Ebony*, November, 168–175.

Berry, J.W. (1983). The sociogenesis of social sciences: an analysis of the cultural relativity of social psychology. In B. Brain (Ed.) *The Sociogenesis of Language and Human Conduct.* New York: Plenum.

Berry, J.W. and Dasen, P. (Ed.) (1974). *Introduction to Culture and Cognition.* London: Methuen.

Bharati, A. (1981). The self in Hindu thought and action. In A.J. Marsella, G. De Vos, and F.L.K. Hsu (Eds) *Culture and Self: Asian and Western Perspectives.* New York: Tavistock, 185–230.

Bhavnani, K., and Phoenix, A. (1994). Shifting identities, shifting racism: An introduction. In K. Bhavnani and A. Phoenix (Eds) *Shifting Identities, Shifting Racism: A Feminism and Psychology Reader.* London: Sage, 5–18.

Billig, M. (1988). Social representation, objectification and anchoring: a rhetorical analysis. *Social Behaviour.* 3, 1–16.

Bohart, A.C., O'Hara, M. and Leitner, L.M. (1998). Empirically violated treatments: Disenfranchisement of humanistic and other therapies. *Psychotherapy Research*, 8, 141–157.

Bolton, P. (1984). Management of compulsorily admitted patients to a high security unit. *International Journal of Social Psychiatry*, 30, (1–2), 77–84.

Boski, P. (1983). Egotism and evaluation in self and other attributions for achievement related outcomes. *European Journal of Social Psychology*, 13, 287–304.

Bourne, J. (1994). Facts and figures. In J. Bourne, L. Bridges and C. Searle (Eds) *Outcast England: How Schools Exclude Black Children*. London: Institute of Race Relations.

Bourne, J., Bridges, L. and Searle, C. (1994). *Outcast England: How Schools Exclude Black Children*. London: Institute of Race Relations.

Boushel, M. (1994). The protective environment of children: Towards a framework for anti-oppressive, cross-cultural and cross-national understanding. *British Journal of Social Work*, 24, 173–190.

Bowlby, J. (1944). Forty-four juvenile thieves: Their characteristics and home-life. *The International Journal of Psychoanalysis*, 25, 19–53.

Bowlby, J. (1951). *Maternal Care and Mental Health*. Geneva: World Health Organization.

Bowles, D.D. (1993). Bi-racial identity: Children born to African-American and white couples. *Clinical Social Work Journal*, 21 (4), 417–428.

Boyd-Franklin, N. (1989). *Black Families in Therapy*. New York: Guildford.

Brandt, L.W. (1979). Behaviorism – The psychological buttress of late capitalism. In A.R. Buss (Ed.) *Psychology in Social Context*. New York: Wiley, 77–99.

Breakwell, G. (1986). *Coping with Threatened Identities*. London: Methuen.

Brennan, J. and McGeevor, P. (1987). *Employment of Graduates from Ethnic Minorities: A Research Report*. London Commisssion for Racial Equality.

Brian, J., and Martin, M.D. (1983). *Child Care and Health for Nursery Nurses*. Amersham: Hulton.

Brian, J., and Martin, M.D. (1989). *Child Care and Health for Nursery Nurses*, 3rd Edn. Thornes: Stanley.

Bronfenbrenner, U. (1979). *The Ecology of Human Development: Experiments by Nature and Design*. Cambridge, Mass: Harvard University Press.

Brown, C. (1984). *Black and White Britain: The Third Policy Studies Institute Survey*. London: PSI/Heinemann.

Brown, C. and Gray, P. (1985*). Racial Discrimination: Seven Years After the Act*. London: Policy Studies Institute.

Brown, P.M. (1990). Biracial identity and social marginality. *Child and Adolescent Social Work*, 7 , 319–337.

Buck-Morss, S. (1979). Socioeconomic bias in Piaget's theory: Implications for cross-cultural studies. In A.R. Buss (Ed.) *Psychology in Social Context*. New York: Wiley, 349–363.

Bulhan, H.A. (1981). Psychological research in Africa: Genesis and function. *Race and Class*, XXIII (1), 25–41.

Bulhan, H.A. (1985). *Frantz Fanon and the Psychology of Oppression*. Boston: Boston University Press.

Burt, C. (1937). *The Backward Child*. London: University of London Press.

Bushell, W. (1992). *Black Children in Care*. London: Ethnic Study Group.

Buss, A. R. (1975). The emerging field of the sociology of psychological knowledge. *American Psychologist*, 30, 988–1002

Cacas, J. M. (1984). Policy, training, and research in counselling psychology: the racial/ethnic minority perspective. In S.D. Brown and R.W. Lent (Eds). *Handbook of Counselling Psychology*. New York: Wiley, 785–831.

Carr, S.C. and MacLachlan, M. (1993). Asserting psychology in Malawi. *The Psychologist: Bulletin of the British Psychological Society*, 6, 408–413.

Carter, R.T. (1991). Racial identity attitudes and psychological functioning. *Journal of Multicultural Counseling and Development*, 19, 105–114.

Central Council for the Education and Training in Social Work (1991). *Rules and Requirements for the Diploma in Social Work*: Paper 30, 2nd Edn. London: CCETSW.

Cheetham, J. (1991). Reviewing black children in care: Introductory note. In S. Ahmed and J. Small (Eds). *Social Work with Black Children and their Families*. London: Batford/BAAF, 117–119.

Ching, C.C. (1984). Psychology and the four modernizations in China. *International Journal of Psychology*, 19, 57–63.

Chomsky, N. (1979). *Language and Responsibility*. Hemel Hempstead: Harvester Wheatsheaf.

Church, A.T. and Katigbak, M.S. (1992). The cultural context of academic motives: A comparison of Filipino and American college students. *Journal of Cross-Cultural Psychology*, 23, 40–58.

Clark, K.B., and Clark, M. (1939). The development of the consciousness of self and emergence of racial identity in Negro pre-school children. *Journal of Social Psychology*, 10, 591–599.

Clark, K.B., and Clark, M. (1947). Racial identification and preference in Negro children, in T.M. Newcomb and E.L. Hartley (Eds) *Readings in Social Psychology*. New York: Holt, Rinehart and Winston, 602–611.

Clark, M.L. (1992). Racial group concept and self-esteem in black children. In A.K.H. Burlew, W.C. Banks, H.P. McAdoo and D. A. ya Azibo (Eds) *African American Psychology: Theory, Research and Practice*. Newbury Park: Sage, 159–172.

Coard, B. (1971). *How the West Indian Child is Made Educationally Sub-Normal in the British School System*. London: New Beacon Books/The Caribbean Education and Community Coworkers Association.

Cohen, R., Parmelee, D.X., Irwin, L., Weisz, J.R., Howard, P., Purcell, P., and Best, A.M. (1990). Characteristics of children and adolescents in a psychiatric hospital and a corrections facility. American Academy of Child and Adolescent Psychiatry, 29, 909–913.

Coleman, J. (1994). Black children in care: crisis of identity. *Runnymede Bulletin*, October, 4–5.

Collins, P. (1990). *Black Feminist Thought: Knowledge, Consciousness and the Politics of Empowerment*. Boston: Unwin Hyman.

Commission For Racial Equality (CRE) (1983). *Ethnic Minority Hospital Staff*. London: Commission for Racial Equality.

Commission For Racial Equality (1984). *Code of Practice in Employment*. London: Commission for Racial Equality.

Commission for Racial Equality (1987a). *Racial Attacks: A Survey in Eight Areas in Britain*. London: Commission for Racial Equality.

Commission for Racial Equality (1987b). *Living in Terror: A Report on Racial Violence and Harassment in Housing*. London: Commission for Racial Equality.

Commission for Racial Equality (1987c). *Employment of Graduates from Ethnic Minorities: A Research Report*. London: Commission for Racial Equality.

Commission for Racial Equality (1987d). *Overseas Doctors: Experience and Expectations: A Research Study*. London: Commission for Racial Equality.

Commission for Racial Equality (1988a). *Learning in Terror: A Survey of Racial Harassment in Schools and Colleges.* London: Commission for Racial Equality.

Commission for Racial Equality (1988b). *Medical School Admission: A Report of a Formal Investigation into St George's Hospital Medical School.* London: Commission for Racial Equality.

Commission For Racial Equality (1988c). *Ethnic Minority School Teachers: A Survey in Eight Local Education Authorities.* London: Commission for Racial Equality.

Commission For Racial Equality (1991). *CRE Annual Report 1991.* London: Commission for Racial Equality.

Commission for Racial Equality. (1995). *Black Children and Exclusion.* London: Commission for Racial Equality.

Connolly, P. (1998). *Racism, Gender Identities and Young Children: Social Relations in a Multi-Ethnic, Inner-City Primary School.* London: Routledge.

Cooley, C.H. (1902) *Human Nature and Social Order.* New York: Scribner.

Coppersmith, S. (1967). *The Antecedents of Self-Esteem.* San Francisco: Freeman.

Costarelli, S. (1993). Gypsy children in Europe: an overview. In S. Costarelli (Ed.) *Children of Minorities: Gypsies.* Florence, Italy: UNICEF, 35–52.

Courtney, M., Barth, R.P., Berrick, J.D., Brooks, D. Needell, B. and Park, L. (1996). Race and child welfare services: Past research and future directions. *Child Welfare*, 75, 99–137.

Coward, B. and Dattani, P. (1993). Race, identity and culture. In K.N. Dwivedi (Ed.) *Group Work with Children and Adolescents: A Handbook.* London: Jessica Kingsley, 245–261.

Cross, W.E. (1978). The Thomas and Cross models on psychological nigrescence: a literature review. *Journal of Black Psychology*, 4, 13–31.

Cross, W.E. (1980). Models of psychological nigrescence: A literature review. In R.L. Jones (Ed.) *Black Psychology*, 2nd Edn. New York: Harper and Row.

Cross, W.E. (1985). Black identity: Rediscovering the distinction between personal identity and reference group orientation. In M.B. Spencer *et al.* (Eds) *Beginnings: The Social and Affective Development of Black Children.* Mahusah, New Jersey: Erlbaum, 155–171.

Cross, W.E. (1991). *Shades of Black: Diversity in African-American Identity.* Philadelphia: Temple University Press.

Dalal, F. (1988). Jung: A racist. *British Journal of Psychotherapy*, 4 (3), 263–279.

Damon, W. and Hart, D. (1988). *Self-Understanding in Childhood and Adolescence.* Cambridge. Cambridge University Press.

Danziger, K. (1979). The origins of modern psychology. In A.R. Buss (Ed.). *Psychology in Social Context.* New York: Wiley, 27–45.

D'Ardenne, P. and Mahtani, A. (1989). *Transcultural Counselling in Action.* London: Sage.

Davey, A.G. and Mullin, P.N. (1982). Inter-ethnic friendship in British primary schools. *Educational Research,* 24, 83–92.

Davis, F.G. (1991). *Who is Black? One Nation's Definition.* University Park: Pennsylvania State University Press.

Dean, C. (1993). *Arguments for and Against Trans-Racial Placements.* Social Work Monograph. Norwich: University of East Anglia.

Demos, V. (1990). Black family studies and the issue of distortion: A trend analysis. *Journal of Marriage and the Family*, 52, 603–612.

Devine, P.G. (1989). Stereotypes and prejudice: Their automatic and controlled components. *Journal of Personality and Social Psychology*, 56 (1), 5–18.

Dien, D.S. (1982). A Chinese perspective on Kohlberg's theory of moral development. *Developmental Review*, 2, 331–341.

Dominelli, L. (1989). An uncaring profession? An examination of racism in social work. *New Community*, 15, 391–401.

Dummett, A. (1984). *A Portrait of English Racism*. London: Caraf.

Durkin, K. (1995). *Developmental Social Psychology: From Infancy to Old Age*. Oxford: Basil Blackwell.

Durojaiye, M.A.O. (1984). The impact of psychology on educational and personnel selection in Africa. *International Journal of Psychology*, 19, 135–144.

Durojaiye, M.A.O. (1993). Indigenous psychology in Africa: The search for meaning. In U. Kim and J.W. Berry (Eds) *Indigenous Psychologies: Research and Experience in Cultural Context*. London: Sage, 211–220.

Dwivedi, K.N., and Varma, V.P. (Eds) (1996). *Meeting the Needs of Ethnic Minority Children: A Handbook for Professionals*. London: Jessica Kingsley.

Ely, P. and Denny, D. (1987). *Social Work in a Multi-Racial Society*. Aldershot: Gower.

Enriquez, V.G. (1993). Developing a Filipino Psychology. In U. Kim and J.W. Berry (Eds). *Indigenous Psychologies: Research and Experience in Cultural Context*. London: Sage, 152–169.

Enriquez, V.G. (1997). Filipino psychology: Concepts and methods. In H.R.S. Kao and D. Sinha (Eds) *Asian Perspectives on Psychology*. New Delhi: Sage, 40–53.

Epstein, S. (1976). The self-concept revisited. *American Psychologist*, 28, 404–416.

Erikson, E.H. (1950). *Childhood and Society*. New York: Norton.

Erikson, E.H. (1959). *Identity and the Life Cycle*. New York: International Universities Press.

Erikson, E.H. (1968). *Identity: Youth and Crisis*. London: Faber.

Erwin, P. (1993). *Friendship and Peer Relations in Children*. Chichester: Wiley.

Esmail, A. and Everington, S. (1993). Racial discrimination against doctors from ethnic minorities. *British Medical Journal*, 306, 691–692.

Essed , P. (1988). Understanding verbal accounts of racism: Politics and heuristics of reality constructions. *Text*, 8, 5–40.

Essed, P. (1994). Contradictory positions, ambivalent perceptions: A case study of a Black woman entrepreneur. In K. Bhavnani and A. Phoenix (Eds) *Shifting Identities, Shifting Racism: A Feminism and Psychology Reader*. London: Sage, 99–118.

Eyman, R.K., Boroskin, A. and Hostetter, S. (1977). Use of alternative living plans for developmentally disabled children by minority parents. *Mental Retardation*,15, 55–61.

Eysenck, H.J. (1971). *Race, Intelligence and Education*. London: Temple Smith.

Eysenck, H.J. (1975). *The Inequality of Man*. Glasgow: Fontana/Collins.

Fanon, F. (1967). *Black Skin, White Masks*. London: Pluto Press.

Farr, R. and Moscovici, S. (Eds) (1944). *Social Representations*. Cambridge University Press.

Fenner, P. (1987). Cognitive theories of the emotions in Buddhism and Western psychology, *Psychologia*, 30, 217–227.

Fernandes, W. (1999). Globalisation, liberalisation and the victims of colonialism. In M. Alamadoss (Ed.) *Globalization and its Victims*. Delhi: Vidyajyoti and Welfare, 2–25.

Fernando, S. (1989). *Race, Culture and Psychiatry*. London: Routledge.

Fernando, S. (1995). Social realities and mental health. In S. Fernando (Ed.)

*Mental Health in a Multi-Ethnic Society: A Multidisciplinary Handbook.* London: Routledge, 11–49.

Figueroa, P. (1991). *Education and the Social Construction of 'Race'.* London: Routledge.

Flaskerud, J.H. and Hu, L.T. (1992). Relationship of ethnicity to psychiatric diagosis. *Journal of Nervous and Mental Disease,* 180 (5), 296–303.

Fogel, A. (1993). *Developing through Relationships: Origins of Communication, Self, and Culture.* New York: Harvester Wheatsheaf.

Forsythe, B. (1995). Discrimination in social work: An historical note. *British Journal of Social Work,* 25, 1–16.

Foster, RoseMarie, P. (1998). The clinician's cultural countertransference: The psychodynamics of culturally competent practice. *Clinical Social Work Journal,* 26 (3), 253–270.

Foster-Carter, O. (1986). Insiders, outsiders and anomalies: A review of studies of identity. *New Community,* 13, 224–234.

Foucault, M. (1979). *Discipline and Punish: The Birth of the Prison.* New York: Vintage.

Freire, P. (1972). *Pedagogy of the Oppressed.* Harmondsworth: Penguin.

Frisby, C.L. (1993). One giant step backward: Myths of Black cultural learning styles. *School Psychology Review,* 22, 535–557.

Furth, H.G. (1995). Self in which relation? *American Psychologist,* 50, 176.

Gantous, P. (1994). Stress drives high suicide rate among native Innu. *Psychology International,* 5, 3.

Garland, A.F. and Besinger, B.A. (1997). Racial/ethnic differences in court referred pathways to mental health services for children in foster care. *Children and Youth Services Review,* 19, 651–666.

Geber, M. (1957). Gesell tests on African children. *Pediatrics,* 20, 1055–1065.

Georgas, J. (1993). Ecological-social model of Greek psychology. In U. Kim and J. W. Berry (Eds) *Indigenous Psychologies: Research and Experience in Cultural Context.* London: Sage, 56–77.

Gergen, K.J. (1979). The positivist image in social psychological theory. In A.R. Buss (Ed.) *Psychology in Social Context.* New York: Wiley, 193–212.

Gergen, K.J., Gulerce, A., Lock, A. and Misra, G. (1996). Psychological science in cultural context. *American Psychologist,* 51(5), 496–503.

Gibbs, J.T. (1987). Identity and marginality: Issues in the treatment of biracial adolescents. *American Journal of Orthopsychiatry,* 57, 265–278.

Gibbs, J.T. and Hines, A.M. (1992). Negotiating ethnic identity: Issues for Black–White biracial adolescents. In M.P.P. Root (Ed.) *Racially Mixed People in America.* Newbury Park: Sage, 223–238.

Gilkey, L. (1976). *Reaping the Whirlwind.* New York: Seabury.

Gill, O. and Jackson, B. ( 1983). *Adoption & Race: Black, Asian and Mixed Race Children in White Families.* Batsford: London.

Gilligan, C. (1982). *In a Different Voice: Psychological Theory and Women's Development.* Cambridge, MA: Harvard University Press.

Giovanni, J.M., and Becerra, R.M. (1979). *Defining Child Abuse.* New York: The Free Press.

Goffman, E. (1959). *The Presentation of Self in Everyday Life.* New York: Doubleday-Anchor.

Gopaul-McNicol, S. (1988). Racial identification and racial preference of black pre-school children in New York and Trinidad. *Journal of Black Psychology,* 14, 65–68.

Graham-Davies, S. (1996). Unpublished. Department of Social Sciences, Lough-borough University.

Greenwald, H.J. and Oppenheim, D.B. (1968). Reported magnitude of self-misidentification among Negro children: Artefact? *Journal of Personality and Social Psychology*, 8, 49–52.

Gregory, J. (1987). *Sex, Race and the Law*. London: Sage.

Gushue, G.V. (1993). Cultural-identity development and family assessment: an interactional model. *Counseling Psychologist*, 21 (3), 487–513.

Guthrie, R. (1976/1980). *Even the Rate was White: A Historical View of Psychology*. New York: Harper and Row.

Hackett, L. and Hackett, R. (1994). Child-rearing practices and psychiatric disorder in Gujarati and British children. *British Journal of Social Work*, 24, 191–202.

Haddon, A.C. and Huxley, J.S. (1936). *We Europeans: A Survey of 'Racial' Problems*. New York: Harper.

Hall, C.C.I. (1992). Please choose one: Ethnic identity choices for biracial individuals. In M.P.P. Root (Ed.) *Racially Mixed People in America*. Newbury Park: Sage, 250–64.

Hall, C.C.I. (1997). Cultural malpractice: The growing obsolescence of psychology with the changing U. S. population. *American Psychologist*, 52, 642–651.

Hall, E.T. (1983). *The Dance of Life*. New York: Doubleday.

Hamill, H. (1996). *Family Group Conferences in Child Care Practice*. Social Work Monograph. Norwich: University of East Anglia.

Haraway, D. (1994). Shifting the subject: A conversation between Kum-Kum Bhavnani and Donna Haraway on 12 April 1993 Santa Cruz, California. In K. Bhavnani and A. Phoenix (Eds) *Shifting Identities, Shifting Racism: A Feminism and Psychology Reader*. London: Sage, 19–39.

Harlow, H. and Harlow, M.K. (1969). Effects of various mother–infant relationships on rhesus monkey behavior. In B.M. Foss (Ed.) *Determinants of Infant Behaviour*. London: Methuen, 15–36.

Heiss, J. and Owen, S. (1972). Self-evaluation of blacks and whites. *American Journal of Sociology*, 78, 360–369.

Herkovits, M.J. (1934). A critical discussion of the negro hypothesis. *Journal of Negro Education*, 401.

Hill, R.B. (1972). *The Strength of Black Families*. New York: Emerson Hall.

Hitch, P. (1983). Social identity and the half-Asian child. In G. Breakwell (Ed.) *Threatened Identities*. Chichester: Wiley, 107–127.

Ho, D. Y.F. (1979). Psychological implications of collectivism: With special reference to the Chinese case and Maoist dialectics. In L.H. Eckensberger, W.J. Lonner and Y.H. Poortinga (Eds). *Cross-Cultural Contributions to Psychology*. Lisse, Netherlands: Swets and Zeitlinger, 143–150.

Ho, D.Y.F. (1993). Relational orientation in Asian social psychology. In U. Kim and J. W. Berry (Eds). *Indigenous Psychologies*. Newbury Park, California: Sage, 240–259.

Holdstock, T.L. (2000). *Re-examining Psychology: Critical Perspectives and African Insights*. London: Routledge.

Home Office. (1981). *Racial Attacks: Report of the Home Office Study*. London: HMSO.

Honeyford, R. (1984) Education and race – an alternative view. *The Salisbury Review*, 6 (winter), 30–32.

Horton, H.D., Thomas, M.E. and Herring, C. (1995). Rural–urban differences in

Black family structure: An analysis of the 1990 census. *Journal of Family Issues*, 16, 298–313.

Howitt, D. (1991). *Concerning Psychology: Psychology Applied to Social Issues*. Buckingham: Open University Press.

Howitt, D. (1992). *Child Abuse Errors*. London: Harvester Wheatsheaf.

Howitt, D. (1995). *Paedophiles and Sexual Offences Against Children*. New York: John Wiley.

Howitt, D., Billig, M., Cramer, D., Edwards, D., Kniveton, B., Potter, J. and Radley, A. (1989). *Social Psychology: Conflicts and Continuities*. Milton Keynes: Open University Press.

Howitt, D., Craven, G., Iveson, C., Kremer, J., McCable, J. and Rolph, T. (1977). The misdirected letter. *British Journal of Social and Clinical Psychology*, 16, 285–286.

Howitt, D. and McCabe, J. (1978). Attitudes do predict behaviour. *British Journal of Social and Clinical Psychology*, 17, 285–286.

Howitt, D. and Owusu-Bempah, J. (1990a). Racism in a British journal? *The Psychologist: Bulletin of the British Psychological Society*, 3 (9), 396–400.

Howitt, D. and Owusu-Bempah, J. (1990b). The pragmatics of institutional racism: Beyond words. *Human Relations*, 43, 885–889.

Howitt, D. and Owusu-Bempah, J. (1994). *The Racism of Psychology: Time for Change*. Hemel Hempstead: Harvester Wheatsheaf.

Howitt, D. and Owusu-Bempah, J. (1995). How Eurocentric psychology damages Africa. *The Psychologist*, 8, 462–465.

Howitt, D. and Owusu-Bempah, K. (1999). Education, psychology and the construction of black childhood. *Education and Child Psychology* 16 (3), 17–29.

Hsu, F.L.K. (1983). *Rugged Individualism Reconsidered*. Knoxville: University of Tennessee Press.

Huang, L.N. (1994). An intergrative approach to clinical assessment and intervention with Asian-American adolescents. *Journal of Clinical Child Psychology*, 23, 21–31.

Hughes, M. and Demo, D.H. (1989). Self-perception of Black Americans: Self-esteem and personal efficacy. *American Journal of Sociology*, 95, 132–159.

Hylton, C. (1997). *Black Families' Survival Strategies: Way of Coping in UK Society*. York: Joseph Rowntree Foundation.

Inada, K.K. (1997). Buddho-Taoist and Western metaphysics of the self. In D. Allen (Ed.) *Culture and the Self: Philosophical and Religious Perspectives, East and West*. Boulder, Colorado: Westview Press.

Jacobs, J.H. (1992). Identity deveopment in biracial children. In M.P.P. Root (Ed.) *Racially Mixed People in America*. Newbury Park: Sage, 190–206.

Jagers, R.J. and Mock, L.O. (1993). Culture and social outcome among inner-city African-American children: An Afrographic exploration. *Journal of Black Psychology*, 19, 391–405.

James, W. (1890). *The Principles of Psychology*. New York: Holt.

James, W. (1950). *The Principles of Pyschology*. New York: Dover.

Jensen, A.R. (1969). How much can we boost IQ and scholastic achievement? *Harvard Educational Review*, 39, 1–123.

Johnson, D.J. (1992). Developmental pathways. Towards an ecological theoretical formulation of race identity in Black–White biracial children. In M.P.P. Root (Ed.) *Racially Mixed People in America*. Newbury Park, California: Sage.

Johnson, P.R., Shireman, J.F. and Watson, K.W. (1987) Transracial adoption and the development of black identity at age eight. *Child Welfare*, 66 (1), 45–55.

Johnson, T.J. (1972). *Professions and Power*. London: Macmillan.

Jung, C.G. (1930). Your negroid and Indian behavior. *Forum*, 83, 193–199.

Kagitcibasi, C. (1984). Socialization in traditional society: A challenge to psychology. *International Journal of Psychology*, 19, 145–157.

Kakar, S. (1978). *The Inner World: A Psychoanalytic Study of Childhood and Society in India*. Delhi: Oxford University Press.

Kakar, S. (1982). *Shamans, Mystics and Doctors: A Psychoanalytic Enquiry into India and its Healing Properties*. Bombay: Oxford University Press.

Kakar, S. (Ed.) (1979). *Identity and Adulthood*. Delhi: Oxford University Press.

Kamin, L.J. (1974). *The Science and Politics of IQ*. New York: Wiley.

Kamin, L.J. (1977). *The Science and Politics of IQ*. Harmondsworth: Penguin.

Kamin, L. (1981). *Intelligence: The Battle For the Mind, H. J. Eysenck Versus Leon Kamin*. London: Macmillan.

Kaplan, S.L. and Busner, J. (1992). A note on racial bias in the admission of children and adolescents to state mental health facilities versus correctional facilities in New York. *American Journal of Psychiatry*, 149 (6), 768–772.

Kashima, Y. and Triandis, H.C. (1986). The self-serving bias in attributions as a coping strategy: A cross-cultural study. *Journal of Cross-Cultural Psychology*, 17, 83–97.

Katz, I. (1996). *The Construction of Racial Identity in Children of Mixed Parentage: Mixed Metaphors*. London: Jessica Kingsley.

Kerwin, C., Ponterotto, J.G., Jackson, B.L. and Harris, A. (1993). Racial identity in biracial children: A qualitative investigation. *Journal of Consulting Psychology*, 40 (2), 221–231.

Kich, G.K. (1992). The developmental process of asserting a biracial, bicultural identity. In M.P.P. Root (Ed.) *Racially Mixed People in America*. Newbury Park: Sage, 304–317.

Kim, U. (1997). Asisn collectivism: An indigenous perspective. In H.R.S. Kao and D. Sinha (Eds) *Asian Perspectives on Psychology*. New Delhi: Sage, 147–163.

Kim, U. and Berry, J. W. (1993). *Indigenous Psychologies: Research and Experience in a Cultural Context*. Newbury Park, California: Sage.

Kim, U., and Choi, S. (1994). Individualism, collectivism, and child development: A Korean perspective. In P.M. Greenfield and R.R. Cocking (Eds) *Cross-Cultural Roots of Minority Child Development*. Hillsdale, New Jersey: Erlbaum.

Kitwood, T. (1983). Self-conception among young British-Asian Muslims: Confutation of a stereotype. In G. Breakwell (Ed.) *Threatened Identities*. Chichester: Wiley, 129–147.

Knappert, J. (1995). *African Mythology: An Ecyclopedia of Myth and Legend*. London: Diamond Books.

Kohlberg, L. (1969). Stage and sequence: The cognitive-developmental approach to socialization. In D.A. Goslin (Ed.) *Handbook of Socialization: Theory and Research*. Chicago: Rand-McNally, 347–480.

Kohlberg, L. (1984). *Essays on Moral Development: The Philosophy of Moral Development*. San Francisco: California: Harper and Row.

Krishnan, L. (1997). Distributive justice in the Indian perspective. In H.R.S. Kao and D. Sinha (Eds) *Asian Perspectives on Psychology*. New Delhi: Sage, 185–200.

Kysel, F. (1988). Ethnic background and examination results. *Educational Research*, 30, 83–89.

Lagmay, A.V. (1984). Western psychology in the Philippines: Impact and response. *International Journal of Psychology*, 19, 31–44.

Landau, S. and Nathan, G. (1983). Selecting delinquents for cautioning in the London metropolitan area. *British Journal of Criminology*, 28, 128–149.

Landrine, H. (1992). Clinical implications of cultural differences: The referential versus the indexical self. *Clinical Psychology Review*, 12, 401–415.

Larkey, L.K., Hecht, M.L. and Martin, J. (1993). What's in a name? African American ethnic identity terms and self-determination. *Journal of Language and Social Psychology*, 12 (4), 302–317.

Leary, K. (1995). Interpreting in the dark: Race and ethnicity in psychoanalytic psychotherapy. *Psychoanalytic Psychology*, 12, 127–140.

Lesser, R.C. (1996). All that's solid melts into air: Deconstructing some psycho-analytic facts. *Contemporary Psychoanalysis*, 32, 5–23.

Leung, K. and Drasgow, F. (1986). Relation between self-esteem and delinquent behavior in three ethnic groups: An application of item response theory. *Journal of Cross-Cultural Psychology*, 17, 151–167.

Levin, R.V. and Bartlett, C. (1984). Pace of life, punctuality and coronary heart disease in six countries. *Journal of Cross-Cultural Psychology*, 15, 233–255.

Lewin, K. (1935). Psycho-sociological problems of a minority group. *Character and Personality*, 3, 175–187.

Lewin, K. (1941). Jewish self-hatred. *Contemporary Jewish Record*, 4, 219–232.

Lindsay-Smith, C. (1979). *Black Children in Care*. London: Allen and Unwin.

Littlejohn-Blake, S.M. and Darling, C.A. (1993). Understanding the strengths of African American families. *Journal of Black Studies*, 23 (4), 460–471.

Littlewood, R. (1992). Psychiatric diagnosis and racial bias: Empirical and inter-pretive approaches. *Social Science and Medicine*, 34, 141–149.

Littlewood, R. and Lipsedge, M. (1989). *Aliens and Alienists: Ethnic Minorities and Psychiatry*, 2nd Edn. London: Unwin Hyman.

Lobo, E. (1978). *Children of Immigrants to Britain: Their Health and Social Problems*. London: Allen and Unwin.

Lomov, F.F, Budilova, E.A, Koltsova, V.A. and Medvedev, A.M. (1993). Psycho-logical thought within the system of Russian culture. In U. Kim and J. W. Berry (Eds) *Indigenous Psychologies: Research and Experience in Cultural Context*. London: Sage, 104–117.

London Association of Community Relations Council (1985). *In a Critical Condi-tion: A Survey of Equal Opportunities in Employment in London's Health Authorities*. London: LACRC.

Longres, J.F., and Torrecilha, R.S. (1992). Race and the diagnosis, placement and exit status of children and youth in a mental health and disability system. *Journal of Social Science Research*, 15, 43–62.

Lykes, M. B. (1985) Gender and individualist vs. collectivist bases for notions of self. *Journal of Personality*, 53, 365–383.

Lyle, S., Benyon, J., Garland, J. and McClure, A. (1996). *Education Matters: African-Caribbean People and Schools in Leicestershire*. Scarman Centre for the Study of Public Order, University of Leicester.

Lyles, M.R., and Carter, J.H. (1982). Myths and strengths of the black family. A historical and sociological contribution to family therapy. *Journal of the National Medical Association*, 74 (11), 1119–1123.

Ma, H.K. (1997). The affective and cognitive aspects of moral development: A Chinese perspective. In S.R. Kao and D. Sinha (Eds) *Asian Perspectives on Psychology*. Princeton University Press, 93–109.

MacDonald, G. (1990). Allocating blame in social work. *British Journal of Social Work*, 20, 525–546.

Macpherson, W. (1999). *The Stephen Enquiry*. London: HMSO.

Mahoney, T. (1988). *Governing Schools: Powers, Issues and Practice*. London: Macmillan.

Maitra, B. (1996). Child abuse: A universal 'diagnostic' category? The implication of culture in definition and assessment. *International Journal of Social Psychiatry*, 42, 287–304.

Malhotra, A.K. (1997). Sartre and Samkhya-Yoga on self. In D. Allen (Ed.) *Culture and the Self: Philosophical and Religious Perspectives, East and West*. Boulder, Colorado: Westview Press, 111–128.

Markus, H.R. and Kitayama, S. (1991). Culture and self: Implications for cognition, emotion, and motivation. *Psychological Review*, 98, 224–253.

Marsella, A.J. (1998). Toward a 'global community psychology'. *American Psychologist*, 53, 1282–1291.

Marsella, A.J., De Vos, G. and Hsu, F.L.K. (Eds) (1985). *Culture and Self: Asian and Western Perspectives*. London: Tavistock.

Martinez, R. and Dukes, R.L. (1991). Ethnic and gender differences in self-esteem. *Youth and Society*, 22 (3), 318–338.

Masson, J. (1989). *Against Therapy: Psychotherapy May Be Hazardous to Your Mental Health*. London: Collins.

Materska, M., Garot, M. and Ehrlich, S. (1987). Les disorganisations de la representation de soi a l'entreé au college. *European Journal of Psychology of Education*, 1, 62–77.

Maximé, J. E. (1991a). Some psychological models of black self-concept. In S. Ahmed, J. Cheetham and J. Small (Eds) *Social Work with Black Children and their Families*. London: B.T. Batsford, 100–116

Maximé, J.E. (1991b). *Black Like Me Workbook One: Black Identity*. Beckenham: Emani Publications.

Maximé, J.E. (1993a). The importance of racial identity for the psychological well-being of black children. *Association of Child Psychology and Psychiatry Review & Newsletter*, 15 (4), 173–179.

Maximé, J.E. (1993b) The ethnographic dimension of race: Its mental health and educational implications. *Educational and Child Psychology* 10 (3), 28–38.

Mays, V.M., Rubin, J., Sabourin, M. and Walker, L. (1996). Moving toward a global psychology: Changing theories and practice to meet the needs of a changing world. *American Psychologist*, 51, 485–487.

Mbiti, J.S. (1969). *African Religions and Philosophy*. London: Heinemann.

McAdoo, H.P. (1978). Self-concept in Black preschool children. In W. Cross and A. Harrison (Eds) *Third Conference on Empirical Research in Black Psychology*. Washington DC: National Institute of Education, 47–64.

McAdoo, H.P. (1988). Transgenerational patterns of upward mobility in African American families. In H.P. McAdoo (Ed.) *Black Families*. Newbury Park, California: Sage, 148–168.

McAdoo. J. (1981a). Black father and child interactions. In L.E. Gary (Ed.) *Black Men*. Beverley Hills: Sage, 115–130.

McAdoo, J. (1981b). Involvement of fathers in the socialization of black children. In H.P. McAdoo (Ed.) *Black Families*, Beverly Hills: Sage, 225–237.

McAvoy, B. and Donalson, L.E. (1990). *Health Care for Asians*. Oxford: Oxford University Press.

McAvoy, B. and Sayeed, A. (1990). Communication. In B. McAvoy and L.J.

Donaldson (Eds) *Health Care for Asians*. Oxford University Press, 57–71.

McFadden, A.C., Marsh, G.E., Prince, B.J. and Huang, Y. (1992). A study of race and gender bias in the punishment of handicapped school children. *The Urban Review*, 24, 239–251.

McGovern, D., and Cope, R. (1987). First psychiatric admission rates of first and second generation Afro-Caribbeans. *Social Psychiatry*, 122, 139–149.

McKenry, P.C. and Fine, Mark A., (1993). Parenting following divorce: A comparison of black and white single mothers. *Journal of Comparative Family Studies*, 24 (1), 99–111.

McRoy, R.G. and Freeman, E. (1986). Racial identity issues among mixed-race children. *Social Work Education*, 8, 164–174.

McRoy, R.G., Zurcher, L.A., Lauderdale, M.L. and Anderson, R.E. (1984). The identity of transracial adoptees. *Social Casework*, 65, 34–39.

Mead, G.H. (1934). *Mind, Self and Society*. University of Chicago Press.

Mehryar, A.H. (1984). The role of psychology in national development: Wishful thinking and reality. *International Journal of Psychology*, 19, 159–167.

Mercer, K. (1984). Black communities' experience of psychiatric services. *International Journal of Social Psychiatry*, 30 (1–2), 22–27.

Miatra, B. (1995). Giving due consideration to the family's racial and cultural background. In P. Reder and C. Lucey (Eds) *Assessment of Parenting: Psychiatric and Psychological Contributions*. London: Sage, 151–166.

Miatra, B. (1996). Child abuse: A universal 'diagnostic' category? The implications of culture in definition and assessment. *International Journal Social Psychiatry*, 42, 287–304.

Milikian, L.H. (1984). The transfer of psychological knowledge to the Third World Countries and its impact on development: The case of five arab gulf oil-producing states. *International Journal of Psychology*, 19, 65–77.

Miller, M. (1997). Views of Japanese selfhood: Japanese and Western perspectives. In D. Allen (Ed.), *Culture and the Self: Philosophical and Religious Perspectives, East and West*. Boulder, Colorado: Westview Press, 145–162.

Miller, R L and Miller, B (1990). Mothering the biracial child: Bridging the gaps between African-American and white parenting styles. *Women and Therapy*, 10, 169–179.

Milner, D. (1975). *Children and Race*. Harmondsworth: Penguin.

Milner, D. (1983). *Children and Race: Ten Years On*. London: Ward Lock Educational.

MIND (1993). *MIND's Policy on Black and Minority Ethnic People and Mental Health*. MIND: London.

Modood, T. (1988). 'Black' racial equality and Asian identity. *New Community*, 14, 397–404.

Modood, T. (1992). *Not Easy Being British: Colour, Culture and Citizenship*. Stoke-on-Trent: Trentham Books.

Modood, T., Berthoud, R., Lakey, J., Nazroo, J., Smith, P., Virdee, S. and Beishon, S. (1997). *Ethnic Minorities in Britain: Diversity and Disadvantage*. London: Policy Studies Institute.

Moncayo, R. (1998). Cultural diversity and the cultural and epistemological structure of psychoanalysis: implications for psychotherapy with Latinos and other minorities. *Psychoanalytic Psychology*, 15(2), 262–286.

Montagu, A. (1974). *Man's Most Dangerous Myth: The Fallacy of Race*. New York: Oxford University Press.

Montagu, A. (1997). *Man's Most Dangerous Myth: The Fallacy of Race*, 6th Edn.

Wallnut Creek: Alta Maria Press.

Morris, H.S. (1968). Ethnic groups. In D.L. Skills (Ed.) *International Encyclopedia of the Social Sciences*, vol. 5, 167.

Moynihan, D. (1965). *The Negro Family in the United States: the Case for Action.* Washington DC: US Govt. Printing Press.

Mullender, A. (1991). The Ebony Project – Bicultural group work with transracial foster parents. *Social Work with Groups*, 13, 34–41.

Munford, M.B. (1994). Relationship of gender, self-esteem, social class, and racial identity to depression in blacks. *Journal of Black Psychology*, 20, 157–174.

Murphy-Berman, V., Berman, J.J. Singh, P., Pachauri, A. and Kumar, P. (1984). Factors affecting allocation to needy and meritorious recipients: a cross-cultural comparison. *Journal 1 of Personality and Social Psychology*, 46, 1267–1272.

Myers, L.J. (1993). *Understanding an Afrocentric World View: Introduction to an Optimal Psychology.* Dubuque, Iowa: Kendal Hunt.

National Association for the Care and Resettlement of Offenders (NACRO) (1986). *Black People and the Criminal Justice System.* London: NACRO.

National Association of Health Authorities (NAHA) (1988). *Action Not Words: A Strategy to Improve Health Services For Black and Minority Ethnic Groups.* Birmingham: NAHA.

National Society for the Prevention of Cruelty to Children (NSPCC). (1999). *Protecting Children From Racism and Racial Abuse: A Research Review.* London: NSPCC.

Nisbett, R.E. and Ross, L. (1980). *Human Inference: Strategies and Shortcomings of Social Judgements.* Englewood Cliffs, New Jersey: Prentice Hall.

Nobles, W. (1980). African philosophy: Foundations for black psychology. In R. Jones (Ed.) *Black Psychology.* New York: Harper & Row, 23–36.

O'Brian, C. (1990). Family therapy with black families. *Journal of Family Therapy*, 12, 3–16.

Ogilvy, C.M., Boath, E.H., Cheyne, W.M., Jahoda, G. and Schaffer, H.R. (1990). Staff attitudes and perceptions in multi-cultural nursery schools. *Early Child Development and Care*, 64, 1–13.

Olson, P.E. (1991). The sexual abuse of boys: A study of the long-term psychological effects. In M. Hunter (Ed.) *The Sexually Abused Male: Prevalence, Impact, and Treatment*, vol. 1. Lexington Books, 137–152.

O'Neil, W.M. (1968). *The Beginnings of Modern Psychology.* Harmondsworth: Penguin.

Orme-Johnson, D.W., Zimmerman, E. and Hawkins, M. (1997). Maharishi's vedic psychology: The science of the cosmic psyche. In S.R. Kao and D. Sinha (Eds) *Asian Perspectives on Psychology.* New Delhi: Sage, 282–308.

Owusu-Bempah, J. (1985). Racism: A white problem? *Community Librarian*, 3, 21–23.

Owusu-Bempah, J. (1989a). The new institutional racism. *Community Care*, 14 September, 23–25.

Owusu-Bempah, J. (1989b). Does colour matter? *Community Care*, 26 January, 18–19.

Owusu-Bempah, J. (1990). Toeing the white line. *Community Care*, November, 16–17.

Owusu-Bempah, J. (1994a). Race, self-identity and social work. *British Journal of Social Work*, 24, 123–136.

Owusu-Bempah, J. (1994b). Theory versus reality. *Community Care*, 1–7 December, 15.

Owusu-Bempah, J. (1995). Information about the absent parent as a factor in the well-being of children of single-parent families. *International Social Work*, 38, 253–275.

Owusu-Bempah, J. (1997). Race: a framework for social work? In M. Davies (Ed.). *Blackwell Companion to Social Work*. Oxford: Basil Blackwell.

Owusu-Bempah, K. (1999a). Confidentiality and social work practice in African cultures. In B. R. Compton and B. Gallaway (Eds) *Social Work Processes*, 6th Edn. Pacific Grove, California: Brooks/Cole, 166–169.

Owusu-Bempah, K. (1999b). Unawareness: A tactical approach within Western psychology? *Psych-Talk: Newsletter for the Student Members of the British Psychological Society*, 22, 32–36.

Owusu-Bempah, K. (1999c). Race, culture and the child. In J. Tunstill (Ed.) *Child and the State: Whose Problem?* London: Cassell, 17–34.

Owusu-Bempah, J. and Howitt, D. (1994). Racism and the psychological textbook. *The Psychologist: Bulletin of the British Psychological Society*, 7, 163–166.

Owusu-Bempah, J. and Howitt, D. (1995). How Eurocentric psychology damages Africa. *The Psychologist*, 8, 462–465.

Owusu-Bempah, J. and Howitt, D. (1997). Socio-genealogical connectedness, attachment theory and childcare practice. *Child and Family Social Work*, 2, 199–207.

Owusu-Bempah, K. and Howitt, D. (1999a). Even their soul is defective. *The Psychologist*, 12, 126–130.

Owusu-Bempah, K. and Howitt, D. (1999b). Defective soul: Response to commentaries. *The Psychologist*, 12, 138–139.

Owusu-Bempah, K. and Howitt, D. (2000). Socio-genealogical connectedness: on the role of gender and same-gender parenting in mitigating the effects of parental divorce. *Child and Family Social Work*, 5, 107–116.

Owusu-Bempah, J. and Howitt, D. (unpublished). *Social Attribution in Inter-racial Situations*. University of Leicester, UK.

Page, R.C. and Berkow, D.N. (1991). Concepts of the self: Western and Eastern perspectives. *Journal of Multicultural Counselling and Development*, 19, 83–93.

Paniagua, F.A. (1994). *Assessing and Treating Culturally Diverse Clients: A Practice Guide*. London: Sage.

Parham, T.A. and Williams, P.T. (1993). The relationship of demographic and background factors to racial identity attitudes. *Journal of Black Psychology*, 19, 7–24.

Park, R. (1928). Human migration and the marginal man. *American Journal of Sociology*, 33, 881–893.

Park, R. (1931). The mentality of racial hybrids. *American Journal of Sociology*, 36, 534–551.

Parrinder, E.G. (1954). *African Traditional Religion*. London: Hutchinson House.

Peagam, E. (1994). Special needs or educational apartheid? The emotional and behavioral difficulties of Afro-Caribbean children. *Support for Learning*, 9 (1), 33–38.

Peavy, R.V. (1996). Counselling as a culture of healing. *British Journal of Guidance and Counselling*, 24, 141–150.

Perez-Foster, R.M. (1993). The social politics of psychoanalysis: *Psychoanalytic Diaglogues*, 3, 69–84.

Petras, J. (1994). Cultural imperialism in late 20th century. *Economics and Politics Weekly*, 29(32), 2070–2073.

Phinney, J.S. (1996). The multigroup ethnic identity measure: A new scale for use with diverse groups. *Journal of Adolescent Research*, 7 (2), 156–176.

Pike, R. (1966). *Language in Relation to a United Theory of the Structure of Human Behavior.* Den Haag: Mouton.

Pollard, D.S. (1989). Against the odds: A profile of academic achievers from the urban underclass. *The Journal of Negro Education*, 58, 297–309.

Porter, C.P. (1991). Social reasons for skin tone preferences of black school-age children. *American Journal of Orthopsychiatry*, 6 (1), 149–154.

Powell-Hopson, D., and Hopson, D.S. (1988). Implications of doll-color preferences among Black preschool children and white preschool children. *Journal of Black Psychology*, 14, 57–63.

Ranger, C. (1989). Race, cultrure and 'cannabis psychosis': The role of social factors in the construction of a disease category. *New Community*, 15, 357–369.

Rao, K.R. (1998). Two faces of consciousness: A look at Eastern and Western perspectives. *Journal of Consciousness Studies*, 5 (3), 309–327.

Rhoner, R. (1984). Toward a conception of culture for cross-cultural psychology. *Journal of Cross-Cultural Psychology*, 15, 111–138.

Richards, K.D. (1995). *A Content Analysis of Texts in a Clinical Setting.* Birmingham: University of Aston.

Richardson, R. (1990). *Daring to Be a Teacher: Essays, Stories and Memoranda.* Stoke-on-Trent: Trentham Books.

Richeport-Haley, M. (1998). Ethnicity in family therapy: A comparison of brief strategic therapy and culture-focused therapy. *The American Journal of Family Therapy*, 26, 77–90.

Riegel, K.F. (1979). Three paradigms of developmental psychology. In A.R. Buss (Ed.) *Psychology in Social Context.* New York: Wiley, 331–348.

Robbins, D. (1986). *Wanted: Railman: Report of an Investigation into Equal Opportunities for Women in British Rail.* London: HMSO.

Robinson, L. (1995). *Psychology for Social Workers: Black Perspectives.* London: Routledge.

Roland, A. (1988). *In Search of Self in India and Japan: Towards a Cross-Cultural Psychology.* Princeton University Press.

Roland, A. (1997). How universal is psychoanalysis? The self in India, Japan, and the United States. In D. Allen (Ed.) *Culture and Self: Philosophical and Religious Perspectives, East and West.* Boulder, Colorado: Westview Press, 27–39.

Root, M.P.P. (1992). Within, between and beyond race. In M.P.P. Root (Ed.) *Racially Mixed People in America.* Newbury Park: Sage, 3–11.

Rosemont Jr., H. (1997). Classical Confucian and contemporary feminist perspectives on the self: Some parallels and their implications. In D. Allen (Ed.) *Culture and the Self: Philosophical and Religious Perspectives, East and West.* Boulder, Colorado: Westview Press.

Rosenberg. M. (1979). Group rejection and self-rejection. *Research in Community and Mental Health*, 1, 3–20.

Rosenberg, M. (1989). Old myths die hard: The case of black self-esteem. *Revue Internationale de Psychologie Sociale*, 2 (3), 357–365.

Rosenberg, N.R. (Ed.) (1992). *Japanese Sense of Self.* Cambridge: Cambridge University Press.

Rossiter, A., de Boer, C., Narayan, J., Razack, N., Scollay, V. and Willette, C. (1998). Towards an alternative account of feminist practice ethics in mental health. *Affilia*, 13 (1), 9–30.

Runnymede Trust (1992). *The Runnymede Trust Annual Report from 1991–1992*. London: Runnymede Trust.

Rushton, J.P. (1990). Race differences, r/K theory and a reply to Flynn. *The Psychologist*, 5, 195–198.

Rushton, J.P. (1992). Cranial capacity related to sex, rank, and race in a stratified random sample of 6,325 U.S. military personnel. *Intelligence*, 16, 401–413.

Russell, D.E.H. (1983). The incidence and prevalence of intrafamilial and extra-familial sexual abuse in female children. *Child Abuse and Neglect*, 7, 133–146.

Russell, K.K. (1994). The racial inequality hypothesis: A critical look at the research and an alternative theoretical analysis. *Law and Human Behaviour*, 18, 305–317.

Russell, R.W. (1984). Psychology in its world context. *American Psychologist*, 39, 1017–1025.

Rutter, M. (1991). *Maternal Deprivation Reassessed*. Harmondsworth: Penguin.

Ryan, W. (1976). *Blaming the Victims*. New York: Vintage.

Salazar, J.M. (1984). The use and impact of psychology in Venezuela: Two examples. *International Journal of Psychology*, 19, 113–122.

Sandfort, Th. G.M. (1988). *The Meanings of Experience: On Sexual Contacts in Early Youth, and Sexual Behavior and Experience in Later Life*. Utrecht: Homostudies.

Sandfort, Th. G.M. (1989) Studies into child sexual abuse: an overview and critical appraisal. Paper presented at the 1st European Congress of Psychology. Amsterdam, 2–7 July.

Sarason, S. B. (1981). An asocial psychology and misdirected clinical psychology. *American Psychologist*, 36, 827–836.

Sastry, J. and Ross, C.E. (1998). Asian ethnicity and the sense of personal control. *Social Psychology Quarterly*, 61 (2), 101–120.

Scarman, Lord. (1981). *The Brixton Disorders: Report of an Inquiry*. London: HMSO.

Schoenfeld, C.G. (1988). Blacks and violent crime: A psychoanalytically oriented analysis. *The Journal of Psychiatry and Law*, Summer, 269–301.

Schwendler, W. (1984). UNESCO's project on the exchange of knowledge for endogenous development. *International Journal of Psychology*, 19, 3–15.

Segal, U.M. and Schwartz, S. (1985). Factors affecting placement decisions of children following short-term emergency care. *Child Abuse and Neglect*, 12, 141–149.

Serpell, R. (1984). Commentary: The impact of psychology on Third World development. *International Journal of Psychology*, 19, 179–192.

Shaikh, A. (1985). Cross-cultural comparison: Psychiatric admission of Asian and indigenous patients in Leicester. *International Journal of Social Psychiatry*, 31, 3–11.

Shearer, S.L., Peters, C.P., Quaytman, M.S. and Ogden, R.L. (1990). Frequency and correlates of childhood sexual and physical abuse histories in adult female borderline inpatients. *American Journal of Psychiatry*, 147, 214–216.

Shiang, J., Kjellander, C., Huang, K and Bogumill, S. (1998). Developing cultural competency in clinical practice. *Clinical Psychology: Science and Practice*, 5(2), 182–210.

Shuinear, N.S. (1993). Growing up a gypsy: Insights from the October 1992 UNICEFCDC Workshop. In S. Costarelli (Ed.) *Children of Minorities: Gypsies*. Florence, Italy: UNICEF, 17–35.

Shweder, R. and Bourne, E.J. (1982). Does the concept of the person vary cross-culturally? In A.J. Marsella and G.M. White (Eds) *Cultural Conceptions of*

*Mental Health and Therapy*. London: Riedel, 97–137.

Silavwe, G.W. (1995). The need for a new social work perspective in an African setting: The case of social casework in Zambia. *British Journal of Social Work*, 25, 71–84

Simpson, E.L. (1974). Moral development research. *Human Development*, 17, 81–106.

Sinha, D. (1984). Towards partnership for relevant research in the Third World. *International Journal of Psychology*, 19, 169–177.

Sinha, D. and Sinha, M. (1997). Orientation to psychology: Asian and Western. In S.R. Kao and D. Sinha (Eds), *Asian Perspectives on Psychology*. Princeton University Press.

Sinha, D. and Sinha, M. (1997). Orientations to psychology: Asian and Western. In S.R. Kao and Sinha, D. (Eds) *Asian Perspectives on Psychology*. New Delhi: Sage, 25–39.

Sinha, J.P.B (1984). Towards partnership for relevant research in the Third World. *International Journal of Psychology*, 19, 169–177.

Sinha, J.P.B. (1993). The bulk and front of psychology in India. *Psychology and Developing Societies*, 5, 135–150.

Skellington, R. and Morris, P. (1992). *Race in Britain Today*. London: Sage.

Small, J. (1991). Transracial placements: Conflicts and contradictions. In A. Shmed, J. Cheetham, and J. Small (Eds) *Social Work with Black Children and their Families: Child Care Policy and Practice*. London: Batford/BAAF, 81–99.

Smith, D. J. (1974). *Racial Disadvantage in Employment*. London: Political and Economic Planning.

Smith, P.B. and Bond, M.H. (1993). *Social Psychology Across Cultures*. London: Harvester Wheatsheaf.

Sowell, T. (1986). *Education: Assumptions versus History*. California: Hoover Institution Press.

Spencer, M.B. (1984). Black children's race awareness, racial attitudes and self-concept: A re-interpretion. *Journal of Child Psychology and Psychiatry*, 25, 433–441.

Spring, J. (1994). *Wheels in the Head: Educational Philosophies of Authority, Freedom and Culture from Socrates to Paulo Freire*. New York: McGraw-Hill.

Stevenson, H.W. (1991). The development of prosocial behavior in large-scale collective societies: China and Japan. In R.A. Hinde and J. Groebel (Eds) *Cooperation and Prosocial Behavior*. Cambridge University Press.

Stevenson, O. (1998). *Neglect: Issues and Dilemmas*. Oxford: Basil Blackwell.

Stonequist, E.V. (1937). *The Marginal Man: A Study of Personality and Culture Conflict*. New York: Russell and Russell.

Sue, D.W. and Sue, D. (1990). *Counseling the Culturally Different*. New York: Wiley.

Sue, S. (1988). Psychotherapeutic services for ethnic minority groups: Some optimism, some pessimism. *American Psychologist*, 43, 301–308.

Sue, S. (1998). In search of cultural competence in psychotherapy and counselling. *American Psychologist*, 53 (4), 440–488.

Swann, Lord (1985). *Education for All: Final Report of the Committee of Inquiry into the Education of Children from Ethnic Minority Groups*. London: HMSO.

Swick, K.J., Brown, M. and Boutte, G. (1994). African American children and school readiness: An analysis of the issues. *Journal of Instructional Psychology*, 21 (2), 183–191.

Terman, L. (1916). *The Measurement of Intelligence*. Boston: Houghton.

Terrell, F., Terrell, S.L. and Taylor, J. (1980). Effects of race of examiner and type of reinforcement on the intelligence test performance of lower-class Black children. *Psychology in the Schools*, 17, 270–272.

Thomas, C.W. (1971). *Boys No More*. California: Glencoe.

Thompson, C.H. (1934). The conclusions of scientists relative to racial differences. *Journal of Negro Education*, 3, 494–512.

Thompson, N. (1993). *Anti-Discrimination Practice*. London: Macmillan.

Thorndike, E.L. (1940). *Human Nature and the Social Order*. London: Macmillan.

Timble, J.E. and Medicine, B. (1993). Diversification of American Indians: Forming an indigenous perspective. In U. Kim and J. W. Berry (Eds) *Indigenous Psychologies: Research and Experience in Cultural Context*: London: Sage, 133–151.

Tizard, B. and Phoenix, A. (1993). *Black, White or Mixed Race*? London: Routledge.

Trepagnier, B. (1994). The politics of white and black bodies. In K. Bhavnani and A. Phoenix (Eds) *Shifting Identities, Shifting Racism: A Feminism and Pyschology Reader*. London: Sage, 199–205.

Triandis, H.C. (1995). *Individualism and Collectivism*. Boulder, Colorado: Westview Press.

Triandis, H.C. (1996). The psychological measurement of cultural syndromes. *American Psychologist*, 54, 407–415.

Triandis, H.C. (1994). *Culture and Social Behaviour*. New York: McGraw-Hill.

Unesco (1967). *Statement on Race and Racial Prejudice*. Paris: UNESCO.

Urquiza, A.J. and Capra, M. (1991). The impact of sexual abuse: Initial and long-term effects. In M. Hunter (Ed) *The Sexually Abused Male: Prevalence, Impact, and Treatment*, vol. 1. Lexington Books, 105–135.

van Beek, W.E. and Blakely, T.D. (1994). Introduction. In W.E. van Beek and T.D. Blakely (Eds) *Religion in Africa: Experience and Expression*. Portsmouth: Heinemann, 1–20.

van den Heuvel, H., Tellegen, G. and Koomen, W. (1992). Cultural differences in the use of psychological and social characteristics in children's self-understanding. *European Journal of Social Psychology*, 22, 353–362.

Van Dijk, T. A. (1987). *Communicating Racism: Ethnic Prejudice in Thought and Talk*. Newbury Park: Sage.

Vandenberg, B. (1991). Is epistemology enough? An existential consideration of development. *American Psychologist*, 46, 1278–1286.

Verkuyten, M. (1989). Self-esteem among Dutch and Turkish children in the Netherlands. *Journal of Social Psychology*, 129, 269–271.

Wakefield, J.C. (1996). Does social work need the eco-systems perspective?: Part 1. Is the perspective clinically useful?. *Social Service Review*, 70, 1–32.

Wallach, M.A. and Wallach, L. (1983). *Psychology's Sanction for Selfishness*. San Francisco: Freeman.

Wallendorf, M. and Anould, E.J. (1988). My favourite things: A cross-cultural inquiry into object attachment, possessiveness and social linkage. *Journal of Consumer Research*, 14, 531–547.

Watkins, C.E. (1990). Psychiatric epidemiology II: The prevalence and aftermath of sexual assault. *Journal of Counseling and Development*, 68, 341–343.

Watts, R.J. (1992). Elements of a psychology of human diversity. *Journal of Community Psychology*, 20, 116–131.

Weidman, H. (1978). Falling-out. *Social Science and Medicine*, 13, 95–112.

Weinreich, P. (1979). Cross-ethnic identification and self-rejection in black adolescents. In G. Verma and C. Bagley (Eds) *Race, Education and Identity*, London: Macmillan, 157–75.

Weinreich, P. (1983). Emerging from threatened identities: Ethnicity and gender in redefinitions of ethnic identity. In G. Breakwell (Ed.). *Threatened Identities*. Chichester: Wiley, 140–185.

Werner, E.E. (1972). Infants around the world: Cross-cultural studies of psychomotor development from birth to two years. *Journal of Cross-Cultural Psychology*, 3, 111–134.

Wertheimer, M. (1972). *Fundamental Issues in Psychology*. New York: Holt, Rhinehart and Winston.

Whaley, A.L. (1993). Self-esteem, cultural identity, and psychosocial adjustment in African American Children. *Journal of Black Psychology*, 19 (4), 406–422.

Whiting, B.B. and Edwards, C.P. (1988). *Children of Different Worlds: The Formation of Social Behaviour*. Cambridge, MA: Harvard University Press.

Wijsen, F. (1999). Beyond the fatal impact theory. Globalization and its cultural underpinnings. In M. Amaladoss (Ed.) *Globalization and its Victims: As Seen by the Victims*. Delhi: Cambridge University Press. 122–131.

Williams, C. (1974). *The Destruction of Black Civilization*. Chicago, Illinois: Third World Press.

Williams, R.L. (1980). The death of white research in the black community. In R.L. Jones Ed. *Black Psychology*, 2nd Edn. New York: Harper and Row.

Willie, C.V. (1993). Social theory and social policy derived from the black family experience. *Journal of Black Studies*, 23, 451–459.

Wilson, A. (1987). *Mixed Race Children: A Study of Identity*. London: Allen and Unwin.

Wooster, A. and Harris, G. (1973). Concepts of self in highly mobile service boys. *Educational Research*, 14, 195–199.

Wright, C. (1987). Black students – white teachers. In B. Troyna (Ed.) *Racial Inequality in Education*. London: Tavistock, 109–126.

Wright, C. (1992). *Race Relations in the Primary School*. London: David Fulton.

Wyatt, G.E. (1990). Sexual abuse of ethnic minority children: Identifying dimensions of victimization. *Professional Psychology: Research and Practice*, 21, 338–343.

Wyatt, G.E. (1990). The sexual abuse of Afro-American and white American women in childhood. *Child Abuse and Neglect*, 9, 507–519.

Yang, K.S. (1986). Chinese personality and its change. In M.H. Bond (Ed.) *The Psychology of Chinese People*. Hong Kong: Oxford University Press.

Yang, K.S. (1997). Theories and research in Chinese personality: An indigenous approach. In H.S.R. Kao and D. Sinha (Eds). *Asian Perspectives on Psychology*. New Delhi: Sage, 236–262.

Zint, M.V. (1963). *Education across Cultures*. Dubuque: William Brown.

# Name index

Akbar, N. 18
Albee, G.W. 189
Alejandro-Wright, M. 100
Allen, D. 38, 39, 40, 113, 201
Amaladoss, M. 118
Amin, K., and Oppenheim, C. 80
Appiah, K.A. 81
Arnold, L., and Babiker, G. 96–7
Azuma, H. 87, 88, 183, 192

Babiker, G., and Arnold, L. 96–7
Bacon, F. 37
Bagley, C., and Young, L. 103
Banks, N. 156, 160, 171
Barn, R. 51
Barnes, E.J. 132–3, 139
Barth, R.P. 91–2
Bartlett, C., and Levin, R.V. 86
Batta, I., and Mawby, R. 51
Batta, I. *et al* 51
Becerra, R.M., and Giovanni, J.M. 57
Beckham, A.S. 109–10
Bennett, L. 53–4
Berkow, D.N., and Page, R.C. 38, 185
Berman, J.J. (Murphy-Berman *et al*) 38
Berry, J.W. 28, 29–30
and Kim, U. 27, 29, 32–3
Best, A.M. (Cohen *et al*) 157–8
Blakely, T.D., and van Beek, W.E. 183
Boath, E.H. (Ogilvy *et al*) 71–5
Boer, C. de (Rossiter *et al*) 83
Bogumill, S. (Shiang *et al*) 26, 43
Bohart, A.C. *et al* 184
Bond, M.H., and Smith, P.B. 192
Boroskin, A. (Eyman *et al*) 159
Boski, P. 187
Bourne, J. 62, 63–5
Boutte, G. (Swick *et al*) 61
Bowlby, J. 47
Bowles, D.D. 142–3
Breakwell, G. 128–30
Brennan, J., and McGeevor, P. 73
Brian, J., and Martin, M.D. 49–50, 52
Bronfenbrenner, U. 115
Brown, M. (Swick *et al*) 61
Buck-Morss, S. 116, 198
Budilova, E.A. (Lomov *et al*) 183
Busner, J., and Kaplan, S.L. 158
Carr, S.C., and MacLaclan, M. 17
Carter, R.T. 138

Cheetham, J. 170
Cheyne, W.M. (Ogilvy *et al*) 71–5
Ching, C.C. 183
Chomsky, N. 116
Clark, K.B., and Clark, M. 97, 100
Clark, M.L. 101–2
Coard, B. 77
Cohen, R. *et al* 157–8
Coleman, J. 52–3, 164–5
Collins, P. 134
Cooley, C.H. 127, 128, 131
Cope, R., and McGovern, D. 17
Costarelli, S. 103
Coward, B., and Dattani, P. 165–6, 173–5
Cross, W.E. 101, 136–8, 139, 169

Darling, C.A., and Littlejohn-Blake, S.M. 55
Dattani, P., and Coward, B. 165–6, 173–5
Davey, A.G., and Mullin, P.N. 98
Dean, C. 111
Demo, D.H., and Hughes, M. 104
Demos, V. 56
Descartes, R. 38–9, 177
Dien, D.S. 118
Dukes, R.L., and Martinez, R. 105
Dummett, A. 93, 141, 197–8
Durkin, K. 167
Durojaiye, M.A.O. 117, 180
Dwivedi, K.N., and Varna, V.P. 62, 90, 198

Edwards, C.P., and Whiting, B.B. 36, 87
Enriquez, V.G. 78, 88, 180
Erikson, E.H. 40, 104–5, 134–5
and Horowitz, E.L. 169
Essed, P. 12–13, 133
Eyman, R.K. *et al* 159
Eysenck, H.J. 80

Fanon, F. 134
Fernandes, W. 121
Fernando, S. 182, 194–5
Figueroa, P. 67–8, 69
Fine, M.A., and McKenry, P.C. 54
Forsythe, B. 91
Foster, R.P. 7, 42, 185–6
Foucault, M. 83
Freeman, E., and McRoy, R.G. 168
Freud, S. 40
Frisby, C.L. 75–6

# Subject index